Empty Labor

While most people work ever-longer hours, international statistics suggest that the average time spent on non-work activities per employee is around two hours a day. How is this possible, and what are the reasons behind employees withdrawing from work? In this thought-provoking book, Roland Paulsen examines organizational misbehavior, specifically the phenomenon of "empty labor," defined as the time during which employees engage in private activities during the working day. The author explores a variety of explanations, from under-employment to workplace resistance. Building on a rich selection of interview material and extensive empirical research, he uses both qualitative and quantitative data to present a concrete analysis of the different ways empty labor unfolds in the modern workplace. This book offers new perspectives on subjectivity, rationality and work simulation and will be of particular interest to academic researchers and graduate students in organizational sociology, organization studies, and human resource management.

ROLAND PAULSEN is a Postdoctoral Research Fellow at the Department of Business Administration, Lund University. Dr Paulsen has received several awards for his work, notably from the Nordic Sociological Association and the International Labor Process Conference. His first book *Arbetssamhället: Hur Arbetet Överlevde Teknologin* [*The Society of Labor: How Labor Survived Technology*] stirred up a national debate in Sweden on the meaning of work.

Empty Labor

Idleness and Workplace Resistance

ROLAND PAULSEN
Lund University, Sweden

CAMBRIDGE
UNIVERSITY PRESS

CAMBRIDGE
UNIVERSITY PRESS

University Printing House, Cambridge CB2 8BS, United Kingdom

Cambridge University Press is part of the University of Cambridge.

It furthers the University's mission by disseminating knowledge in the pursuit of education, learning and research at the highest international levels of excellence.

www.cambridge.org
Information on this title: www.cambridge.org/9781107066410

© Roland Paulsen 2014

First published 2014

Printed in the United Kingdom by Clays, St Ives plc

A catalogue record for this publication is available from the British Library

Library of Congress Cataloguing in Publication data

ISBN 978-1-107-06641-0 Hardback

Contents

Figures

Foreword

The significance and positive nature of paid labor is taken for granted in many societal debates and also most research. Of course, "bad" working conditions are always seen as bad, but work in itself is for most seen as something positive, even essential to the needs and wants of most people. Unemployment is highly problematic, even when welfare societies ease the financial strain of not being employed. Full or near-full employment is the ideal, to avoid people's suffering from lack of activity or meaningful existence associated with work, often equated with paid labor. So is the case even in advanced economies, half a decade after the arrival of affluent society and well into post-affluence, where technology takes care of most of the production. Needless to say, the social value of the outcomes of work is often debatable.

At the same time it is common to express worries about many people working too much or being exposed to high demands on performances. Boundaryless work, harsh work tempo, stress, uncertain, temporary employment conditions, and low tolerance for underachievers are common themes in debates and research. In contemporary capitalism, competition is hard, and people in the labor force are facing tough demands in an increasingly squeezed working life. So we are often told.

Within the sociology of work, it is tempting and common to adhere to this template for truth-telling and join the mainstream. But without denying that these descriptions often make sense, there are other stories to be told. Not all parts of the labor market are driven by fierce competition intensifying people's work days.

Roland Paulsen's book falls outside the mainstream of labor studies. He does not buy the assumptions of the blessing of work (as long as it is liberated from bad conditions) and neither the thesis that a rationalized economy and working life put hard pressure on employees to work intensively and risk health and work satisfaction. His point of departure is rather the opposite: work (paid labor) is an antithesis to freedom, but it is not necessarily so that tight control and intense pressure to work characterize the average work day for most people.

Paulsen suggests that researchers may not understand so much of the inner dynamics of working life. They may be caught in their own work ideology and in the production of knowledge that benefit themselves: here is the thesis of the significance of work and problematic work conditions as a popular point of departure. And what researchers assume, they tend to find and confirm. In his study, Paulsen proceeds from an original, interesting and very productive idea – the study of empty labor. This refers to individuals who during paid work hours do not engage in – for the employer – productive activity, but are concerned with private matters – taking a nap, surfing on the net, or chatting with colleagues or friends. The study of empty labor leads him to a quite different image of contemporary working life than the one that is salient in the mainstream of labor studies. A great deal of people are not so positive about their work and are not so formed and constrained by labor contracts, work ideology, or a repressive management holding a tight grip over the labor process.

The basic problem addressed is about resistance and agency within paid employment in relationship to the ideological and practical demands of work society and its organizations.

Key questions then become: How do we deal with work society? What do we do with our wish to work less and live more? Does *status quo* necessarily mean acceptance? Or what happens with the unrealized longings for another life?

The book connects to the research area *organizational misbehavior* – the complex relationship between resistance and adaptation in workplaces. The empirical subject matter is to describe and understand motives for empty labor, e.g. for not working while being paid for doing so. According to a number of international studies, the work day for many people is characterized by quite a lot of empty labor. There are indications that between 1.5 and 3 hours per day are spent on non-work. This has inspired Paulsen to ask two sets of questions, within the overarching aim of understanding the links among empty labor, subjectivity, and worker resistance:

How? How is it possible to get away with working half of your working hours or less? Is it an individual pursuit or is there collective organization? Is it known to management or is it concealed? How do you manage not getting noticed? How do you spend the hours freed by empty labor?

Why? What motivates empty labor? Do slackers themselves conceive of it as an expression of dissent or just laziness? Is it something that you can mention to your colleagues, your friends or is shame involved? Is it politically motivated and in that case, how – against management, the firm, work itself, or what?

Central for good research are good research questions. They call for creativity, critical distance, and an ability to go against conventional thinking. These are important qualities in this book. Not only the questions, but also by the very nature of social science, the always tentative answers provided in this book demonstrate these qualities. So does the careful, reflective, sometimes ironic writing style, a text full of clever remarks and observations and many inspiring thoughts and suggestions for further research questions. Paulsen demonstrates that this is indeed a rich area to explore further.

Having read a great deal during my 30 years as a researcher I very often feel that new texts do not add much in terms of new insights. Paulsen's book is definitively an exception. It represents social science when it is at its best: it has something important to say and it says it with credibility and elegance.

Mats Alvesson, Lund University

Preface

I write this with a fine view of the Indian Ocean. I can hear splashing noises from the pool behind, children laughing and screaming, and beneath me the pulse of crashing waves. I read the freeze has knocked out the railroad lines in Sweden again. It is early February and at this time of the year it usually gets dark around 3.30 p.m. back home. People are now waiting on the platforms, in the cold, with tingling fingers, numb feet, silently suppressing that deep rage that is so hard to put into words. Where I am now, life is quite different. The Balinese workers' main concern seems to be to sweep away the flowers that keep falling from the trees. This is our second time at this island, and we will probably stay another week or so. Officially, we are on a conference trip to Bangkok. Unlike my wife, who also works as a researcher, I have not informed anyone at work that the trip includes a five-week stay in Indonesia. Why should I? As I see it, where, when, and how I work is of no importance as long as I do it. The question that recurs to me, particularly at moments like this, is rather whether I work at all.

If pressing these keys is "work," it certainly is different from the work I watched my parents do as I grew up. Sometimes, mostly with the sense of being a fraud, I find myself thinking of my father, his thick-skinned hands and the burn-marks on his forearms from that half lifetime spent in the kitchen. During my PhD studies they would often return to it: "but what will you do for work once you're finished?" Today, I can still appreciate a vague sense of disbelief on their end – vague, but justified. Clearly, it cannot be right that some people continue to "work" on far-flung beaches with the wind in their hair, idly pondering how to best formulate something in a language they have not really mastered, whereas others have to "work" with things that no one would do voluntarily, damaging both mind and body while trying to normalize stress levels that most academics could scarcely fathom.

Every now and then I hear colleagues saying that academic research is not only work, but *hard* work, that you can get *burned out* if you are not careful. My experience is very different. Yet I sympathize with those who are less content with this job than I am. If truth be told, right now I would rather try windsurfing than writing this preface. But my body does not even react to those impulses anymore. "Work" in the abstract sense – as compulsion, as morality – is always present, like a twinge of guilt, like a John Calvin figurine planted on my right shoulder, continually asking me: "Do you *really* deserve this? Is it *really* okay for you to take time off right now?"

Most sociologists know of discipline, both personally and theoretically. We have studied it for more than a century, and there is no sphere of life where we have not observed its manifestations. In some sociological classics, you might even get the impression that discipline is the most prominent characteristic of the modern worker. This book will yield another understanding of today's employees. Even if discipline is there, it is never absolute. The universal capacity to establish a cynical distance to whatever power we obey is now so well documented that it has itself been described as a form of ideology. Sometimes discipline is very real – cognitively, behaviorally or both – other times, it is no more than a charade. This should not surprise anyone; wage labor is to a large extent constituted by a set of well-rehearsed charades. Yet, as the expanding research on organizational "misbehavior" illustrates, there is another reality beyond. Slacking off at work is doubtlessly the most widespread form of organizational misbehavior. It is also a misbehavior that must remain particularly covert in order to recur. This clandestine existence may be a reason why so few have studied it.

Another reason may be that sleeping employees represent a theoretical challenge to the supposed rationality of wage labor. The general assumption, from which I myself suffered when initiating this project, seems to be that "there is always work if you want it"; that productivity losses stem from individual misfits lacking in work commitment, from mere aberrations in an otherwise efficient machine. This study reveals that there are other rationales than "instrumental reason" regulating the modern workplace. Most fundamentally, I would like to stress the fact that hard work does *not* necessarily pay off. What you produce, how much you contribute to your organization, will not allow you to reap any rewards unless your work is recognized by others. At work, it is not what you do, but how you *look like* you are doing it. This order will always disadvantage the humble – and stimulate illusion tricks.

Under such simulacric conditions, withdrawing from work – at work – becomes an equivocal act. Is it resistance, adjustment or something in between? Unfortunately, there is a tendency in the research on organizational misbehavior to answer questions of this type with no regard for the different contexts in which the misbehavior takes place. As the reader will discover, there is indeed, under certain circumstances, an element of silent defiance at play. This observation should, however, not be exaggerated into a rejection of the very phenomenon of discipline. What I want to suggest is simply that the disciplinary power of work is far from uncontested and that the rationality that we often attribute to work is ill-founded. Even if the phantasm of work cannot be eradicated under present conditions, I hope that this book will inspire some of you to act against it.

This study emerged from a range of interviews which I conducted over a period of three years. I am indebted to many people, from both academia and "the real world" outside. Without the generosity and kindness of all the interviewees who gave me their valuable time, there would have been nothing to write about. Thank you all for sharing your stories, and thanks to the Maska.nu Crew for allowing me to advertise for participants on your website.

While writing, I was very fortunate to be able to visit two institutions outside Sweden. For my three-month stay at the Department of Human Resource Management, Strathclyde University, I want to thank Dora Scholarios and Paul Thompson, who received me in the best possible way. As the reader will notice, Paul has had a tremendous impact on how I approached the subject of this book, and I feel very privileged to have met and discussed earlier drafts and ideas with him. My one-year visit at the Department of Sociology, Cornell University, was one of the best experiences of my life. Thank you, Richard Swedberg, for tutoring me in the art of theorizing and for being such a shining example of how great intellect can be combined with great humility.

I have also benefited from the efforts of a number of Swedish colleagues who have commented on this manuscript and earlier versions of it. There are too many to mention here, but I would particularly like to thank Michael Allvin, Mats Alvesson, Patrik Aspers, Ugo Corte, Erik Hannerz, Kaj Håkanson, Jan Ch. Karlsson, Rafael Lindqvist, Vessela Misheva, Lennart Räterlinck, and Lena Sohl.

Two sections of the book were previously published in altered forms, and I thank the publishers for permission to reuse parts of those articles. Chapter 4 is derived from "Non-work at Work: Resistance or What?" in *Organization* (Forthcoming, 2014), and Chapter 6 is a reworking of "Layers of Dissent: The Meaning of Time Appropriation" in *Outlines – Critical Practice Studies* 1 (2011): 53–81.

Since several of the people I have thanked here would find the less "neutral" passages of this book quite disturbing (not to mention all the failings of which I am not yet aware), I should point out that although they have contributed to my formation and the completion of this project, I am the only one responsible for the final outcome. If anyone else should be blamed, it would have to be my love, muse, partner in crime, and most devoted reader, Anna Lindqvist. Thank you, Anna, for all that you are, and for giving me the idea to initiate this study that eventually, as an absolute proof of the absurdity of work, took so much of our spare time. I dedicate this book to you.

1 | *Introduction*

The main part of this book is about how and why people spend large amounts of their working hours on private activities. Why is this worth studying? Well, that is the other part of the book. There are two threads running throughout the study: One is theoretical – how can we conceive of resistance at work and why have we heard so little about it? The other is empirical – do the rather large proportions of our working hours that we spend on private activities signify a hitherto unrecognized type of resistance against work? Of course, the two threads will intertwine as we move along, but initially I will keep them separate for pedagogical reasons.

1.1 The theoretical problem

Part of the problematic of this book derives from what I have tried to capture in another book (Paulsen, 2010), namely *the critique of work*. The critique of work has a long tradition and is becoming increasingly relevant as productivity grows and the eulogized ambition to "create jobs" echoes more and more hollowly. There are conservative elements in the critique of work dating back to Plato and Aristotle, in which the stupefying effects of work have long been scrutinized (see Applebaum, 1992; Beder, 2001; Tilgher, 1931). There are anarchist elements in the critique of work in which the inherent power structure of wage labor is criticized for being incompatible with a life of freedom and dignity (Black, 2009; Illich, 1978; Kropotkin, 1927 [1892]). The critique of work can be found in mainstream sociology (Bauman, 2004; Beck, 2000; Wright, 2010). It is at the core of (early) critical theory (Adorno and Horkheimer, 2010 [1956]; Marcuse, 1955), and yet well practiced outside the boundaries of continental philosophy (cf. Keynes, 1991 [1931]; Leontief, 1986; Russell, 1996 [1935]). It is also vital in both the ecology movement (Gorz, 1994; Jackson, 2009; Schor, 2010) and

1

the radical feminist movement (Méda, 2008; Solanas, 1967; Weeks, 2011).

In most of its variations, the critique of work represents one of the darker streams in social theory. In it, you find the most depressing accounts of social life, including advanced explanations of why work society survives its own technology and why it is so hard to break the symbolic spell of work. A fundamental argument is that work is not merely external, not merely a threat *against* life – *work infiltrates life*. It structures time, thought and emotion. According to some commentators, the colonizing aspects of work have become so intense during later years that work is even *absorbing life*. The spheres in which we can forget our work-based identities and in which there is no (disguised) imitation of the principles of work are steadily shrinking. Consequently, we lose contact with non-submissive, spontaneous, and recalcitrant ways of being, and instead of championing autonomy, we fear it.

There are several concrete tendencies in working life supporting these gloomy contentions. "Work without boundaries" (Allvin et al., 2011) is not only a psychological concept denoting faint tendencies of "work becoming life"; it is also about more tangible phenomena such as longer working hours, endless responsibilities, fleeting operational procedures, rapid precarization, and a capsized "work–life balance" (see also Hochschild, 1997). Central to this development is the tendency towards more *immaterial labor* in which workers' sensorial capacities are no longer required (Gorz, 1989; Sennett, 1998), a deskilling process (Braverman, 1998 [1974]) that runs parallel to greater demands on attitudes and personalities. With these demands and the growth of the service industries, work becomes more and more perverted in the sense that we are being paid for things that appear less and less as "work" in any substantial sense. A subject dear to the sociology of work is *emotional labor*, i.e. work in which we are not paid for production of either commodities or services, but for the display of emotions (see Hochschild, 1983; Mills, 1951). More recently we have also become aware of *aesthetic* or *sexualized labor* gaining ground on the labor market, i.e. work in which employer demands are not only concerned with work performance and emotion, but with employee corporeality including look and "sex appeal" (see Warhurst and Nickson, 2007, 2009). These and other tendencies are often cited when "work absorbing life" arguments are defended, and rightfully so.

Considering the amount of time we spend "working for the man," it is hard to overstate the impact that these changes have on our lives.

Yet there are gaps in the pessimistic line of reasoning that makes the generalized notion of the absorbed worker appear somewhat exaggerated. Most fundamentally: if we are all so absorbed by work, how can there be a critique of work? The typical old-school critical-theory answer is that capitalism absorbs everything, including its own negation (cf. Adorno, 2005 [1951]; Marcuse, 1955). Today, we also see veiled forms of neo-functionalism pushing the argument a bit further (cf. Contu, 2008; Fleming, 2009; Žižek, 2009); not only can capitalism integrate just about every form of symbolic negation, it also derives its nutriment from this very critique: "This is the time in which grim and downtrodden employees at the heart of corporate hegemony proclaim to be communist. And even the CEO agrees work sucks. Capitalism persists, not despite, but *because* of this mode of critical awareness," Carl Cederström and Peter Fleming (2012: 29) assert. But how can we know whether the employee proclaiming to be communist is just "incorporated" by the firm, or slowly awakening? Is it not easy to reject all types of employee resistance as – "in fact" – harnessed and "co-opted" forms of managerial discourse?

If we put aside the argument that everything happening within capitalism strengthens it, the everyday negations of work society become hard to ignore. The child's stubborn refusal to sit still, the teenager's truancies from school, the depressed forty-year-old doubting the meaning of his or her career, are all examples that anyone can either recognize in themselves or notice in their surroundings. In several major economies (including the US, the UK, Germany, Israel, Belgium) a growing majority of the working population says that they would quit their current jobs if they had the economic possibility to do so (for an overview, see Paulsen, 2008). Worldwide, only 13 percent of employees actually like going to work, according to a recent Gallup study. Sixty-three percent are "not engaged" the study says – these employees are essentially "checked out" – and the remaining 24 percent are not just unhappy at work; they are "more or less out to damage their company" (Gallup, 2013: 17). In Sweden, there is also a growing majority saying that they prefer future productivity gains to be cashed in as reduced working hours rather than higher wages (Sanne, 2007: 50). Many are even prepared to negotiate their current level of material wealth in order to free more time: 40 percent of fulltime working mothers say that they want to reduce their working hours even if it means decreased incomes (Larsson, 2010: 8). When the wish to weaken the obligation to work is so strong, it is odd, to say the least, that the main endeavor of our most powerful political parties is to "create jobs." Concerning the non-existence of a significant, formally organized countermovement, the pessimism of some of the authors referred to above seems well founded. The question, then, becomes: How do we survive work society? What do we do with our wish to work less and live more? Does *status quo* necessarily mean acceptance? And what happens with the unrealized longings for another life? In the laudable attempt to explain why people do not resist, the critique of work has made it harder to see how anyone could resist.

The relatively small literature on oppositional practices that we find elsewhere usually ignores labor and economic power. It is focused on symbolic and quite harmless types of resistance, or on singular acts of open defiance that sooner or later are knocked down. With the growing insight that these are far from pre-revolutionary times, we see a greater interest in so-called passive resistance (see Certeau, 1984; Graeber, 2004; Scott, 2012). As Federico Campagna puts it in *The Last Night*: "This is not the time for assaults, but for withdrawal." There may be a day in the future when we will see "the heroism of open battlefields" (Campagna, 2013: 44), but for now, efficient resistance entails other tactics.

The expanding research field of *organizational misbehavior* (see Ackroyd and Thompson, 1999; Thompson and Ackroyd, 1995) offers extraordinary insight into what these tactics can look like in the sphere of labor. It is not only relevant to organizational theorists, who too easily tend to assume that employees readily internalize whatever managerial dictates fall from above; it is also, and for similar reasons, relevant to critical theorists. The study of workplace sabotage, theft, effort bargaining, and other types of misbehaviors suggests longings and frustrations that seem incompatible with the concept of the absorbed worker. When I began working on this study, the explicitly political ambition was to add to this knowledge about everyday negations of work society. A vague intuition, bolstered by my pilot interviews, told me that people not working while "at work" was key to our understanding of how life can strike back at work, and more generally, how subjectivity can flourish in the very institution around which our most oppressive power structures are constructed. What I found, however, was a much more complex phenomenon, challenging not only clear-cut distinctions between "resistance" and "adjustment," but also the notion of the rational firm.

1.2 The empirical problem

Empty labor is everything you do at work that is not your work. All who work know what empty labor is. We all take breaks; we all go to the bathroom. Many of us also make private phone calls, write private e-mails, and surf the web for our own purposes while at work. Most of us spend a great deal of time on this type of non-work-related activities. Different reports suggest that the average time of empty labor per employee is between 1.5 to 3 hours a day (Blanchard and Henle, 2008; Blue et al., 2007; Bolchover, 2005; Carroll, 2007; Gouveia, 2012; Jost, 2005; Malachowski and Simonini, 2006; Mills et al., 2001). By measuring the flows of electronic audience between indexed internet sites, it has also been observed that 70 percent of the US internet traffic which by the turn of the millennium passed through pornographic sites did so during working hours and that 60 percent of all online purchases were made between 9 a.m. and 5 p.m. (Mills et al., 2001: 3). This kind of "cyberloafing" is not restricted to the US (in which most of the surveys have been conducted), but is also prevalent in nations such as Singapore (Vivien and Thompson, 2005), Germany (Rothlin and Werder, 2007), and Finland (Grahn, 2011).

Despite these survey results, there have been very few studies of empty labor, and even fewer (if any) conducted by a non-management scholar (i.e. without the managerial aim of learning how to control, reduce or gain from empty labor). Considering the recent media attention that the phenomenon has received, this is indeed a considerable "gap" in working life studies. As a result, the way work is publicly discussed seems to differ noticeably from how working life scholars study it. Why this discrepancy?

Consider the following headlines: "Swedes laze away their working hours" (*Dagens Nyheter*), "Facebook labelled a $5b waste of time" (*Sydney Morning Herald*), "You're wasting time at work right now, aren't you?" (*TIME*) (see West, 2007; White, 2012; Zenou, 2011). Although it is not a new phenomenon, the media attention is slowly making empty labor more and more evident to the collective mind. There may be many reasons for this. For instance, social media have made our engagement in private matters during working hours much more public. Each time we send an e-mail, update our Facebook status or twitter away a message, *when* and sometimes even *where* we do it is visible for all recipients, and so what used to be private may well become blown out of proportion. It may also be that there are companies with vested interests in keeping up employer demand for filtering and monitoring software that lie behind the "studies" on which some of the newspaper articles are based. Especially when inquiring into articles that present estimates on how much cyberloafing generally costs employers, I have often been unable to get access to more than press releases that reveal very little about how the studies were conducted.[1] The ill-concealed purpose of this pseudo-science business is at times appalling, and explaining how they time and again manage to get into some of the more respected newspapers may itself be subject for another book.[2]

Nevertheless, there is enough evidence to assume that not all headlines are taken out of thin air. Most of the more reliable studies of empty labor come from organizational psychology and (uncritical) management studies. The partiality of these studies is often evident already in the terms they use to describe the phenomenon. "Time waste" is probably the most frequently used term, which in itself judges what is "waste" and what is not. Otherwise, empty labor has also been referred to as: "anti-social behavior" (Penney et al., 2003), "counter-productive work behavior," "poor quality work" (Ones and Viswesvaran, 2003), "deviant behavior" (Vivien and Thompson, 2005), "shirking," (Henle and Blanchard, 2008), and "futzing" (Mills et al., 2001).

---

[1] According to Dan Verton (2000), 30 to 40 percent in productivity losses may be the result of cyberloafing, and Dan Malachowski and Jon Simonini (2006) attracted much media attention when asserting that time waste may cost US employers up to $544 billion annually. Based on similar calculations, Richard Cullen (2007) estimates that the collective working hours spent on the interactive internet site facebook.com cost Australian businesses $5 billion a year. In the US it has also been suggested that water-cooler conversations about the Super Bowl have the potential of costing employers up to $821.4 million in lost productivity (D'Abate, 2005: 1011).

[2] A typical example: in a relatively long article in a Swedish newspaper under the headline of "They put price tag on the drivel," the CEO of a firm called Before states that drivel at the workplace generally costs the average company one million dollars a year but that they have developed "a model" to push down the costs to $400,000. This was not an advertisement (Gianuzzi, 2008).

A central reason why empty labor has not been more studied by sociologists who share other partialities is that it is hard, though by no means impossible, to integrate the phenomenon of empty labor into the popular framework that speaks of *work intensification*. My study does not falsify the widespread impression, evident from an abundance of quantitative studies, of increasing work-related tension and strain, and more technically, of an average increase in the proportion of effective work performed for each working hour. What I suggest is that, behind these data, the intensity of work is stratified in layers that remain to be specified. For the moment, the measures most commonly used to measure work intensity suffer from several shortcomings. Tony Elger, who has written extensively on work intensification, contends that "any assessment of trends in effort and work pace is notoriously difficult as there is little appropriate aggregate data" (Elger, 1990: 83). Francis Green, who is one of the few who have conducted nationwide surveys in this field (mainly in Britain), also acknowledges that there are other problems associated with these studies (Green, 2001, 2004). For one, the type of subjective reports that are most frequently employed, makes for a considerably less precise measure than the time-based estimates referred to above. Survey questions like "Has there been any change in this workplace compared with 5 years ago in how hard people work here?" which are given five response alternatives along the Likert scale (Green, 2004: 723), can only reveal changes in the subjective experience of work intensity. Now that busyness has become the new "badge of honour" (Gershuny, 2005), we might suspect a desirability bias in how people respond (cf. Harpaz and Snir, 2002). Yet, when one looks closer at the statistics gathered by Green, these subjective experiences vary a lot. In one of his surveys (Green and McIntosh, 2001: 295), about 30 percent of the respondents claimed to be "working at very high speed" more than half of their working hours, whereas 30 percent said they "never" did so, and 17 percent "almost never." While the majority seems to enjoy relatively calm working days, we thereby have a thin segment that works at the pinnacle of its capacity all the time. When this segment grows from including 7 percent to 10 percent of the working population, there is an average intensification of work. But this intensification does not affect everyone.

My focus is on the opposite extreme, on those who never work hard. Why has so little, if anything, in the sociology of work been written about this group, whereas the articles and books about the stressed-out fraction of humanity can be counted in the thousands? The major part of my theoretical discussion will be concerned with this issue. Certainly, unperturbed slackers constitute less of a social problem, but might they not tell us something valuable about working life, something that might even help us to understand the intensification of work on a deeper level?

1.3 The (ir)rational institution

Modern sociology, both in critical and legitimizing versions, has a long tradition of emphasizing the *rationality* of capitalist production. This emphasis can even be observed in the study of workplace misbehavior; whereas management tends to be depicted as an anonymous, almost impersonal force, those resisting management are *individuals* with emotions and frustrations – irrational and human. This divide between the rational structure and the irrational individual was unfortunately also quite present in my pre-understanding as I approached the field of empty labor. This study will present an abundance of examples where it is rather "the structure," represented by the organization of the labor process, that appears to be irrational. For a while, I strongly believed that what the interviewees told me was spectacular. Now, I am not sure if anyone outside the tribe of social scientists would find any of my results surprising.

Returning to the media reports, the scandals concerning employees' online activities have succeeded each other at increasingly short intervals. During 2010 in Sweden, twenty municipalities reported having fired employees for "inappropriate" internet usage (Lindström, 2010). When it came out that a public authority like the Swedish Migration Board had had some employees surfing the web for private use up to 40 hours a month, there was a great deal of moralizing concerning employee behavior (Brattberg, 2007; otherwise, the debates following these scandals have mainly treated the degree to which employers have installed electronic surveillance devices to control their employees). Less has been said about the apparent possibility of surfing long hours on the web without any noticeable decline in performance.[3]

---

[3] Of course, the debate on workplace surveillance is most legitimate and of almost global relevance. In 2005, the American Management Association survey found that 76 percent of companies monitor which websites their

Take for example the Swedish Civil Aviation Administration, where seven persons lost their jobs after it was revealed that some of them had been visiting pornographic websites during up to 75 percent of their working hours: whereas the dismay mainly concerned the most obvious offense, that they had visited *pornographic* websites, there was no reflection on the fact that well-educated professionals to all appearances could spend 75 percent of their working hours on (very) private activities without anyone outside the automated monitoring system taking notice (cf. Roos Holmborg, 2009). Why so?

My guess is that what may appear as an empirical outrage to many sociologists could be more of a triviality to the "unenlightened masses." Not only in the sociology of work, but also in the wider "conflict tradition" (cf. Collins, 1994) of sociology, the phantom of rationality has long been assumed to govern production. The notion of a ruthless capitalist rationalization process that, as if governed by an anonymous law of nature, speeds production and colonizes human societies (until the system implodes) was already present in Karl Marx. Marx was among the first to predict the intensification of labor, or, as he put it, that once "a normal working-day whose length is fixed by law" was legally established we would see a "closer filling up of the pores of the working-day, or condensation of labor to a degree that is attainable only within the limits of the shortened working-day" (1976 [1867]: 534). In Max Weber, who is best known for his "iron cage" of rationality, we find many examples of the same belief in modern rationality, and outside the conflict tradition, Émile Durkheim happily praised the "order" of this system which, at least in his early theory, was derived from the division of labor. With such great grandfathers, it is no wonder that sociologists have been so occupied by trying to discern different rationalities (ranging from cold instrumentality to the all-embracing principles of functionalism) in our institutions and especially in work. But what if work is no more than a bad joke for many employees? What if the very idea that work should necessarily have anything to do with production is unfounded?

Anyone familiar with a fraction of the last fifteen years of western popular culture will know that there is a great gap between how

employees visit and that 65 percent use filtering software to block certain websites (Riedy and Wen, 2010: 87). It has also been estimated that 27 million online employees are monitored internationally (Ball, 2010: 88).

sociologists write about work and how work is depicted in more crowd-pleasing productions. Consider a sitcom television series like *The Office*, or a cult film like *Office Space*. Although these accounts are parodies, it is precisely the lack of both rationality and meaning in office work that makes for the satire. "Put the key of despair into the lock of apathy," Ricky Gervais says through one of his characters in *The Office*, "turn the knob of mediocrity slowly and open the gates of despondency – welcome to a day in the average office." This is a pretty clear message, and even if part of the purpose is to provoke laughter it might be said that "humor is also a way of saying something serious" (T.S. Eliot). In fact, some of the most influential works on working life that we have seen recently (i.e. that reach a public) have indeed been humorously written, and most successfully by office workers themselves. In her bestseller *Bonjour Paresse*, Corinne Maier offers a valuable inside perspective on the corporate world that according to her is "shrouded in mystery." Maier opens the book (that eventually cost her job) by declaring that social science has miserably failed to understand the mechanisms of office work: "Millions of people work in business, but its world is opaque. This is because the people who talk about it the most – and I mean the university professors – have never worked there; they aren't *in the know*" (Maier, 2006: 4).

Maier's contention is that work is increasingly reduced to "make-believe," that at the office, "image counts more than product, seduction more than production" (Maier, 2006: 49). Under these circumstances, pretended obedience and fake commitment become part of the labor process in which the slightest dissociation from simulation may result in the collective embarrassment of everyone. As she recalls:

One day, in the middle of a meeting on motivation, I dared to say that the only reason I came to work was to put food on the table. There were fifteen seconds of absolute silence, and everyone seemed uncomfortable. Even though the French word for work, *'travail,'* etymologically derives from an instrument of torture, it's imperative to let it be known, no matter the circumstance, that you are working *because you are interested in your work*. (Maier, 2006: 34)

Whereas "the absorbed worker" is thus recognized *as a role*, it is precisely the difference between what we say we do and what we actually do that Maier highlights. This gap between image and substance is also a recurring theme in Scott Adams' *Dilbert* series. Again and again,

Adams seems to question not only the link between work and rationality, but also the relation between work and productivity: "Work
can be defined as 'anything you'd rather not be doing.' Productivity
is a different matter" (Adams, 1996: 95). In the preface to *This is the
Part Where You Pretend to Add Value*, Adams open-heartedly gives
his personal impressions of sixteen years of employment at Crocker
National Bank and Pacific Bell:

If I had to describe my sixteen years of corporate work with one phrase,
it would be 'pretending to add value.'... You might have noticed that corporations hum along no matter who is sick, vacationing, or recently dead.
Any one person's value on any particular day is vanishingly small. The key
to career advancement is appearing valuable despite all hard evidence to the
contrary.... If you add any *actual* value to your company today, your career
is probably not moving in the right direction. Real work is for people at the
bottom who plan to stay there. (Adams, 2008: 6)

The list of office workers who have presented the same type of analysis can be made much longer. In *The Living Dead*, David Bolchover
laments "the dominance of image over reality, of obfuscation over
clarity, of politics over performance" (Bolchover, 2005: 68), and in
City Slackers, Steve McKevitt, a disillusioned "business and communications expert," gloomily declares: "In a society where presentation is everything it's no longer about what you do, it's about how
you look like you're doing it" (McKevitt, 2006: 32). The simulation, the glossing over, the loss of meaning, the jargon, the games, the
office politics, the crises, the boredom, the despair, and the sense of
unreality – these are ingredients that often reappear in popular
accounts of working life. The risk when they only appear in popular
culture is that we begin regarding them as metaphors or exaggerations
that may well apply to our own jobs but not to work in general. But
what would happen if we started taking these "unserious" accounts of
working life more seriously?

Consider the last novel by David Foster Wallace, *The Pale King*,
in which it is described how an IRS worker dies by his desk and
sits there for days without anyone noticing that he is dead (Wallace,
2011: 27). This might be read as a brilliant satire of how meaningless
work sucks out life until no one notices whether you are dead or alive.
However, in the strict sense of the word, it was *not* satire. In 2004, a tax
office official in Finland died in exactly the same way while checking

tax returns. Although there were about 100 other staff on the same floor and some thirty employees at the auditing department where he worked, it took them two days to notice that he was dead. None of them missed his services; he was only found when a friend stopped by to have lunch with him (BBC, 2004). If all we see are helpless individuals vainly resisting or being crushed under the forces of rationalization and work intensification, how can we explain the unheeded existence of this dead body during its first two days at work?[4]

1.4 Aims and scope

The following two chapters will be devoted to critical inquiry into the notion of the rational iron cage in which submissive employees are but victims of managerial dictates and intensification programs. This preparatory work is not only necessary to approach the phenomenon of empty labor from a perspective in which worker resistance and the irrationality of management are but anomalies, it also addresses a long, still ongoing, debate in critical workplace studies with deep roots in critical theory. My main argument is that this debate lacks a clear concept of the subject that recognizes every individual's capacity for autonomy – a capacity that is first and foremost realized in the act of resistance to different power centers. Among theorists who have elaborated this concept, there are many questions left unanswered. Most fundamentally, the subject has mainly been theorized outside the sphere of wage labor. Since wage labor represents a type of sociality in which power is always present (e.g. between employer and employee), we cannot expect the same expressions of subjectivity there as elsewhere. As I will argue, the notion of resistance and submission as *either/or* phenomena has greatly impaired the study of workplace

---

[4] In an interview for AFP, Anita Wickström, who was then director at the Helsinki tax office, provides her own explanation: "He was working alone very much and often visiting companies, while his friends and colleagues who used to have lunch or coffee with him were busy in meetings or outside the office at the time" (AFP, 2004). When I contacted Wickström (eight years after the incident) to verify that the story was not an urban legend, she also said that the tax official did not belong to the team of accountants; he had his own field of expertise in which he worked closer to clients than to his colleagues. To be fair, he could have been utterly busy doing a job whose consequences were not immediate but still of great value. His death proves nothing – it just raises questions.

resistance. The first part of this book will be devoted to outlining an approach allowing the study of empty labor with a less categorical pre-understanding.

I have already defined empty labor as the part of our working hours that we spend on other things than our job. Of course, this definition can be expanded and endlessly elaborated. A problem that immediately suggests itself is how to define "work," "labor" or "a job" (see Applebaum, 1992; Arendt, 1958; Karlsson, 1986; Kosík, 1979). I have tried to be as pragmatic as possible by proceeding from what workers themselves conceive of as "work" and "not work" in their own context. The empirical material consists of interviews with employees who spend large proportions of their working hours on empty labor. In the selection of interviewees I have tried to go around the monstrous semantics of "work" by excluding researchers, journalists, and other "entrepreneurs" who flatter themselves by saying that they "always work." Certainly, the problem has not been entirely avoided by this pragmatic circumvention, which is why I return to it towards the end of the book, yet it works for my purposes. I have so far encountered very few (no one amongst the interviewees) who find it hard to draw a line between empty labor and things "you'd rather not be doing" to return to Adam's concept of work.

With the publications of *All quiet at the workplace front?* and *Organizational misbehaviour*, Paul Thompson and Stephen Ackroyd managed to turn the tables regarding the negligence of workplace resistance by collecting and synthesizing a wide range of studies (mainly belonging to the school of labor process studies) and by formulating a field that they chose to call "organizational misbehaviour" – defined as "anything you do at work you are not supposed to do" (Ackroyd and Thompson, 1999: 2) – as opposed to the established discipline of "organizational behavior." Ackroyd and Thompson argue that the labor process is the result of a constant struggle between employees and management in which several factors or "appropriations" are at stake – the appropriation of identity, product, work, and time. Empty labor covers all their examples of time appropriation, including small time perks and more serious time wasting. Yet there is an important difference: empty labor does not necessarily imply organizational misbehavior. Whereas time appropriation requires a subject, i.e. an employee actively taking back the time that officially belongs to the employer, empty labor can emerge for other reasons. Due to my own preconceptions concerning the rationality of work, what I did not consider when beginning this research project was that at some workplaces, not working was not as much of an offense as at other workplaces. In many cases, empty labor was in a gray area, not entirely legitimate, but harmless enough for the employer or manager to "turn a blind eye" to it.

With the overarching aim of understanding the links between empty labor, subjectivity, and worker resistance, I have conducted the study with two leading questions:

How? How is it possible to get away with working half of your working hours or less? Is it an individual pursuit or is there collective organization? Is it known to management or is it concealed? How do you manage not getting noticed? How do you spend the hours freed by empty labor?

Why? What motivates empty labor? Do slackers themselves conceive of it as an expression of dissent or just laziness? Is it something that you can mention to your colleagues, your friends or is shame involved? Is it politically motivated and in that case, how – against management, the firm, work itself, or what?

The why-questions were initially of most interest to me. When I started doing my interviews, the idea was to map out a "heterology" (Certeau, 1986) of employee dissent, to discern a form of workplace resistance that had largely been neglected in working life studies and hear how employees themselves regard the work that they are so good at avoiding ("give voice!"). Eventually the how-questions and especially the complex interaction between the time-appropriating employee and the rest of the organization came into focus. How can the same "goofing off" that Frederick Winslow Taylor once described as "the greatest evil with which the working-people of both England and America are now afflicted" (Taylor, 1919: 14) today be tacitly accepted at some workplaces? And what consequences does it have for our understanding of subjectivity and workplace resistance?

1.5 Disposition

Beginning with broader theoretical issues concerning subjectivity and resistance, I gradually concentrate the analysis on the empirical phenomenon at the center of the study. The reader whose main interest is in the different expressions of empty labor may jump directly to

Chapter 4. The more empirical chapters are, however, structured with the goal not only of describing the dynamics of empty labor but also of understanding it in the broader context referred to above.

In Chapter 2, I develop the opening thoughts of this introduction relating to how power at work has generally been analyzed in critical theory with relation to the concept of the subject. The chapter also introduces the reader to relevant debates in labor process studies and critical management studies and elaborates the theoretical interests in studying different forms of workplace resistance and dissent. In Chapter 3, I discuss the most advanced attempts at rediscovering the resistant subject and why studies of organizational misbehavior including empty labor still constitute a missing piece in "Grand Theory" discussions of subjectivity. The overemphasis on open (as opposed to covert) forms of resistance and the dichotomist notion of resistance and adjustment are two factors, beside the rationalist conception of work, that contribute to this situation.

In Chapter 4, I break down the concept of empty labor into four categories according to which the three chapters that follow are organized. I argue that each case of empty labor differs with respect to how much it (a) emanates from the active recalcitrance on the part of the worker, and (b) stems from a lack of work tasks for the individual worker. Chapter 5 is based on recalcitrance versions of empty labor. In the form of five propositions on how to appropriate time while at work, I address the how-questions mentioned above. Chapter 6 discusses the same type of empty labor, but now in relation to the why-questions. Why are employees so eager not to work and how do their answers advance previous discussions of subjectivity?

In Chapter 7, I turn to the real surprise in the empirical material, namely to the type of empty labor that stems from lack of work tasks. How is such a lack possible in these times of increasing work intensification and anorectically slim organizations? And how does it happen that some employees who sustain long periods of empty labor may do so against their will? What is wrong with them, and why is it so difficult to start working again once your job is permeated by empty labor? Chapter 8 is, in part, also an attempt at answering these questions, but this time in relation to the issue of whether empty labor, in all its variations, is yet another example of "incorporated resistance" that gives the employee a sense of "fooling the system" while leaving the same system intact. While offering a critique of this type of analysis, I return to the question of power at work. To call something resistance, we must know what the resistance is directed against, and to the extent that there is no rationale of maximal efficiency in one's job, empty labor can indeed be yet another example of how work loses its meaning. In Chapter 9, I conclude by posing some final questions on the meaning of "work" and what resisting it might entail.

2 | *Power at work*

In this chapter, I further the study by challenging some theoretical notions that have not only prevented the study of empty labor, but also of organizational misbehavior as such. Generally in sociology, studies of subjectivity and acts of resistance have largely ignored the sphere of labor. It is as if we lose our capacity to think and react as soon as we enter the workplace, whereas we are able to resist all types of domination as soon as we step out. How could work become such a black box? Why is it still assumed to be the stronghold of instrumental reason?

One of few attempts to explain this can be found in Thompson and Ackroyd's writings where the "virtual removal of labour as an active agency of resistance in a considerable portion of theory and research" (1995: 615) is mostly related to "the shift in radical theory to Foucauldian and post-structuralist perspectives" (1995: 622). But Thompson and Ackroyd write very little about how other post-structuralist perspectives than the Foucauldian one have contributed to this tendency, and they hardly consider other theoretical influences. This is unfortunate for two reasons: firstly, their analysis fails to acknowledge a more widespread tendency that links versions of Marxism, critical theory and labor process theory to structuralism and Foucauldianism, namely the overriding emphasis on the invincible domination of the power apparatus and the hopeless obedience of the worker collective. Secondly, it limits the sociological relevance of organizational misbehavior while reducing the study of it to yet another distinctive mark between labor process theory and critical management studies. As has become clear after the intervention of Thompson and Ackroyd, researchers from both schools are in fact perfectly able to study acts of resistance and dissent. Nevertheless, we still have a few subject-denying concepts that influence all schools which can be termed "critical" (i.e. that share an emancipatory interest). These are the concepts that I address in this chapter.

To begin with, labor process theory has from the beginning, and particularly in the pioneering work of Harry Braverman, tended to emphasize the ruthless rationality of the labor process that, in the process of "deskilling," reduces the worker to a cog in the machinery. This notion stretches back to Marx and even earlier to Adam Smith's theory of the division of labor. Before returning to Michel Foucault and his reformulation of "the subject," I discuss the early Frankfurt School and the notion of "false consciousness" that influenced both Braverman and the young school of critical management studies. I argue that each of these three theoretical notions has nurtured the view of labor as an institution of obedience rather than struggle, and I also give examples of how this view is expressed in critical workplace studies.

But first, I will briefly mention a more general denial of "the subject" as defined by Alain Touraine. Touraine early challenged the pessimism emanating from structuralism and the first generation of the Frankfurt school, and he did so by studying different examples of what it means to be a subject. In order to avoid the great confusion that surrounds the concept of "the subject," I will present Touraine's definition which is the one that I will base my analysis upon and eventually attempt to develop. As I will argue in the next chapter, beneath apparent consensus and recognition there may be many practices of resistance that take place "undercover." In order to see them, we must not only do empirical research that looks beyond the immediately observable; we must also become aware of conceptions of domination that have been around for so long that we sometimes take them for granted.

2.1 The denial of the subject

E.P. Thompson once summarized the argument of this chapter with the following words:

Whether Frankfurt School or Althusser, they are marked by their very heavy emphasis upon the ineluctable weight of ideological modes of domination – domination which destroys every space for the initiative or creativity of the mass of the people – a domination from which only the enlightened minority of intellectuals can struggle free. No doubt this ideological predisposition was itself nurtured within the terrible experiences of Fascism, of mass indoctrination by the media, and of Stalinism itself. But it is a sad premise from which Socialist theory should start (all men and women, except for us, are originally stupid) and one which is bound to lead on to pessimistic or authoritarian conclusions. Moreover, it is likely to reinforce the intellectual's disinclination to extend himself in practical political activity. (Thompson, 1995 [1978]: 250)

While both the Frankfurt School and Louis Althusser are poor examples of lack of political activity, many have criticized the elitist elements of their theories and the tendency to neglect both individual and collective resistance. One of the most vigorous critics is Touraine, who attributes this tendency not only to radical – or "Socialist" – theory, but to the very project of science: "The whole history of social sciences – and even more of natural sciences – could be summed up as the elimination of the concept of the subject" (Touraine, 2005: 199). The same critique of sociology in particular can be found in many versions, notably (and ironically) from the same Frankfurt philosophers that Thompson and Touraine criticize (see especially Horkheimer, 1995 [1937]; Marcuse, 1941). As Hans Skjervheim contends, "the dominating sociological portrayal of man is 'man without transcendence,'" a man "subordinated to social facticity" (Skjervheim, 1971: 59). What separates Touraine from other critics is his elaboration of a theoretical framework centered on the opposite notion: "man *with* transcendence," a social being which is not *only* social but also capable of resisting the social.

Touraine here represents a portion of twentieth century French philosophy that is considerably less à la mode in critical workplace studies than the post-structuralist school associated with Michel Foucault. Whereas the latter has his very own notion of "the subject" (to which we shall return) and a competing notion can be found in empirical phenomenology (primarily denoting the experience of meaning, see Schutz, 1967), Touraine proposes a *sociological concept of the subject* derived from the existentialist axiom of human agency. Here, the capacity to negate the existing order is not only acknowledged but the very fundament for the analysis of social action. From this perspective, workplace resistance, misbehavior, recalcitrance, dissent etc. become less anomalistic than in other philosophical anthropologies; they are simply signs of life and all the more likely to occur in the hierarchic organization characteristic of wage labor. The Althusserian interest for "ideology" and "order" is thus reversed in what remains of French existentialism. "The question of the subject has remained central for me, as it was for Sartre," Gorz (2010: 3) comments. "We are born to ourselves as subjects – in other words, as subjects irreducible to what other people and society ask us to be and allow us to be." What else we choose to be is not only an "existential question" for the individual, but also open for sociological study; a perpetual movement through which social change (or the lack of it) can be understood. The subject is thus Touraine's answer to the question that lies at the very heart of sociology:

> Notwithstanding those schools of thought that reduce social action to ratio-nal choices of an economic nature, or to the manifestation of cultural pat-terns or social institutions considered to be determinants of individual and collective action, we constantly face the question: how does the distancing from established norms lead to creative freedom, rejection of old rules or non socially regulated emotions and finally to the creation of new norms? (Touraine, 2000a: 901)

I cannot sufficiently stress how radically Touraine's concept of the subject differs from other subject definitions. Touraine describes the subject as a type of intentionality that always results in action – it should not be understood ontologically as a certain creature, nor essentially as a quality of the "self" of the individual. The subject is fundamentally an anti-essentialist concept, but at the same time the opposite of the docile, submissive "body" that Foucault associated with being a subject.[1] Touraine defines the subject as the will (or sometimes "attempt") of the individual to become an actor (cf. Touraine, 1995: 207; 2000b: 13). The subject should not be confused with the ego, Touraine says: "nothing could be more antithetical to the Subject than the consciousness of the Ego, introspection or that most extreme form of the obsession with identity: narcissism" (Touraine, 1995: 210). The human subject is rather a resistor of the established

---

[1] The vagueness of the term "essence" has generated a confused debate between structuralists and existentialists concerning which school is the most "essentialist" (for a recent example, see Berardi, 2009). Although the existentialist school emanating from Martin Heidegger and branching off to Herbert Marcuse, Jean-Paul Sartre et al. began as a critique of universal concepts of human nature, it might be argued that the notion of the human being as a creature that projects itself into potentiality itself assumes some type of essence (free will). The question then becomes in what sense the denial of a situated freedom of the will represents a critique of essentialism. Since I do not wish to engage in the debate, I will leave that question open.

order; it is the negation of both the world of economic rationality and the world of community by which individuals and groups engage in self-creation struggles and alternative value settings.

Whereas subjectivity traditionally was incorporated in the notion of deity (a god who created the universe as an act of will), modernity can be described as an age of anthropocentrism followed by the scientific undermining of this anthropocentrism yielding to the growing belief in natural and social laws. With Charles Darwin and Sigmund Freud, it was established that impersonal processes taking place behind our backs rule the world. In social science, the concept of "structure" took a central place in Marx, Durkheim, and Weber, and also the notion of an ongoing rationalization that over the years has become increasingly anonymous in sociology and economy. These two notions were well integrated in critical theory which, according to Touraine, permeated continental sociology when it was at its most influential: "Mid-century European sociology was clearly dominated by critical theory, even if at the same time it was deeply influenced by Talcott Parsons' work, as the last great thinkers of 'classical' sociology" (Touraine, 2005: 201).

The elimination of the concept of the subject was first announced by Touraine in the 1980s but is still a compelling analysis that does not only denote Grand Theory sociology, but also libido-centered Freudianism and recent forms of chemico-neurological naturalism. Everywhere the authority of Science points at evidence against agency, that we are governed by external powers. When internalized, this notion tends to become self-fulfilling – withdrawal, cynicism, and political apathy are not only due to the elimination of *the concept* of the subject but indicative of how the subject as such is withering. In reaction, Touraine reformulates sociology as "the science of social action" which aims at raising the awareness of how *actions* – not nature, essence, instinct, desire or any other type of *being* – constitute the basic elements of society.

Touraine's early empirical work includes a number of case studies of the May movement (Touraine, 1971a), the Polish Solidarity-movement (Touraine, 1983a), and the anti-nuclear movement (Touraine, 1983b). He is most prominent in the sociology of social movements but referred to less in studies of the workplace. In recent years, the challenges of globalization have occupied his writings, still highlighting the potentiality of and threat against the subject: "A main obstacle to this subject-centered approach is the idea that, in a globalized economy, we are helpless; we cannot do anything against powerful financial and economic transnational corporations," Touraine (2005: 209) writes. Although this idea is highly central to critical workplace studies of today, there are other ideas at play behind the scholarly marginalization of organizational misbehavior. Before moving on to developing the notion of the subject and its relevance for a critical sociology of work in the next chapter, I will discuss the three most relevant to critical management studies and labor process theory. Firstly, the idea that the worker has been transformed into an appendage of the machine. Secondly, the idea that we are being manipulated and induced with false consciousness. Thirdly, the idea that the subject is in fact an object. The aim is not to refute the validity of these accounts – they are all legitimate analyses of sociality and working life, in particular the more empirically founded deskilling thesis. My aim is to demonstrate how they have been exaggerated into what may be regarded as the intellectual denial of the subject.

2.2 The appendage of the machine

One explanation of why studies of work intensification have been conducted with the one-sided focus on average trends described in the introduction is because work intensification is congruent with the modern conception of work as an efficient, rational machine. A central, if not *the* central, part of its rationality is to constantly eliminate empty labor from the labor process, to make workers work harder. Critics have generally not been concerned with questioning the exact workings of this rationality, and especially not with distinguishing spheres where it has no bearing, but rather with demonstrating its domination and ferocity. This is not only a trait of early Marxism and today's Foucauldian working life studies, it can also be said about the school from which most studies of organizational misbehavior have issued.

In Thompson and Ackroyd's discussion of organizational misbehavior, one might easily get the impression that struggle and resistance has been at the "core" (Thompson, 1983) of labor process theory from the beginning, whereas critical management studies, having introduced Foucault into the analysis, are more prone to bring out mechanisms of discipline and domination. Others have pursued this thesis even further; in John Hassard et al. (2001: 339) it is claimed that "whereas Braverman attempted to restore confidence in the potential of the working class to fulfill its Marxist destiny to lead a revolutionary transformation of society, any such confidence in the second coming of communism has long since evaporated from critical management studies." However, as Thompson and Ackroyd themselves point out, the founder of labor process theory was not terribly interested in indicating how this revolutionary potential was expressed in the everyday life of the working class (Ackroyd and Thompson, 1999: 47). What we see in *Labor and Monopoly Capital* is rather an analysis of how craft work, and with it, the agency of the worker are crushed under the industrial machine, or in Braverman's words, how

the remarkable development of machinery becomes, for most of the working population, the source not of freedom but of enslavement, not of mastery but of helplessness, and not of the broadening of the horizon of labor but of the confinement of the worker within a blind round of servile duties in which the machine appears as the embodiment of science and the worker as little or nothing. (Braverman, 1998 [1974]: 134)

In a wider perspective, it might even be argued that this theme stretches back to the roots of social science. Before Braverman formulated the deskilling thesis, C. Wright Mills (1951: 228) lamented "the historical destruction of craftsmanship" in *White Collar*, and long before Mills published his classic study, Weber, Durkheim, and Marx were all concerned with the division of labor and the social pathologies it entailed among workers and bureaucrats. Marx most famously announced how the worker "becomes an appendage of the machine" and how "it is only the most simple, most monotonous, and most easily acquired knack, that is required of him" (Marx and Engels, 1998 [1848]: 17). Even before Marx, Joseph Proudhon made a very similar analysis in *What Is Property?* where he claimed that "the laborer who consumes his wages *is* a machine which destroys and reproduces" (Proudhon, 1876 [1840]: 210, emphasis added). To reduce the "laborer" to a machine was even more *comme il faut* among the founders of liberalism (with the notable exception of John Stuart Mill (cf. Bauman, 2004)). The people produced in factories that Marx described as "monsters," "stunted" and "crippled," as ruled by "an entirely military discipline," were already in Smith known as "semi-imbeciles" (see Gorz, 1982: 26). Smith, who was fundamentally positive about the division of labor, believing that "education" could solve some of its mind-numbing effects for "the great body of the people," did not mince his words when it came to actually describing it:

The man whose whole life is spent in performing a few simple operations, of which the effects, too, are perhaps always the same, or very nearly the same, has no occasion to exert his understanding, or to exercise his invention, in finding out expedients for removing difficulties which never occur. He naturally loses, therefore, the habit of such exertion, and generally becomes as stupid and ignorant as it is possible for a human creature to become. The torpor of his mind renders him not only incapable of relishing or bearing a part in any rational conversation, but of conceiving any generous, noble, or tender sentiment, and consequently of forming any just judgment concerning many even of the ordinary duties of private life.... His dexterity at his own particular trade seems, in this manner, to be acquired at the expense of his intellectual, social, and martial virtues. (Smith, 2007 [1776]: 506)

Smith's cynicism concerning the division of labor is remarkably similar to that of the man who devoted his entire life to fragmenting work into pieces. Taylor's cynicism is, however, inverted in the sense that whereas Smith assumes that labor dulls the intellect, Taylor takes for granted that the worker is, or at least should be, stupid from the beginning. This becomes particularly blatant in his description of the mental requirements for an industrial worker:

Now one of the very first requirements for a man who is fit to handle pig iron as a regular occupation is that he shall be so stupid and so phlegmatic that he more nearly resembles in his mental make-up the ox than any other type. The man who is mentally alert and intelligent is for this very reason entirely unsuited to what would, for him, be the grinding monotony of work of this character. Therefore the workman who is best suited to handling pig iron is unable to understand the real science of doing this class of work. He is so stupid that the word 'percentage' has no meaning to him, and he must consequently be trained by a man more intelligent than himself into the habit of working in accordance with the laws of this science before he can be successful. (Taylor, 1919: 59)

Returning to Braverman, much of his critique of Taylorism is effectively articulated just by quoting Taylor himself (although he must have missed the passage above). For Taylor, the destruction of craft work was an important step towards efficiency not only because it made the optimization of each operation possible, but also because it entailed taking power from the worker collective with its "natural" inclination towards "soldiering," and giving it to management – or as Taylor would have it, to Science. Although Braverman (1998 [1974]: 104) noted that beneath the "apparent habituation, the hostility of workers to the degenerated forms of work which are forced upon them continues as a subterranean stream," it is not an exaggeration to talk about "Braverman's success at depicting a progressively de-skilled and decidedly non-revolutionary working class" (Tanner et al., 1992: 440). His psychology was primarily concerned with the degradation of both work and workers lamenting the lost "unity of thought and action, conception and execution, hand and mind" (Braverman, 1998 [1974]: 118).

Braverman also made reference to Marcuse who before him analyzed the relation between technology and sensorial alienation which he, in his turn, mainly took from Heidegger (see Feenberg, 1991). That theme has become increasingly popular in combination with Touraine's concept of the post-industrial society. It is at the core of Richard Sennett's (1998) notion of the "corrosion of character" and is even more central in André Gorz's critique of immaterial labor which "disqualifies the senses, steals the certainties of perception, takes the ground from under our feet" (Gorz, 1999: 113) and makes the human body dependent upon "chemical prostheses to 'tranquilize' its nervous system stressed as it is by the violations it endures" (Gorz, 2003: 112, my translation). Like Marcuse, Braverman does not consider the Taylorist degradation of work an unavoidable element of technological development. Technology does not have to constrain the worker in the labor process and it is not size, complexity, or speed that is the problem but the manner in which the worker is controlled through technology. "The application of power to various hand tools such as drills, saws, grindstones, wrenches, chisels, rivet hammers, staplers, sanders, buffers, etc. has not changed the relation between worker and machine," Braverman (1998 [1974]: 130) notes. These tools are in the hands of the workers and might even lead to an increase in skills required by the operator. The deskilling process begins and evolves when the machine fixes the motion path of the operation, when we have multiple function machines predetermining the sequence of operations, and later with the remote control of the machine, with numerical control and machines which automatically record and correct the performance of the worker (Braverman, 1998 [1974]: 130–54). This is how the worker becomes "subject to discipline," or to put it differently, this is how work becomes the hub of social order (cf. Gorz, 1989; Offe and Heinze, 1992; Paulsen, 2010). With the ideology of work that grew out of industrialism, craft and skill were superseded by the virtue of obedience. Consequently, any individual impairment or obstacle to work became "feared because they cast their victims outside the reach of the panoptical drill on which the maintenance of social order relied; people out of employment were also masterless people, people out of control – not surveilled, not monitored, not subjected to any regular, sanctions-fortified, routine" (Bauman, 2004: 18). This view of the ideology of work was also adopted by the early Frankfurt philosophers who, for the same reason, made work and its infiltration into all spheres of culture and society the main target of their critique – "concentration camps are a key to all these things" Theodor Adorno said, "in the society we live in all work is like the work in the camps" (Adorno and Horkheimer, 2010 [1956]: 34).[2]

In a similar vein, Jürgen Habermas made "work" the analytical category representing instrumental rationality and the opposite of "interaction." Although Habermas has written almost nothing about work more concretely, as an ideal type "work" constitutes the core of "the system" that in his analysis colonizes the lifeworld. The colonization thesis was fundamentally a clever abstraction of Marcuse's critique of technology. Like Gorz, Marcuse argues that modern organizations are too complex to be governed by communicative reason and that instead of trying to humanize labor, alienation should rather be "completed" by "general automatization of labor, reduction of labor time to a minimum, and exchangeability of functions" (Marcuse, 1955: 152). An important difference between Habermas and Marcuse is that whereas Marcuse regards this as the consequence of interests of capital – or to use the term preferred by Marcuse, "the rationality of domination" – being materialized in technology (see Marcuse, 1955, 1998, 2009 [1968]), Habermas naturalizes the technological development by deriving it from pure instrumentality. Based on a very weak

---

[2] And to this Max Horkheimer replied: "Take care, you risk coming close to the idea of enjoying work. The uselessness of the work and derision deprive people of the last bit of pleasure they might obtain from it, but I do not know if that is the crucial factor. No ideology survives in the camps. Whereas our society still insists that work is good" (Adorno and Horkheimer, 2010 [1956]: 34). It should be noticed that this probably is the most extreme criticism of work that I have encountered.

analysis (mostly taken from Arnold Gehlen), Habermas argues that "there is an immanent connection between the technology known to us and the structure of purposive-rational action." This connection is manifest in the history of technology and its gradual replacement of human action:

At first the functions of the motor apparatus (hands and legs) were augmented and replaced, followed by energy production (of the human body), the functions of the sensory apparatus (eyes, ears, and skin), and finally by the functions of the governing center (the brain). Technological development thus follows a logic that corresponds to the structure of purposive-rational action regulated by its own results, which is in fact the structure of *work*. (Habermas, 1971: 87)

"Realizing this" he continues, "it is impossible to envisage how ... we could renounce technology, more particularly *our* technology, in favor of a qualitatively different one" (ibid.).

It might be argued that Habermas in this early text sowed the seed to a new type of critical theory that has little concrete to say about technology and the institution where the majority of adults spend most of their waking hours (cf. Carleheden, 1996; Feenberg, 1991). Habermas would later stop referring to "work" as the opposite of interaction "in order to avoid a too concrete apprehension of his action theory" according to Mikael Carleheden (1996: 52), yet the functionalist naturalization of both work and technology remains in the very dichotomization between lifeworld and system. As in the tradition of "Grand Theory" (Mills, 2000 [1959]: 25–50), work is a black box that can be studied in terms of its input and output, but whose internal workings are simply assumed to be rational or, at best, unknown.

The idea that resistance and democratization will more likely take place in civil society than in the sphere of labor has gathered momentum since 1968 and the intellectualist "disaffection with the working class" (Hassard et al., 2001: 343) in mainstream sociology. It is also noticeable in the works of Touraine and the sociology of social movements. Within this referential framework, any sign of subjectivity at work becomes an anomaly – thus supporting conventional organizational psychology and management studies in which phenomena such as "social loafing" or "cyberslacking" are turned into "dysfunctional behaviors" that with the help of Science should be eradicated (cf. Griffin et al., 1998; Miller, 2007; Vivien et al., 2002). The study of subjectivity at work is therefore of importance not only to the sociology of work, but also to general sociology.

2.3 The imprint of false consciousness

In his critique of the Marxist concept of ideology, James C. Scott (1991) makes a distinction between thin and thick theories of false consciousness. I discussed the thin theory in the previous section: the idea that the dominant ideology achieves compliance by control mechanisms and the practice of power so that subordinate groups are convinced that the existing social order is "natural" or inevitable. The thick theory of false consciousness goes a bit further: "the thick version claims that a dominant ideology works its magic by persuading subordinate groups to believe actively in the values that explain and justify their own subordination" (Scott, 1991: 72). In other words, whereas the thin version sees resignation, the thick version claims consent.

Sometimes there may be good reasons for assuming that either type of false consciousness is actively induced from above. The problem occurs when false consciousness becomes a theoretical precept that predetermines our empirical observations rather than the other way around. With the coming of "post-Fordism" during the 1980s, in which industrial, service, and professional work was infused with "theory Y" notions emphasizing how individuals will be more productive if less controlled (McGregor, 1960) and promoting traditionally humanist discourses of self actualization and esteem (Maslow, 1943), labor process theory experienced a "cultural turn" that soon resulted in the formation of critical management studies as a school of its own. So-called soft human resource management, or what Hugh Willmott (1993) calls "corporate culturism," came into focus, and the overwhelming power that HR gurus sometimes claimed (doubtlessly to promote their own professional careers) was not questioned as such but rather used to advance a thick theory of false consciousness. "The guiding aim and abiding concern of corporate culturism," Willmott writes, "is to win the 'hearts and minds' of employees: to define their purposes by managing what they think and feel, and not just how they behave" (Willmott, 1993: 516). Although critics argued and continue to argue that there is not much support for the cultural impact thesis (see Thompson, 2011), "seduction," "internalization of self-regulation," and "colonization of the affective domain" are still popular themes that re-actualize old notions in critical theory (cf. Casey, 1995; Grant et al., 1998; Townley, 1993).

One such notion is that of "the cheerful robot." In *The Sociological Imagination*, Mills poses a question that to his mind constitutes the largest social problem of our time:

> We do not know how profound man's psychological transformation from the Modern Age to the contemporary epoch may be. But we must now raise the question in an ultimate form: Among contemporary men will there come to prevail, or even to flourish, what may be called The Cheerful Robot? . . . It will no longer do merely to assume, as a metaphysic of human nature, that down deep in man-as-man there is an urge for freedom and a will to reason. Now we must ask: What in man's nature, what in the human condition today, what in each of the varieties of social structure makes for the ascendancy of the cheerful robot? And what stands against it? (Mills, 2000 [1959]: 171)

Mills contends that he knows of "no idea, no theme, no problem that is so deep in the classic tradition" (ibid.) and indeed this is also the subject that binds together Mills' disparate contributions to sociology. As mentioned in the introduction, it is at the heart of Marx's earlier essays on alienation, of Weber's notion of the iron cage and the locked-up nullity, and, as Mills points out, it is the chief concern of Georg Simmel's (1981) essay on the metropolis. But no school has been more occupied with this issue than the first generation of the Frankfurt School.[3]

According to the two major representatives of critical management studies, Mats Alvesson and Willmott (2003: 2), for early contributors to critical management studies "the tradition of Critical Theory,

---

[3] Although I here focus on the remnants of critical theory, which indeed is the school most associated with "false consciousness," Mills is right in asserting that this theme denotes the whole classic tradition. Beside Weber and Marx, we may also notice the ghost of Durkheim who, somewhat less critically, endorsed the human herd mentality thesis. Making no reference to the Frankfurt School or to Foucault in her article *The Last Frontier of Control*, Carol Axtell Ray argues that corporate culture represents the last complement to the bureaucratic control described by Weber and the humanistic control encouraged by Elton Mayo and Douglas McGregor. Mostly based on Durkheimian concepts, Ray's thesis is that the development of "corporate consciousness" based on the active manipulation of myths, rituals, and ceremonies that she and Durkheim regard as the fundament for "moral involvement," may finally integrate people entirely while viewing them as the "emotional, symbol-loving, and needing to belong to a superior entity or collectivity"–creatures that they really are (Ray, 1986: 295).

established in Frankfurt in the 1930s [was] the chief, though by no means exclusive, inspiration." They also mention "Horkheimer, Benjamin, Adorno, Marcuse, Fromm and, most recently, Jürgen Habermas" (ibid.). Unfortunately, these are names that are seldom mentioned when the theoretical foundation of critical management studies is scrutinized. Their legacy is particularly noticeable in the critique of corporate cultures where more psychoanalytical notions are employed. Already in the early empirical studies on authoritarianism that were to be published under the title of *The German Workers under the Weimar Republic* (which never happened due to a quarrel between Horkheimer and Erich Fromm), a great discrepancy between avowed beliefs and actual personality traits among German workers was observed (see Jay, 1973: 116–18). "The authoritarian worker" (a concept that was formulated before the Nazis took power) became a recurring figure in all the major works of the Frankfurt philosophers (see especially Adorno, 1950; Fromm, 1973; Marcuse, 2008 [1964]). Fromm, who contributed the most to this theme, worried for the same reason as Mills; "*robotism*" (Fromm, 2008 [1955]: 354) ultimately represented the undermining of democracy: "How can people express 'their' will if they do no have any will or conviction of their own, if they are alienated automatons, whose tastes, opinions and preferences are manipulated by the big conditioning machines?" Fromm asked (2008 [1955]: 180). Being the only major member of the *Institut für Sozialforschung* who practiced psychoanalysis, Fromm also observed how the fear of not fitting in weakened the moral integrity of individuals: "How then can ethics be a significant part of a life in which the individual becomes an automaton, in which he serves the big It?" (2008 [1955]: 168).

While not denying the possibility of human agency a priori, the Frankfurt School has been largely pessimistic concerning the prospects of a free subject resisting the repressions of late capitalism. Especially at the heart of the early Frankfurt School lies the assumption that adaptation to labor is increasingly becoming the meta-function of all social institutions. Yet in contrast to more orthodox Marxists, the Frankfurt philosophers laid the foundation for what has become the overarching theme of most critical theory, namely the critique of culture and consumption. Rather than studying the power structures at the workplace, critical theorists have been more interested in studying their reflection in other areas of everyday life – for instance as in Adorno's controversial analysis of jazz as an entertaining repetition of the factory drill

(Horkheimer and Adorno, 2002 [1944]: 101) or in Marcuse's notion of repressive desublimation, i.e. the development of an illusively liberated sexuality that is increasingly tied to the rationality of domination (Marcuse, 2008 [1964]). The "distorted emphasis on identity and the management of culture" that Thompson (2011: 364) accuses critical management studies of links to a long tradition.

The Frankfurt School has had a fundamental impact on how sociologists have studied domination that is not only visible in critical management studies. The problem with the cheerful robot is that it is cheerful and therefore unmotivated to become something other than a robot. This "euphoria in unhappiness" (Marcuse, 2008 [1964]: 7) is vividly described by Guy Debord who coined the term "the society of spectacle" to draw attention to how consumerism reduces interaction to mediated forms of one-way communication. In contrast to later theorists in the burgeoning industry of cultural studies, Debord maintained that "the spectacle is not a collection of images; it is a social relation between people that is mediated by images" (Debord, 2002 [1967]: §4). This relation, Debord argued, could most appropriately be described as *power*.[4]

The power that proponents of thick theories of false consciousness make reference to is not the violent one – even if violence is ultimately what all power relies upon. As Steven Lukes (2005) theorizes, power operates on three different levels. It can be the brute force of coercing someone to do something against that person's will – the first dimension. It can also be the suppression of potential issues by "nondecision-making" of people in authority – the second dimension. The third dimension of Lukes' power concept is *the ideological power* over people's wishes and thoughts that prevent them from realizing their *real interests* – the type of power that breeds the cheerful robot.

It is easy to raise epistemological questions concerning whether this type of manipulative power can be externally observed.[5] That,

---

[4] Again, the same associations can be found much earlier, even before the birth of sociology, here from *Queen Mab* published in 1813 by Percy Bysshe Shelley: "Power, like a desolating pestilence / Pollutes whatever it touches; and obedience / Bane of all genius, virtue, freedom, truth, / Makes slaves of men, and, of the human frame, / A mechanized automaton" (Shelley, 1839: 817).

[5] Lukes' third power dimension has been much criticized. In relation to his own concept of "sour grapes," Jon Elster is particularly critical of the idea that

however, is not my concern here. The question is rather what the alternative to false consciousness is. If you take an act of resistance like time appropriation, does it require some type of radical or oppositional consciousness that questions the whole of work society? Or are there other types of consciousness in between that both accept and negate that which is, at the same time? Unless we have a clear picture of what the alternative to false consciousness could be, it is all too simple to capriciously project the falseness onto virtually everyone (with the typical exception of those belonging to the same theoretical subtribe).

2.4 The subject as object

Although he would later regret it, Thompson (1983: 249) early on addressed the question of the "missing subject" in labor process theory. In his introduction to the debates on the labor process where he attempts to formulate a "core theory," Thompson noticed that little had been written about how subjectivity conditions and is conditioned by the labor process, that there was no theoretical foundation for doing so, and that this was "a major problem." According to Damian O'Doherty and Willmott this has remained a weakness of orthodox labor process theory: "Bravermanian analysis marginalizes, and indeed aspires to exclude, consideration of the role of consciousness and action in the reproduction and transformation of the interdependent, though asymmetrical, relations of capital and labor" (O'Doherty and

ideological submission can be intentionally induced. Describing the process of adaptive preference formation as "a strictly endogenous causality" (Elster, 1996: 116) – as a trick of the mind – Elster criticizes Lukes for the assumption that rulers have the power to produce certain beliefs and desires in their subordinates; instead, resignation and conformity should be considered as "essentially by-products" (Elster, 1983: 116). In response to Elster, Lukes points out that power does not always have to take the form of deliberate intervention. Power relations can be unintended and even unconscious to both "masters" and "slaves," but this does not rule out the possibility that resignation can be intentionally induced (Lukes, 2005: 136). A more serious critique is that Lukes, by referring to real interests, commits "the unforgivable sin of essentialism" (Lukes, 2005: 117); that he assumes that there is something *real* in each person – beyond the socially constructed – which he as a social scientist can make claims about. This is the post-structuralist critique, which emanates from the assumption that the subject fundamentally is an object open for endless reconstructions.

Willmott, 2001: 459). The Foucauldian framework offers valuable tools for approaching this issue while avoiding (or so it claims) essentialist reasoning and classic dualisms such as power-freedom, structure-agency, nature-culture, heteronomy-autonomy, and control-resistance. Accordingly, while O'Doherty and Willmott sympathize with Thompson's suggestion to theorize workplace subjectivity, they claim that "in the 'evolution' of his work there is a retreat to a more orthodox position" expressing the "unwillingness or incapacity to think outside or beyond structure-agency dualism" (O'Doherty and Willmott, 2001: 461). Foucauldian analysis can answer the questions posed by Thompson at the end of *The Nature of Work*, they claim, namely why "workers get attached to routines that are seemingly devoid of self-expression" and how "gender identities shape and constrain individual opportunities at work" (ibid.). However, they do not quote the first question from the same passage in Thompson, namely "why workers defend their skilled identities even after 'technical' deskilling" (Thompson, 1983: 250).

The emphasis among organizational Foucauldians has remained on the mechanisms of consent in which "the external power may throw off its physical weight" (Foucault, 1977: 203) – not on the study of resistance. The most popular theme is, of course, that of the panopticon and the disciplinary gaze that recur in different shapes. The phenomenon of corporate culturism, which was discussed in the section above, tends to be analyzed with special attention to observation, examination, and normalization mechanisms reiterating the relatively modest contribution of Foucault himself to the sociology of the workplace in *Discipline and Punish* (cf. Marsden, 1993; Townley, 1993, 1997). Another trend that Foucauldians have jumped upon is that of teamworking and its quite explicit rationales of peer pressure and self-surveillance. Teams, James Barker contends, now create "a nearly perfect form of control. Their attendance behavior (and in a way their human dignity) was on constant display for everyone else on the team to monitor: an essentially total system of control almost impossible to resist" (Barker, 1993: 430; see also Sewell and Wilkinson, 1992). In relation to this, the "construction of identity" is a theme that has experienced an expansion, not to say explosion, in critical management studies. A twist to the Foucauldian analysis can here be found in David Knights and Willmott (Knights and Willmott, 1989; Willmott, 1993) where the existential insecurity of the human being (as analyzed by Fromm, 1994 [1941]) is assumed to boost the discursive absorption of the individual and the potency of managerial power. Another boost of surveillance and discipline is the electronic eye of information technology, especially as it is employed in total quality control (TQM) and just in time (JIT) production, but also in service jobs such as call-centers, which now constitute a sub-discipline of its own in critical workplace studies (cf. Sewell et al., 2012).

The Foucauldian providing of the "missing subject" is, to say the least, ambiguous since the attempt to dissolve the individual-structure dualism rather seems to consume the subject. Such an interpretation may, however, be too hasty. As Touraine comments, Foucault's work is "too rich to be doctrinaire" (Touraine, 1995: 169) and to this, one might also add: too vague. What some may call "Foucault's emphasis upon the freedom of subjects" (Newton, 1998: 428), others may celebrate as the questioning of "the humanist concept of autonomy ascribed to subjects" (Alvesson and Willmott, 2003: 2). To be fair, the emphasis among the interpreters of Foucault is, however, on the absence of freedom: "The free subject cannot be conceptualized as a thinking, choosing or reflecting one" Stanley Deetz (2003: 40) contends, "the illusionary 'free' subject as a part of the disciplinary practice must be rejected.... Agency is not dependent on a newfound internal will, but a recovery of the demand on the outside, of 'otherness.'"

This could be regarded as a clever solution to the structure-agency dualism; it may also be regarded as pretty much identical with the structuralist theory of Althusser in which the subject is but an ideological construction (see especially Foucault, 1971). The use of Foucault can thus be said to address the problem of the missing subject only to the extent that it substantially eradicates it while semantically replacing the (conventional) meaning of "subject" with that of "object": "Since the subject largely appears as a function of power-knowledge practices... the problem of the subject largely disappears" (Newton, 1998: 440). And since it is assumed that the subject is but an effect of power, studies of organizational discourse sometimes pay little or no attention to the actual behaviors of employees. "Many discourse studies proceed from the assumption of the inseparability of language-meaning-cognition-action-practice," Alvesson and Dan Karreman (2011: 1142) comment in a critique of how the constitutive effects of discourse are presumed rather than empirically proven. Consequently, "labour processes have been moved to the periphery while talk and text have taken center stage" (Alvesson and Karreman, 2011: 1125). As we shall see, the idea that discourse constitutes reality and that there is no subjectivity beyond discourse may easily develop into a circular argument. If, for instance, someone observes that employees do not internalize the values promoted in a corporate culture but are indignant and critical of their employer, then "cynicism" may instead be described as the dominating discourse (cf. Contu, 2008; Fleming, 2009; Mumby, 2005). Thus, "one gets the impression that Discourse is the thought and action system within which it all occurs; if one then finds something that departs or deviates from it then, per definition, another Discourse must do the trick" (Alvesson and Karreman, 2011: 1131).

One might question whether this method is a consequence of a bad reading of Foucault or an unavoidable consequence of the application of his theory. Although it will not be possible to investigate this issue here, Lukes' reading is that "Foucault was, characteristically, not investigating actual disciplinary practices but their *design*. His purpose was to portray their idealized form – describing not how they work, or ever worked, but an ideal type of how they are meant to work" (Lukes, 2005: 93). On the other hand, it is commonly argued that in his later years, Foucault became more preoccupied with stressing that "where there is power, there is resistance" (Foucault, 1978: 95), yet without empirically demonstrating it as he otherwise was so eager to do. Touraine contends that although Foucault's work contains many pages "in which we hear the rumble of rebellion in social life" (Touraine, 1995: 170), *subjectivation* (defined by Touraine as the internal will to individuation) remains in Foucault's framework primarily a matter of *subjection*.

Here it is necessary to return to the concept of power again. Despite the fact that Foucault's concept of power has been celebrated as the most penetrating of social science, it is very unclear. The closest we get to a definition is in a lecture from 1976:

Power must be analyzed as something which circulates, or rather as something which only functions in the form of a chain. It is never localized here or there, never in anybody's hands, never appropriated as a commodity or piece of wealth. Power is employed and exercised through a net-like organization. And not only do individuals circulate between its threads; they are always in the position of simultaneously undergoing and exercising this power. They are not only its inert or consenting target; they are always also the elements of its articulation. In other words, individuals are the vehicles of power, not its points of application. (Foucault, 1980: 98)

Beside the Althusserian connotations of the individual as a puppet of power – also quite conspicuous in the statement that "the individual is an effect of power" (ibid.) – this model makes the distinction between power and resistance unnecessary. Foucauldians may argue that power is impossible to localize and that no one really "has" power, but that both the oppressed and the rulers ultimately are vehicles of this anonymous, almost divine form of circulating energy. Since both "parts" of this false dualism in fact have power, the study of power may thus be said to always (implicitly) include the study of resistance. Commenting on this obscure, not to say discursive, notion of power, Ackroyd and Thompson contend:

Of course, in practice, power or control and resistance interpenetrate rather than mechanically produce one another. But separating them, as in labour process theory, has been a necessary heuristic device that enables us to 'see' the reciprocal actions. Without such a separation one merely collapses into another and we are left with the confusing and opaque results observed in the work of Foucault and followers. (Ackroyd and Thompson, 1999: 158)

What Ackroyd and Thompson do not discuss is the criticism of Foucault on this point among allegedly Foucauldian scholars. In an effort to provide for a theoretical (albeit post-humanist) fundament that may bring agency back into organizational analysis, Willmott early pointed out the contradiction in Foucault's position, that "all power relations must be undermined; and yet there is no escape from power relations" (Willmott, 1994: 114). This very strange concept of power that threatens to empty itself of meaning – if power is everywhere how can we separate it from sociality? – might have been tolerable if Foucault had offered any normative criteria for evaluating "good" and "bad" forms of power, but since he does not, Willmott accuses him of painting himself into a corner. The Foucauldian critique of power thus becomes "capricious, individualistic and ultimately nihilistic," while not offering any lead "on how any new, de-subjected form of subjectivity is to be realized" (Willmott, 1994: 115).

Whereas the interest in practices of resistance and the interaction between subject and discourse has been expressed by both Foucault and his devotees, the fact remains that "though Foucauldians may

note the freedom of subjects, their emphasis is largely upon the rationalities of discursive programmes" (Newton, 1998: 429). In Lukes'
analysis of Foucault's own writings, the acknowledgment of the existence of resistance appears "merely to posit the conceptual necessity of resistance" (Lukes, 2005: 95). Beyond the conceptual frames,
Foucault never offered any detailed account of how this resistance
could play out empirically. In a feminist critique of Foucault, Allen
observes that "the only social actors in these works are the dominating
agents; there is no discussion of the strategies employed by madmen,
delinquents, schoolchildren, perverts or 'hysterical' women to modify
or contest the disciplinary bio-power exercised over them" (in Lukes,
2005: 96). The lack of analysis of what may happen at the interface of individual and discourse thus makes the Foucauldian model
incomplete; as Newton contends: "noting the problematic relationship between the subject and discourse is not equivalent to explaining
how the subject relates to discourse" (Newton, 1998: 428, emphasis
omitted).

In this chapter I have discussed the major recurring themes of power
at work and their roots in "grand theory." To summarize, the concepts of power move along a ladder where the Bravermanian "coercion through technology" represents the mild form of power, and the
Foucauldian "big D discourse" (Alvesson and Karreman, 2011: 1129)
represents the all-encompassing, supernatural type of power that no
one can escape. In these analyses, there is a gradual shift from body, to
consciousness, to discourse, and although most Foucauldians would
vehemently protest, I would also say from historical analysis to meta-
physics. That the worker is reduced to an appendage to the machine
does not necessitate any assumptions of what the worker thinks about
work, the employer, society etc. Power is here a question of the organization of the labor process. When referring to a false consciousness
on the other hand, we do not have to care so much about the labor
process in order to explain the impotence of workers. Then, the subjective aspects move center stage and the task of management becomes
more a matter of fostering the right ideology than of organizing labor
in a certain way. In the Foucauldian framework, the analysis becomes
even more abstract in the sense that actions nearly disappear from the
analysis privileging the focus on discourses (which sometimes include
actions, depending on how "discourse" is defined).

The difference between German and French versions of critical theory here becomes clear. Even if Adorno belongs to the most pessimistic
writers through history, with notions such as the "amorphous and
malleable mass" (Adorno, 2005 [1951]: 139) of "standardized and
organized human units" (Adorno, 2005 [1951]: 135), following the
"line of least resistance" (Adorno, 2005 [1951]: 57), there is also a
good portion of despair in his writings, which emanates from the idea
that "it should be otherwise" (Adorno, 1980: 194). Since the Frankfurt philosophers do not conflate subject with object, the horror of
objectification and power becomes all the more intolerable in their
writings. They do not naturalize power; they still assume that the subject (as defined by Touraine) may reawaken even if it now appears
just as dead as in Foucault's analysis. As David Hawkes comments in
Ideology: "The consequences of this position are so frightening that
it is easy to understand why many thinkers, including Althusser and
Foucault, recoil from them, and take refuge in the notion that the
subject was actually an object all along" (Hawkes, 2003: 175).[6] Of
course, it might be argued that the Frankfurt School's conception of
the subject was "noticeably impregnated with humanism of a Marxist
type" (Foucault and Trombadori, 1991: 120), and that this humanism
is the most discursive metaphysical assumption of Western culture, but
then again it becomes hard to integrate practices of resistance into the
anti-humanist framework of Foucault.

In the next chapter, I will argue that we need to develop an alternative theory of subjectivity in order to effectively study workplace
resistance. I will briefly discuss what the outlines of such a theory
might look like and why the study of workplace resistance and empty
labor in particular can help us to develop the sociological conception
of subjectivity.

---

[6] In his analysis of "the dialectic of selfhood" in critical theory, Lauren Langman
   comes to a similar conclusion: "the Frankfurt School understanding of how
   domination becomes internalized, remains a major, and enduring contribution
   to the understanding of domination, and a far more nuanced understanding
   than similar arguments of Althusser or Foucault whose frameworks, devoid of
   affect, agency or resistance, reproduce the very domination they would
   critique" (Langman, 2009: 278).

3 | *Subjectivity at work*

In this chapter I discuss how resistance has been debated generally in critical sociology and more concretely how we can approach some of the issues raised in this debate by studying workplace resistance. I will begin with one of the broadest questions in social science – what does it mean to be a subject? – then narrow the scope while localizing the theoretical relevance of workplace resistance and empty labor in particular.

"Resistance" can and has been defined in a number of ways. Almost all fruitful definitions include some dimension of subjectivity, but let us begin by looking at an exception: Ackroyd and Thompson use the terms "resistance" and "misbehavior" rather interchangeably and they define the latter term as: "anything you do at work you are not supposed to do" (Ackroyd and Thompson, 1999: 2). When reading through their examples, one quickly realizes that their definition is too broad. Ackroyd and Thompson write nothing about employees mistakenly slowing down production, having accidents, or anything else unintentional that they are not supposed to do. In a later article by one of the authors, misbehavior is defined as "self-conscious rule-breaking" and distinguished from "resistance" which is assumed to have "connotations of behaviour that is overt, principled, and perhaps formally organized" (Collinson and Ackroyd, 2005: 306). A similar but more elaborate distinction has been provided by Jan Ch. Karlsson, who defines workplace resistance as "anything you consciously are, do and think at work that you are not supposed to be, do and think and which is directed upwards through the organizational hierarchy" (Karlsson, 2012: 185).[1]

---

[1] I only mention this distinction to illustrate how subjectivity has been assumed in different definitions of misbehavior and resistance. As the reader will notice, I make no difference myself between misbehavior and resistance for the simple reason that I have so far not seen a single example of an "undirected" or "unconscious" type of oppositional behavior that one might call

What these definitions express is how subjective intent must always be considered when analyzing resistance (at or outside the workplace). Some have made this point more explicitly. As Lauraine Leblanc argues, "accounts of resistance must detail not only resistant acts, but the subjective intent motivating these as well" (in Hollander and Einwohner, 2004: 542). Take a typical case of empty labor that I will return to: a man leaving early from work without the knowledge of his employer. He might do this accidentally because he has lost track of time, he might do it because he knows that there is no more work for him to do for the day, or he might do it as an act of revenge, to give his manager a hard time, or to "steal back" time he feels his employer has taken from him. Not all these scenarios depict an act of resistance. As Scott has argued, the subjective dimension is even more important than the actual outcome since resistance might not always have the effects we intend it to have (Scott, 1985: 290). Resistance requires a subject.

Here, I will discuss how others have approached this subject, both in general sociology and in critical workplace studies. Before elaborating the relevance of Touraine's subject theory to the study of workplace resistance, I will briefly present his argument in a bit more detail and also some of the criticism it has received. A problem with Touraine and other grand theorists who are writing about social movements and other types of resistance is their overemphasis on open (as opposed to covert) forms of resistance, which is conducive to their theorizing resistance everywhere but at work. Even in their theory, work remains an island of instrumental rationality, inaccessible to human agency, governed by anonymous laws. Socialists, anarchists, and radical plant sociologists who romantically celebrate the practice of sabotage are on the other hand often too willing to attribute to workplace resistance a

"misbehavior." One could include behaviors that are not necessarily hierarchical such as bullying or sexual harassment, but then, the oppositional aspect that most scholars writing about organizational misbehavior seem to assume, disappears. One could also make a gradual distinction between misbehavior and resistance, as in David Collinson and Ackroyd, where the misbehavior is "self-conscious" and resistance is "principled", but as long as there is no clear criteria for how to separate the two, we risk the entrapment of the old Sorites paradox – when is a heap a heap? Is it enough to put two grains together or do we need three or four for it to count as a heap? Similarly, one may ask how "principled" an act has to be to count as resistance and not as misbehavior.

tinge of revolt that its practitioners may not necessarily identify with. Empty labor is a perfect example. It can be a trap; it can be a way of coping, a personal pleasure, or a type of sabotage, depending on the organizational context and the subjective intent of the employee.

3.1 Subjectivity as resistance

In his critique of the Frankfurt School and Marcuse in particular, Touraine points out the paradox that the culmination of "radical despair," promulgated from the abyss that Georg Lukács mockingly named *das Grand Hotel Abgrund*, incited a movement that would later become synonymous with "the late sixties":

How can anyone fail to notice that Marcuse's book [*One-Dimensional Man*] was published in 1964, the year in which the student movement first exploded with the Free Speech Movement at Berkeley, and at the beginning of a decade which, in both the United States and other countries, was to be dominated by campaigns for black civil rights, and women's equality, by protests against the war in Vietnam and by great student uprisings? The fact that these movements turned to critical theory or to structural Marxism, to Marcuse or to Althusser, does not alter the fact that their actions, which were often in contradiction with their consciousness, proved that a mass society had not finally eliminated social actors. (Touraine, 1995: 160)

Even if it "was the rapid collapse of these student movements that led to the triumph of schools of thought which deny that social actors can intervene in society" (ibid.), Touraine's argument still holds: society cannot be reduced to a labor camp as the early Frankfurt philosophers in their more cynical moments would have it; the empirical evidence against such assumptions, including social movements, is too vast even to accept them metaphorically. Touraine's notion of the subject is therefore a valuable reaction to both the pessimism described in the previous chapter that allows us to theorize subjectivity beyond the one-dimensional man of Marcuse, or "the subject" of Foucault. Yet it is more a contribution in terms of articulation than in substance. Touraine's subject is not a new invention; it can at least be traced back to Søren Kierkegaard and is, as I have already hinted, quite endorsed by some of the targets of Touraine's critique. Assuming a subject is precisely what separates Habermas from the first generation of the Frankfurt philosophers.[2]

The hope that Jean Fourastié and others expressed vis-à-vis the coming of the "tertiary civilization," in which the growth of the service sector gradually would eliminate industrial labor and with it the humiliations of Taylorism described in the previous chapter, was never shared by Touraine. With the "programmed society" – a concept that he uses interchangeably with "post-industrial society" (Touraine, 1971b) – there is "a transition from the administration of things to the government of men" (Touraine, 1995: 244). Managerial power is now no longer exclusively concerned with controlling the labor process, but also with "predicting and modifying opinions, attitudes and modes of behaviour, and in moulding personalities and cultures" (ibid.). Rather than focusing on utility, it is now also involved in the creation and implementation of social norms.

This analysis repeats some of the arguments mentioned in the previous chapter; at first glance the differences between Touraine and the Frankfurt philosophers may not appear significant. Touraine devotes much of his critique to how identities can be colonized in a way that is also reminiscent of Foucault's analysis. But in Touraine's analysis, "identity" or "ego" is not synonymous with the "I" or the "subject." The will to meaning and to become an actor is a much more fundamental force of human existence that goes "beyond identity" and is constituted precisely in resisting power: "The normalization and objectification of human beings produce the Self whereas the I is constituted through resistance to power centres" (Touraine, 1995: 167). Hence,

---

[2] Marcuse's (Heideggerian) concept of "essence" (see Marcuse, 2009 [1968]) comes close to Touraine's subject. Both rely on the existentialist idea that the human being first and foremost projects himself into potentiality (the only real human essence that Marcuse acknowledges) and that this projection, under present conditions, must take place in conflict with power. Unlike Habermas, in whom the subject is either absorbed in the lifeworld or systems of instrumental reason, Adorno also stressed the "non-identity" that allows the subject to resist, challenge and refuse the social roles or instrumental functions that are imposed on us (Adorno, 1973 [1966]). What would mark the theory of the early Frankfurt School was their experience of National Socialism representing history's worst downfall of the working class. As Gorz contends, critical theory, interpreted as the scientific reflection of "emancipatory actions in whose 'pre-scientific' reality its truth would be grounded," thus lost its "anchorage in conflicts and actions that challenged the system" (Gorz, 1999: 127–28).

as Gorz comments, it is in the interstices of domination, in its misfir-ings and margins, that "autonomous subjects emerge, through whom moral questions may be posed. At the origin of such questions, there's always that founding act of the subject which consists in rebellion against what society makes me do or undergo" (Gorz, 2010: 5).

In his later writings, Touraine also asserts that the "I" is under attack, but here the problem is not that of excessive integration or manipulation but of fragmentation and of decay, of the separation of culture and economy that on an individual level is experienced as the "divorce between acts and meaning" (Touraine, 1995: 99). Touraine's "two faces of modernity," rationalization and subjectivation, can no longer counterbalance each other when the individual loses faith in his capacity to be an actor and with it his subjectivity (defined as the attempt to be an actor). This represents a serious threat to modernity: "For a long time, the repressive weight of prohibitions and the law was the main pathological factor. We are now experiencing a very different pathology: the impossibility of formulating an 'I'" (Touraine, 2000b: 55).

Touraine here strikes a chord with the existentialist notion of alien-ation as defined by Sartre and elaborated by Gorz. As Gorz (1967) contends in *Le Socialisme Difficile*, alienated individuals are not nec-essarily oppressed in the sense that they are forced to obey structural imperatives – their freedom is degraded, constrained, and negated by their own accomplishments. There is no fixed state of alienation to be in; just as subjectivity is a question of self-directedness, we *are* not alienated; we produce and reproduce our alienation by retreating from our subjectivity and by yielding to resignation and cynicism.[3] Both in Gorz and in Touraine we find the notion of a "dual society" that, although his duality came later, mostly has been associated with Habermas. Gorz conceptually separates the "sphere of autonomy" from "the sphere of heteronomy," where the first is the arena for what

---

[3] To illustrate the alienation of the modern worker, Gorz (1959: 99) gives the example of traffic congestion. The individuals drive with the aim of enhancing their own autonomy. They want to be independent of the fixed timetables, slow pace, and discomfort of public transport. The more drivers on the roads, however, the more their aims will be thwarted. The collective result of their independent actions is congestion, decreasing vehicle speed, and taking the long view, a more dangerous and polluted city etc. The drivers are thus alienated from the social product of each other's actions, while at the same time producing and reproducing what is required for this social order.

Hannah Arendt (1958) calls *praxis* (action for the action's own sake) and the second sphere is defined as "the totality of specialized activities which individuals have to accomplish as functions co-ordinated from outside by a pre-established organization" (Gorz, 1989: 43). In Touraine, the duality is between the subject and the "anti-subject" or the "logic of apparatuses and power" (Touraine, 1995: 274) where the contraction of subjectivity comes close to Gorz's notion of alienation.

While there are similarities between the dualisms of Gorz and Touraine, they are far removed from the lifeworld-system model of Habermas. Touraine opposes all types of communication theories where intersubjective communication precedes individual consciousness. "Like Sartre," Wolfgang Knöbl (1999: 418) observes, "Touraine refuses to treat subjectivity as something derivative and to thus presuppose for it an 'a priori intersubjectivity.'" Whereas "communicative action takes place within a lifeworld that remains at the backs of participants in communication" and is "present to them only in the prereflective form of taken-for-granted background assumptions and naively mastered skills" (Habermas, 1984: 335), the Tourainian subject is a "non-social principle," resistant both to socialization and to social expectations. "We can no longer contrast the lifeworld (*Lebenswelt*) with the strategic action of instrumental rationality" according to Touraine. "The Subject comes into being only by rejecting both instrumentality and identity, because identity is no more than a debased and introverted lived experience that is in a state of decay" (Touraine, 2000b: 56). The conception of the subject as preceding sociality is important since it, as Gorz argues, provides the foundation of negativity without which critical theory and its "unfolding of a single existential judgment" (Horkheimer, 1995 [1937]: 227) appears unfeasible.[4]

"The subject of emancipation" (the activist) and "the subject of theory" (e.g. the sociologist) should in Touraine's theory be recognized

---

[4] As Gorz contends: "[I]f the space for communicative action is restricted and its very possibility jeopardized by the destructive inroads of the logic of systems, how can communicative reason fight off the system's infringements upon a life-world which, according to Habermas, 'is its infrastructure'? Does the crisis of the latter not necessarily entail the crisis of communicative co-operation and understanding? Is social critique, waged in the name and on the basis of communicative reason, not an external critique waged by a subject – the sociologist – positioning him/herself outside the society in which socio-cultural life-worlds are breaking down?" (Gorz, 1999: 131).

as complementary sides of the same structure. This in many ways challenges traditional sociology and the tendency to explain the individual as the product of society where the latter becomes a subjective and yet mysteriously anonymous force. The challenge is also methodological. Subjectivity is not only necessary to transcend the lifeworld, but also to study the subject as such. Since the subject is "a non-social principle" or as Gorz puts it, "a self-founding and self-creating point of departure, not of arrival" (1999: 137), it cannot be externally deduced with methods of positivistic sociology. In order to understand subject-actors' movements not only as objects of study but as bearers of the meaning of their own action, the sociologist must be a partisan. Touraine's reconsideration of sociological methodology runs completely contrary to the usual standards of validity. The sociologist as a participating analyst finds his or her *raison d'être* in crystallizing the meaning of the subject, Touraine argues, and whether this succeeds can be decided only by the subject itself: "If the group, siding with the analysis, makes their hypotheses its own, because they increase the intelligibility of what it is undertaking, then the pertinence of those hypotheses is confirmed" (in Gorz, ibid.). This view of sociology, which I share, has later been elaborated by Michael Burawoy (2005) in his notion of "public sociology," to which I shall return.

There are several problems with Touraine's subject theory; I will mention only those relevant to this study. The most problematic aspect is the ambition to explain all forms of social transcendence with a single concept that both seems to move on the micro and macro level melting the "for-itself," the "praxis" and "project" of Sartre, into a single super category. On the one hand, Touraine defines the subject as "the individual's quest for the conditions that will allow him to become the actor of his own history" (Touraine, 2000b: 56); on the other hand, the only subject that Touraine really has studied is the "the subject as a social movement" (Touraine, 1995: 243, emphasis omitted). It is only by acting collectively, Touraine asserts, that we can become actors and change the conditions of our situated existence. The subject as individual and the subject as social movement are, however, quite different entities and it is not hard to imagine how the two may collide: people engaging in a social movement, or to relate to what I am studying here, people engaging in the same type of resistance, may do it for very different reasons depending on biography and individual situation. Yet in Touraine's vocabulary they are still part of the same "subject."

In relation to this, the reader might have noticed both rational and romantic overtones in some of the quoted passages. Touraine depicts the dissident as the exemplary figure of the subject: "The dissident bears witness, even without any hope of being heard, against the powers that take away his freedom. The Subject is Speech, and its act of witness is a public one, even if no one can hear it or see it" (Touraine, 2000b: 75). The picture that comes to mind is a group of protesters marching the streets and expressing a unified message. This is an unnecessary reduction of the "subject" concept, which might be an effect of Touraine's endeavor to expand Sartre's group theory into *"une sociologie de la liberté"* (Knöbl, 1999: 407). With his macro-approach to the social, Touraine has apparently lost interest in the individual and often irrational expressions of subjectivity that Sartre, and before him, Kierkegaard and Fyodor Dostoyevsky spent so much of their writings analyzing.[5] In relation to the "conspicuous neglect of institutional analysis" that Knöbl (1999: 411) sees in Touraine, this becomes especially problematic if we want to study subjectivity at work. Here, where fragmentation and specialization make collective action extremely difficult and where "Voice" may represent the safest way to lose your job, non-unionized subjectivity of any lasting kind almost seems impossible. To be able to make sense of subjectivity in this area, we must extend its relevance to covert and individual forms of resistance.

3.2 Barrier reefs of resistance

What I have elsewhere described as the spreading of *economic activism*, a type of activism whereby individuals reduce their participation in

---

[5] A general theme here is the individual's urge to act irrationally in order to resist modernity's celebration of the rational. "Out of love for mankind" Kierkegaard writes, "and moved by a genuine interest in those who make everything easy, I conceived it as my task to create difficulties everywhere" (Kierkegaard, 2004 [1846]: 87). The endeavors of some of Dostoyevsky's characters appear even more idiosyncratic. In the attempt to prove themselves alive they engage in the most absurd activities in order to break with the established and supposedly rational order. Typical examples include Kirillov's suicide in *Demons* (Dostoyevsky, 2000 [1872]), Raskolnikov's murder in *Crime and Punishment* (Dostoyevsky, 1964 [1866]), the attraction of the game in *The Gambler* (Dostoyevsky, 2003 [1867]), and the long monologue from the first part of *Notes from Underground* (Dostoyevsky, 1994 [1864]) where the individual's need to become a subject is analyzed at length and in somewhat less humanist terms than in Touraine.

commercial production and consumption, would probably not be considered an expression of subjectivity in the strict sense of Touraine since
this activism often takes place covertly and is too heterogeneous to be
associated with a single "Speech" (see Paulsen, 2010: 205–20). The
third of the Swedish population that has engaged in illegal file sharing
of copyright material (Gustafsson, 2009) might be regarded as a social
movement depending on definition, but it is clearly different from the
French anti-nuclear movement for instance. Squatters, freegans, slackers are all subjects in the sense that they resist power centers, but in
economic activism, including workplace time appropriation, the resistance is not purely symbolic; there are immediate material gains in it
for the individual, and whereas some might engage in it as a symbolic
act, others might do it for nothing more than their own material gains.
Economic activism, which includes some of the workplace fiddles that
Gerald Mars describes, can also have an element of excitement that
some workers may value even more than the symbolic or the material:
"When a worker feels that by bringing off a fiddle he is beating the system, and is in control of his fate, his rewards are more than monetary"
(Mars, 1982: 35).

As Touraine himself points out, the "idea of the Subject does not
grow in over-protected greenhouses; it is a wild flower" (Touraine,
2000b: 58). Beside the sociology of social movements, there have
been several attempts to theorize subjectivity where false consciousness and hegemony were earlier assumed to reign supreme. Some of
these attempts have grown into sub-disciplines of their own. Concerning the issue of the culture industry, the field of cultural studies has
been utterly concerned with media-reception theory since the emer-
gence of the Birmingham School (cf. Hall, 1980; Skeggs and Wood,
2008; Wood, 2005) whereas sexual repression and micro-resistance
constitute one of the most debated subjects within feminist studies (cf.
Allen, 1999; Greer, 2006; Solanas, 1967). In great (and sometimes
excessive) detail, these disciplines have managed to bear empirical
evidence of Henri Lefebvre's (1991 [1958]: 40) notion that even if
behaviors of everyday life undeniably bear witness to domination and
passivity, they also "contain within themselves their own spontaneous
critique of the everyday."

The most serious attempt to collect these practices in a universal
anthropology has been offered by Scott, whose main thesis is that we,
often under the facade of blind obedience, practice advanced forms of
micro-resistance that together form an inevitable part of social reality:

"Just as millions of anthozoan polyps create, willy-nilly, a coral reef, thousands upon thousands of petty acts of insubordination and evasion create a political and economic barrier reef of their own" (Scott, 1989: 20). Scott uses the term "hidden transcript" to describe the type of "discourse that takes place 'offstage' beyond direct observation of powerholders" (Scott, 1991: 4). The official transcript with its "formulas of subservience, euphemisms, and uncontested claims to status and legitimacy" usually is not openly criticized since "it ordinarily serves the immediate interests of subordinates to avoid discrediting these appearances" (Scott, 1991: 87). Taking Foucault's claim that "where there is power, there is resistance" more seriously than Foucault himself did, Scott argues that we all know about the difference between the official and the hidden transcript in our own context; it is only when one observes another circle that the official transcript appears hegemonic. The reason why resistance often must remain hidden is because subordinate actors understand that they would risk losing an open struggle where both parts mobilized all their resources. It is when there is a "shift in the balance of power or a crisis" (Scott, 1991: 16) that the hidden transcript can be overtly declared and acted upon.

The theory of hidden transcripts represents the extreme opposite to the gloominess of early critical theory and has been criticized in its turn. Lukes (2005) argues that Scott uses an exceptionally interpretative method in his analysis of folkloric symbols and that his focus on the historically most oppressed groups in the world may not necessarily be generalizable to societies where power is more manipulative. Scott writes very little about workplace resistance and the only passage where he comments on typical work-related subjects such as "theft, pilfering, feigned ignorance, shirking or careless labor, foot-dragging, secret trade and production for sale, sabotage of crops, livestock, and machinery" (Scott, 1991: 188) is in relation to (non-wage) slavery. More importantly, Lukes contends that Scott's "either-or" terminology makes the discussion as simplistic as ever before: "[T]he alternatives of 'consent' and 'resignation' look like a hopelessly impoverished schema for describing and explaining the gamut of the remaining human responses to conditions of powerlessness and dependence" (Lukes, 2005: 132). This argument clearly does not take into account Scott's careful elaboration of all the manifestations of the hidden transcript, but it does call for an analytic framework that distinguishes between reactions along the spectrum from compliance to resistance.

A different account can be found in Michel de Certeau, whose interest lies precisely in the plurality of reactions to power where hidden resistance remains preferable to open revolt. Mostly in reaction to Foucault, whom he criticizes for reducing "the functioning of a whole society to a single, dominant type of procedure" (Certeau, 1986: 188), i.e. the panoptical and disciplinary drill, Certeau elaborates on a "heterology" of tactics that we employ in our everyday life to evade complete submission and to provide a sense of dignity. While these practices remain "unprivileged by history," they become hard to ignore when social theories are applied practically. A well-known problem for city planners that Certeau expands upon is the impossibility of predicting how the flows of individuals will react to a certain structure – where they will gather, what shortcuts and meeting places they will invent etc. As Charlie Chaplin "multiplies the possibilities of his cane ... the walker transforms each spatial signifier into something else," Certeau (1984: 98) argues.

This "pedestrian speech act" comes close to the act of time appropriation. Perhaps his most recognized example of an everyday tactic is the type of empty labor that in France is called *la perruque* ("the wig") in which "the worker's own work [is] disguised as work for his employer" (Certeau, 1984: 25). *La perruque* is neither pilferage since no product is stolen, nor plain absenteeism since the worker stays at the workplace; it is rather the autonomous appropriation of "time (not goods, since [the worker] uses only scraps) from the factory of work that is free, creative, and precisely not directed toward profit" (ibid.). Exemplifying this phenomenon, Certeau mentions the secretary's writing of a love letter during working hours and the cabinetmaker's borrowing a lathe for turning a piece of home furniture. To Certeau, this represents one of the clearest examples of individual manipulations of imposed spaces, an "enunciatory act" as he terms it:

In the very place where the machine he must serve reigns supreme, he cunningly takes pleasure in finding a way to create gratuitous products whose sole purpose is to signify his own capabilities through his work and to confirm his solidarity with other workers or his family through spending his time in this way. (Certeau, 1984: 25–26)

There is no need, Certeau says, of turning to the past, the countryside, or to "primitive" peoples to find examples of tactics whereby individuals find ways of bending the order of things to their own ends. They exist "in the heart of the strongholds of the contemporary economy" (Certeau, 1984: 25). As I have already mentioned, this is precisely what gives empty labor its sociological relevance: in the workplace where so often it is assumed that the machine we must serve "reigns supreme," every type of spanner in the works deserves a study of its own.

Another difference between Certeau and Scott can be seen in Certeau's insistence that despite the fact that all people whether consciously or not engage in micro diversions, these acts cannot be forced into a meta-narrative and assimilated into one "Voice" – "there is no unique unity among the sounds of presence that the enunciatory act gives a language in speaking it. Thus we must give up the fiction that collects all these sounds under the sign of a 'Voice,' of a 'Culture' of its own – or of the great Other's" (Certeau, 1984: 132).

For a proper understanding of Scott's barrier reefs of resistance, each little polyp should thus be taken into account and analyzed on its own terms. This requires empirical analysis beyond the interpretation of text. Strangely, studies of workplace resistance have so far been ignored in the "grand theory" of subjectivity. Even in Touraine, work remains a domain in which subjectivity is not theorized. After the false prediction in his early work that the technical intelligentsia of the new professions would form an oppositional class of their own (cf. Knöbl, 1999: 411), work has remained associated with control and manipulation in his theory. Instead of relating the issue to the most central institution of power in our time, the study of everyday resistance has too often focused on struggles in other epochs, under slavery or totalitarian regimes with clear connotations of exoticism (also in Certeau). Sociologists of work have, on the other hand, done very little to relate their findings to the general discussion on power and resistance.

3.3 Workplace resistance: from Romanticism to functionalism

While open resistance and collective mobilization were more of an issue in industrial sociology when Touraine published his earlier studies on the post-industrial society and the Solidarity-movement, the gradual weakening of trade unions has changed the rules for subjectivity at work. As Mars contends, "unions in Western industrial societies have become so enmeshed in our emergent corporate states that their role has been reduced to that of mediators rather than workers' champions"

(Mars, 1982: 198). Regardless of whether they can even be conceived of as mediators, it is clear that there has been a shift in research focus where the study of informal workplace behaviors appears to be more relevant to our understanding of employee subjectivity.[6]

Romantic notions of workplace resistance are as old as syndicalism. Time appropriation has always been part of this resistance, but more often than "soldiering" the term used for it has been "sabotage." The often referred to etymology of "sabotage" – "to work clumsily as if by sabot blows" (Pouget, 1913 [1898]: 17, emphasis omitted) – denotes the reduction of production including "[g]oing slow, workers' decisions to cut down on hours, working without enthusiasm, absenteeism, labour turnover and simply not working" (Dubois, 1979: 57). Pierre Dubois even argues that this is the essence of the concept: "'Sabotage' primarily means working slowly and lowering the quality of what is produced" (Dubois, 1979: 103). According to Thorstein Veblen, the "sinister meaning" of sabotage "as denoting violence and disorder, appears to be due to the fact that the American usage has been shaped chiefly by persons and newspapers who have aimed to discredit the use of sabotage by organized workmen" (Veblen, 2001 [1921]: 4). Émile Pouget (1913 [1898]: 18) traced industrial sabotage to the Scottish expression "ca'canny" which literally means "go slow" (see also Ackroyd and Thompson, 1999: 32) – a tactical misbehavior that often was employed when the official strike was over (see also Brown, 1977). For Pouget, sabotage signified a covert, everyday type of revolutionary rehearsal whereby workers asserted their subjectivity:

Every one knows how much a guerilla warfare develops individual courage, daring and determination – the same may be said of *sabotage*. It keeps the workers in training, preventing them from relaxing into a pernicious sloth – and as it requires a permanent, restless action, it naturally obtains the result

---

[6] Whereas Sweden often stands out as exemplary when it comes to worker organization, it should be noted that it has also experienced a significant decline in union membership and union activity all together (Allvin and Sverke, 2000; Kåks Röshammar, 2008; Sverke and Hellgren, 2002). Unlike France and the UK (see Stewart, 2008: 57), the Swedish "spirit of consensus" has furthermore prevented a radicalization of the movement politically and the employment of strike action. The interest in spontaneous types of workplace resistance grew particularly strong in the 1970s, when "[l]abour's recalcitrance and potential for radicalism was seen to be ill-served by the dominant brand of economistic, defensive and sectional trade unionism" (Ackroyd and Thompson, 1999: 45) while direct action provided new ground for optimism.

of developing the worker's initiative, of training him to act by himself and of stirring his combativeness. (Pouget, 1913 [1898]: 35)

A feminist version of the same romanticism can be found in Valerie Solanas, who even praised sabotage as a revolutionary practice in its own right. By "systematically fucking up the system, selectively destroying property, and murder" the Society for Cutting Up Men (SCUM) would take over the US within a year, she argued. The "fucking up the system" part interestingly involved a practice that she called "unwork":

- SCUM will become members of the unwork force, the fuck-up force; they will get jobs of various kinds and unwork. For example, SCUM salesgirls will not charge for merchandise; SCUM telephone operators will not charge for calls; SCUM office and factory workers, in addition to fucking up their work, will secretly destroy equipment.
- SCUM will unwork at a job until fired, then get a new job to unwork at. (Solanas, 1967: 22)

A less spectacular but still romantic conception of sabotage is that it is "bound up with the private ownership of the means of production" and will disappear only "when we have finally achieved socialism with freedom" (Dubois, 1979: 213). What is especially noticeable is the tendency to see sabotage and other forms of misbehavior as a *constant*, just as inescapable as the discontents of work: "As long as people feel cheated, bored, harassed, endangered, or betrayed at work, sabotage will be used as a direct method of achieving job satisfaction – the kind that never has to get the bosses' approval" (Sprouse, 1992: 7). There is also the notion that sabotage is a *reaction* against managerial strategies: "The more control exerted over people's time, the more the individual is tempted to squander it" (Mars, 1982: 50).

After Thompson and Ackroyd published their studies on organizational misbehavior, sabotage and other signs of subjectivity entered the main stage of critical workplace studies. As Fleming and André Spicer (2007: 2) put it, "according to Thompson and Ackroyd, resistance was always there, be it in the form of organized action, or subtle subversion around identity and self, with humor, sexuality and skepticism being key examples. Others soon chimed in." In Thompson's (2009) own account, this brief "hero-time" of workplace resistance escalated in theory-heavy analyses and occasionally enthusiastic celebrations of milder forms of organizational misbehavior such as "offstage gestures" (cf. Gossett and Kilker, 2006; Korczynski et al., 2006; Taplin, 2006), "cynicism" (cf. Cooke, 2006; Fleming, 2005b, 2005a) and "irony" (cf. Sewell, 2008; Taylor and Bain, 2003; Warren and Fineman, 1997).

Inspired by *The Good Soldier, Švejk* by Jaroslav Hašek, Fleming and Graham Sewell offer a typical example in their formulation of "Švejkism" – a term used for "subtle forms of subversion that are invariably 'invisible' to his superiors (and often to his peers too)" (Fleming and Sewell, 2002: 859). In their reading of resistance studies, earlier "approaches have limited the definition of resistance to formalized, organized acts, dependent upon some transcendental principle" (Fleming and Sewell, 2002: 862). The notion of "Švejkian transgressions," they argue, can help us to detect hidden forms of resistance "even under the most claustrophobic cultural hegemony," which has become all the more important now that "subjectivity is the very terrain that is being contested" (Fleming and Sewell, 2002: 863).

When the "hero time" of resistance studies was over and the Švejkian transgressions had been analytically (and massively) dissected, "post-structuralists" began "reclaiming the land of gloom" as Thompson (2009) puts it. Many did it on good grounds; as Dennis Mumby contends: "It seems a very hollow victory to celebrate the ability of social actors to engage in irony, parody, mimicry, and so on, while neglecting the extent to which the lives of organization members are becoming more oppressive, more heavily surveilled, and generally more insecure" (Mumby, 2005: 39). Others have driven the same argument to the point where almost nothing can be counted as "real" resistance. A typical example is Alessia Contu (2008), who argues that what is commonly called "resistance" is in fact a "decaf resistance" that neither entails any risk-taking on the part of the resisting employees, nor leads to any significant change of the fundamental oppression.[7] This is the incorporation argument: the idea that what we conceive of as

---

[7] The idea that subtle forms of misbehavior, such as irony or humor, become more important as the possibilities to overtly engage in collective resistance diminish, has also been questioned: "I cannot see why workers, whatever their profession, would be more funny today than before only because unions have weakened or disappeared," Paul Stewart (2008: 55, my translation) contends. Instead of concentrating on the meaning of different actions in relation to subjectivity, he suggests that we should focus more on what workplace struggles can tell us about the contradictions of capitalist production (Stewart, 2008: 62).

workplace resistance is in fact just a safety valve for worker frustration that leaves the power structures of work intact. In some versions, this argument can also have a functionalist touch, the system is reproduced not *despite*, but *because* this safety valve exists. This is an interesting argument since it challenges the very relevance of subjectivity. Could it be that the *attempt* to become an actor is decoupled from *being* an actor? That we believe we resist when in fact this belief makes us accept the fundamental oppression?

The seducing force of the incorporation argument may easily lead to endless abstraction where the sense of what resistance could look like withers away. Since we have no concrete phenomenon to apply it to yet, I conclude that it is too early to treat it here. The reader might, however, keep the question in mind as the analysis of empty labor proceeds: resistance or triviality? Until Chapter 8, where I return to this question, the focus will be on the subjective and practical dimensions of empty labor.

Two issues that have been confused in the debate on workplace resistance and that are central to the empirical analysis of empty labor are first, the subjectivity of workers and their ability to resist the types of "thought control" referred to in the previous chapter, and second, whether the signs of transgression and dissent that have been studied *really* can be called "resistance." While the first question comes close to individually-centered attitude research, the second features the gravity of the resisting act in relation to its organizational context.

Although various notions of "the death of the subject" are still widely embraced, particularly in critical theory, there is today enough theoretical and empirical foundation to refute this idea. However, there is still much left to desire from the literature where critical theorists have intervened in the pessimist discourse. As I have read Touraine, his main contribution is his reformulation of the subject from an existentialist (i.e. non-essentialist) perspective and in direct reaction to the subject-denying tendencies of earlier critical theory. Touraine addresses the classic issues of "Grand Theory" such as the macro-micro debate, the integration problem and the participatory role of sociology, but he has very little to say about the individual's expressions of subjectivity. In Touraine's empirical research, it is collective action, mostly done in public, that remains in focus. In Scott's studies of resistance, it is still collective forms of actions and narratives that constitute the empirical material, but now with a focus on hidden forms of subjectivity and dissent. Yet for both Scott and Touraine, subjectivity is an either/or phenomenon; they write very little (especially Touraine) about the grey areas where people may adopt some bits of the ideology and resist others, and they both tend to subsume a certain movement under a single voice. This tendency was actively resisted by Certeau, whose main interest was precisely the multitude of tactics employed in everyday life for a multitude of reasons.

Although Certeau mentions a type of time appropriation – *la perruque* – none of these grand theorists has presented any solid theory about resistance in the modern workplace. In this sense, the notion that the ideology of work remains unchallenged has not really been refuted. Most critical theorists would willingly acknowledge that western capitalism can absorb symbolic opposition and everyday negations of any kind as long as the protesters go back to work on Monday. A central reason why Marcuse criticized the new left movement was precisely because parts of it (the hippie scene, the dropout scene) were "based on the confusion of personal with social liberation" (Marcuse, 2005: 140) leading to the "drug culture, the turn to guru-cults and other pseudo-religious sects" (Marcuse, 2005: 185) – precisely the petit bourgeois type of revolts that have now been incorporated into working life (cf. Cederström and Fleming, 2012; Fleming, 2009). Workplace studies of misbehaviors have on the other hand done little to address the debate on subjectivity. Apart from a few romantics (among whom none is active today) who assumed that all types of sabotage were a rehearsal for more drastic revolt, the focus has been on praxis and in what way (if at all) these misbehaviors can be regarded as resistance in relation to organizational power.

As I argue in the appendix, the type of ethnography that still constitutes the standard method of these studies may seem like a good way to approach the practical aspects of organizational misbehavior, but it could also be argued that it is the main reason why the bulk of workplace studies have focused on "petty acts"; indeed, they have now more than saturated the academic market. These days, ethnographers rarely have time to do field research for more than half a year. Therefore, it is quite impossible for them to penetrate into the backstage where radical forms of time appropriation, sabotage, and pilferage may take place. Discourse analyses and the observation of group interaction are cheap in terms of the scarcest resource we have, namely time, but they

have the disadvantage of providing "thick" descriptions only of surface phenomena, whereas more radical expressions of subjectivity tend
to be ignored.

The focus of this study is on different voices of subjectivity that
underpin the practice of empty labor. Empty labor is sometimes mentioned (under different names) in critical workplace studies, but it has
for various reasons not been studied *per se*. This is a "gap" that I think
should be filled, partly because there are statistics proving a wide prevalence but less of a qualitative understating of it, and partly because time
appropriation might represent something more than "decaf resistance"
since it provides us with the scarcity I just mentioned – time. Whether
it is only for this reason that people engage in it or whether there are
still aspects of "sabotage" to it etc., deserves to be further explored.
Again, a lead question is *why*?

Relating to the other question – *how*? – the organizational context
of empty labor is also an issue that should be further elaborated,
particularly since most studies of time appropriation are based on
shop floor ethnographies, where labor processes can be very different
from office work with regard to surveillance, autonomy, complexity
etc. The limitations and advantages of approaching this subject doing
interviews are discussed in the Appendix.

4 | *Mapping out empty labor*

As Scott has put it, there is a "double conspiracy of silence" shrouding acts of insubordination in anonymity. For the perpetrators, safety lies in their invisibility. For the officials, interest lies in not encouraging others and calling attention to the fragility of their moral sway (Scott, 2012: 8). This makes the study of organizational misbehavior exceeding mere triviality somewhat challenging. At the beginning of this research project, I had heard of some extreme examples of empty labor through friends and acquaintances. I found these to be exceptionally intriguing, almost like counterexamples of everything I had learned as a student of sociology. When I embarked on the empirical study, the extreme cases still interested me the most. But it was not only personal fascination that urged me to do the selection I did. The most important reason was that empty labor tended and still tends to be reduced to banality in the literature. The notion of blurring boundaries between work and leisure suggests that what we do not do at work evens itself out when considering all the work we do from home (see Allvin et al., 2011; Hochschild, 1997). Short "breaks," we are told, can even prove to be beneficial for productivity in the long run (see Garrett and Danziger, 2008; Ivarsson and Larsson, 2012). To be sure to evade these comments, which otherwise can be very hard to falsify, I decided to concentrate on *employees who spent half or more of their working hours on private activities.*

Those interested in how I managed to find such employees may refer to the Appendix. All in all, I interviewed twenty women and twenty-three men. Since I had only one selection criterion, I garnered wide occupational variety in the sample. Interviewing employees from very different working environments – e.g. marketing, finance, software development, logistics, sales, pharmaceutical production, social work, archival work, manufacturing industry, mining industry, service industry – enabled me to develop a multifaceted analysis of empty labor that a standard ethnography would not have allowed. Still the variety should not be exaggerated. For instance, it should be noted that I did *not* interview any hospital nurses, or fast food or assembly line workers. Researchers, journalists, artists, farmers, and others for whom the working time tends to merge with the spare time were furthermore avoided for reasons of validity. Yes, sometimes it can be very hard to tell what is work and what is not, but with the exception of a privileged few, it is fairly easy. A tougher distinction was between those who withdraw from work voluntarily and those who are enduring it against their will.

When I began searching for interviewees the term I used for what would later become "empty labor" was the Swedish word *maskning*. *Maskning* (noun for the verb *maska*) could most easily be translated into "masking" in the sense of concealing something – in this case, what you do at work. But it has a twofold meaning. It denotes "soldiering" or "footdragging," the type of oppositional behavior or sabotage in industrial settings described in Chapter 3, but it is also the term you use when referring to "doing nothing / not working while at work." The difference may not appear great, but is crucial when it comes to the question of resistance.

It first dawned on me during an interview with a florist. "We never argue about me having too much," she said about her employer, "but about how I can get more things to do." She worked for a big furnishing company that recently had decided to sell flowers and she received two or three clients a day. The shop was neatly ordered, she put effort into the arrangements, the cleaning, and all she could to make it "look good," but since no clients turned up, it was impossible to fill a whole day with meaningful work. The afternoons were often spent at a café nearby where she read and played with her cell phone while keeping an eye on whether any potential client would pass by. She reproached her employer for not knowing anything about "doing business."

When listening to her story, I realized that I could not possibly frame all sorts of empty labor as resistance or as expressions of subjectivity. At that moment I was not acquainting myself with someone slacking off as a protest or because she did not care about her work, I was approaching what might be called *the absurdity of work*. More specifically there was a great difference among the interviewees in how they experienced their workload, or rather how much they could actually do. This, together with what turned out to be another variable – how much work they wanted to do – allowed me to discern four types of empty labor that I will present in this chapter. Before describing the outlines of each type, I will analytically explain the two dimensions of empty labor.

4.1 Potential output

Wilhelm Baldamus (1961) early developed conceptual tools for understanding how the conflict between managerial and worker interests appears on the organizational level and how the "effort bargain" is at the core of each employment relation. Even if Baldamus' model needs to be updated, several of his concepts are relevant to the study of empty labor – particularly the notion that the relation between output (i.e. the quantity and quality of that which is being produced) and effort (defined as "the sum total of physical and mental exertion, tedium, fatigue, or any other disagreeable aspect of work" (Baldamus, 1961: 29)) always constitutes a source of uncertainty in the labor process. While it often is assumed that output and effort can be rationally measured against each other, Baldamus convincingly demonstrates that this is not even possible in the most Taylorized firm. The difficulty of estimating when workers produce at the top of their capability and how much new technology can increase their productivity was the reason why Taylor never managed to eliminate soldiering but created a new game between the "Methods Department" and the workers (cf. Roy, 1953). Attempts to go around this uncertainty are futile, Baldamus contends, and he illustrates his argument with this example:

[A] collective agreement between the Federated Associations of Boot and Shoe Manufacturers and the National Union of Boot and Shoe Operatives (January 1954) requires from the employer to 'pay the full rates of wages for all output', and from the employees, 'to use their trade skill and productive ability to the best advantage and fullest capacity and with no restriction of output following a change of organization or machinery'. But who can define ability, restricted output, capacity ('fullest' or otherwise)? (Baldamus, 1961: 90)

I would suggest that the answer to his question is the worker, but that is beside the point. What Baldamus argues is that "the formal contract between employer and employee is *incomplete* in a very fundamental sense" (ibid.). While it often is assumed that there is no limit to the amount of work that the employee can engage in, sometimes the *potential output* may settle on a very low level in relation to effort. In the case of the florist, her main task, to keep the shop in order and take care of clients, turned out to require a low effort vis-à-vis the time she had available. Therefore, after her morning routines there was not much for her to do except waiting for new clients. In other jobs the main task may be equally undemanding but coupled with various "extras," i.e. jobs for which the employee has no real responsibility but that he or she may choose to do anyway. When I define the potential output as low, as in the case of the florist, the main task requires little effort in relation to time whereas extra tasks are either not available or so distant from the employees' responsibilities that it would put them in trouble if they were to engage in them. Here, the expectations of clients, colleagues, and management play a central role. The potentiality should thus be considered in an organizational context – to be sure, you can always devise work that is of no use to anyone, including the firm. In some cases, empty labor may take place despite the employee, as an effect of the organizational structures rather than of the employee's initiative. On the other hand, when the potential output of a job is high, i.e. when the main task of the employee requires a higher effort in relation to time, or when there is plenty of extra work readily at hand, empty labor can come about only if the employee actively withdraws from work.

What I have described here is a scale for how to understand the organizational context of empty labor based on the single variable of potential output. Needless to say, the reality of organizational life is rarely that simple. There are often transitions from one level to another in which the employee may be highly involved. Organizational structures are precisely what the act of time appropriation must manipulate to be successful, and this also involves defining one's tasks and responsibilities. Sometimes the job and particularly the extras may be very loosely defined, and management may express different attitudes and expectations concerning employee initiative. Potential output is, in other words, a dynamic concept. One could question the whole meaning of it and argue that "there is always work" if only the employee communicates understimulation to the manager, or is "creative" enough to invent new tasks etc. My argument, which will be developed in Chapter 7, is that such notions tend to underestimate the complexities in the management-worker relationship and overestimate the rationality of the firm.

4.2 Work obligations

What Baldamus calls the "sense of work obligation" is captured in a survey question dealing specifically with the attitude towards "extras" that he quotes: "You probably do certain things in your job not actually specified in your contract. Suppose you are justifiably dissatisfied but can do nothing about your grievance short of finding another job. Would you, in the meantime, drop the extras?" (Baldamus, 1961: 85–86). The sense of work obligation can be defined as the employee's inclination to work within the frames of the firm regardless of collegial and managerial pressures. Weak work obligations can result in soldiering, strong work obligations can result in inventing more or less meaningful work when the potential output is low. According to Baldamus, "the whole complex of obligations to work [appears] to be surrounded by feelings of guilt, a variety of rationalizations, and, often a marked reluctance to articulate these attitudes into definite statements" (Baldamus, 1961: 87). Unlike many other sociologists of work, he cares little about the supposed manipulation of feelings towards work and performance. Sentiments "cannot be measured" he argues, and "the techniques that attempt to change them can only be inferred from overt behavior" (Baldamus, 1961: 42). Work obligations go much deeper, to primary socialization, which is proved, he claims, by the fact that the two most significant variables that affected the answer to the survey question were income and social origin: the more you earned and the higher the social class you came from, the more probable that you would not drop the extras.

Although Baldamus discerns an important factor of the labor process, my take on work obligations is different. As Martin Sprouse (1992: 4) contends in his interview study of sabotage, "each person's choice of sabotage and reasons for using it were as much a reflection of their character as of their jobs. The motives behind the acts covered the spectrum between altruism and revenge." Like Sprouse, I believe that these motives may be more than the effects of class and income and worth analyzing on their own terms, i.e. as verbalized by employees regardless of position and background (Chapter 6 offers such an analysis). Also, it is important to stress that just as potential output

	Low potential output	High potential output
Strong work obligations	Enduring	Coping
Weak work obligations	Slacking	Soldiering

Figure 4.1 Empty labor according to work obligations and potential output.

must be understood in an organizational context, work obligation here means obligation to work *for the firm*. Most of the interviewees who are categorized as having weak work obligations are very productive when it comes to self-initiated work or studies. In many cases, it is precisely these other types of work that supersede the work that the employee is supposed to perform.

As we see in Figure 4.1, high or low levels of work obligations and potential output make for four types of empty labor. *Enduring* refers to an involuntary form of empty labor, whereas *soldiering* refers to the intentional type of "output restriction" commonly analyzed in labor process theory. *Coping* is a form of empty labor that may be called "recreational" in a non-euphemistic sense. It differs from soldiering in that the employee's intention when coping is to remain at a productive maximum. *Slacking* signifies the happy marriage between weak work obligations and low potential output. Here, the employees enjoy periods of empty labor with less conflicting feelings than in enduring.

Again, empty labor is rarely static enough to stay within one of the squares above. There are movements between the types to which I shall return. The difference between enduring and slacking can simply be a matter of changing moods from day to day – the sense of freedom and autonomy that some associate with empty labor may soon change into boredom. Similarly the potential output is not a constant that remains unaffected by the employee's actions. If someone has been soldiering for a while, thus withdrawing from what could be done, the extras may have moved to the (unofficial) responsibilities of someone else, thus shrinking the potential output of the individual worker (see Chapter 7).

Before analyzing the organizational conditions and individual motivations behind the different types of empty labor, I will briefly describe what they may look like. The idea is not to give a full account but rather a sense of how they differ from each other; therefore the few examples I give in this chapter are intended only as illustrations. Questions such as why those enduring empty labor do not ask their bosses for more work or whether slacking can be viewed as a collective form of soldiering etc. will be saved for the following chapters.

4.3 Slacking

In his theory of the leisure class, Veblen (2008 [1899]) questions the utility perspective that still dominates economic theory while pointing out irrational and, as he excessively argues, primitive elements in the economic behavior of the upper classes. According to Veblen, the modern leisure class was not liberated from work; instead it participated, but only in a minor, highly symbolic, and still conspicuous manner. More importantly, the leisure class not only consisted of the noble and priestly classes; especially when it came to "conspicuous waste," their "retinue" also played an important part. The "vicarious leisure" that some duties of the servant class entailed, served, according to Veblen, the function of "imputing pecuniary reputability to the master or to the household on the ground that a given amount of time and effort is conspicuously wasted in that behalf" (2008 [1899]: 25). In this study, we will probably not find any clear-cut representatives of today's leisure class; this "subsidiary or derivative leisure class" is on the other hand well represented among the interviewees.

A web designer describes the Swedish office of the international broadcasting company she works for as a "big playground for adults." Greeted by a massive aquarium in the shape of a reception desk, the visitor is guided through an open plan office where each department has been markedly designed to correspond to a metropolis. In the glittering Dubai section that the web department occupies, the real work constitutes approximately *one hour* of working hours, whereas the rest of the time is devoted to slack. For instance, the web developers take turns at being "disc jockey" to the music streaming through the headsets that they all wear; through Messenger they silently exchange web links, internal jokes, and lengthy discussions about where to eat lunch, but most of all, they surf the web for their own pleasure. If she

wanted to work more than is required of her, she would not know
what to do, she claims. "If I started asking for work the whole day
they would probably wonder what's wrong with me."

She came in directly from high school. A friend that she knew from
an internet forum had asked whether she would be interested in working for a widely renowned firm where he then was employed. She said
yes without really believing that there would come something out of
it. She had no education – "I was just a hobby designer" – and she
had never had "a real job." When her current boss first called her, he
wanted her to come for an interview on the same day.

So there I was, dressed in sweatpants, at the cool, cool [company]. I felt
really awkward and when I met my boss he was like: 'okay?' . . . Then he
drew a diagram and said: 'if we say that you are here now, where would you
like to be in two years?' And I just thought, what? Then he drew a line: 'this
is the development of [the company]. I think that in two years, you should
be here.' I just stared, like is this for real? Then, afterwards I've understood
that he was pulling my leg. *He just wanted to know if I was good-looking
or not.*

Clearly, this is a milieu where Weber's conception of the "purely impersonal character of the office, with its separation of the private sphere
from that of the official activities" (Weber, 1978 [1922]: 968, does
not apply. Yet it is more than a "culture of fun" where employees are
encouraged to express their personalities and think about their work
as "play" (cf. Fleming, 2005a). This is a job where a large proportion
of the working hours *is* devoted to play – play that has nothing to
do with designing websites. The designer does not have any sense of
work obligation whatsoever and is happy that her boss seems to share
her disloyalty to the company: "I remember one time when he said
'now I have 600 unread mails in my inbox.' Then he marked them and
pressed delete. 'Now I have zero.'"

A common understanding among those who are slacking (and soldiering) is that "as long as the client is pleased, nothing else matters"
(the same observation was also made in D'Abate, 2005: 1023). But
not even with that credo can empty labor take place in the open. The
closest manager may accept or even be involved in the activities that fill
empty labor, but that does not mean that one can let colleagues from
other departments know what is going on; one must always appear
busy. Yet as long as you are in front of a screen, that is not very difficult

according to the designer: "Think of a mom, or just anyone who has recently learned Outlook. They don't have a clue about what is happening on the screen as long as it is full of color and looks advanced." Even if slack is the only form of empty labor where there is no conflict between the employee's work obligations and the potential output, that does not mean that anything goes. It is still crucial to not reveal how much empty labor you have. The difference between slacking and soldiering is that in slacking, management, colleagues, or clients do not expect more of you than what you actually do. In order to get more work, you have to expand your area of responsibility, which may not always be the easiest thing to do. While some enjoy this type of slacking, others merely endure it.

4.4 Enduring

One condition that seems necessary for a weak sense of work obligation is that the employee benefits from some type of external activity that she or he perceives as more meaningful than the job. It can take the form of writing a dissertation, but it can also be indulging in movies or music. An instrumental attitude to work, i.e. to appear at work not for the sake of the productive performance *per se*, but for the salary (cf. MOW International Research Team, 1987), is dominant among slacking interviewees in this study. But as many commentators have pointed out, traditional work ethics are far from eradicated. Whether valued as part of an identity project or as a meaningful activity in itself, wage labor is still a major source of self-esteem for many people (cf. Bauman, 2004; Beder, 2001). As the case of the florist illustrates, empty labor can be of more trouble than gain to these people, sometimes leading to a state of intense apathy and boredom (also known as "boreout," see Chapter 7).

Here, we should draw a parallel to the extensive research on various survival strategies at work. A common observation among ethnographers who have experienced the monotony of the majority of wage labor jobs is how it forces the worker to create games whose autonomous character renders psychological investment possible (Burawoy, 1979: 72; Ditton, 1977: 76; Roy, 1953: 5). Today the games at work are no longer bound to the labor process – they can be more than distractions. Strange as it may sound, blogging, chatting, studying, reading, are activities with intrinsic values that people also perform outside of work. As defined here, "enduring" signifies the failure of fully engaging in such games. To the endurer, time awareness acquires another meaning than the economically oriented one described by sociological classics such as Weber (1992 [1904]) and E.P. Thompson (1967). The endurer's awareness of time implies time as an agonizing dimension of life that needs to be repressed (while working).

A key accountant desk manager has worked at a logistics company for five years. His task is to track deliveries of the company's most important clients whenever anything goes wrong. Work comes in waves: some days, he works nonstop all of his working hours, other days, he works less than one hour. The calls usually come in between 2 and 3 p.m., before and after that period it is up to him to do follow-ups and "go through the routines." However, that type of "overwork" usually takes very little time. This is the difference between his current position and the job he earlier had at the same company: "Then, there were always things to do. I worked at the complaint department and we were always lagging behind."

He does not share his responsibilities with someone else, but he has noticed that he is not the only one at the office who spends his time on other things than work. "The guy beside me mostly plays web games and speaks on the phone... But there are not that many options." His superiors, who have no insight into his work and who do not even share an office with him, know nothing about the effort required for what he does, but they seem to have noticed that the internet is used for other things than work. On the pretense that too much web surfing slows down the network, some web pages have been "proxy blocked." "Facebook was down for a while, then they turned it on again. They figured that it might be a good way of networking. Which is interesting. Now everyone seems to have become tired of Facebook so we're no longer there the whole day. *Aftonbladet* [a Swedish daily newspaper] is also blocked, but not between eleven and one."

Like the florist, he has done nothing, except applying for a new position, to free his working hours from work. When asked whether there are any chances that he might get more job tasks, he seems negative: "No. This is a fairly new post so it's just one client at a time. In the beginning I had very little to do, but now there are more clients, and the more goods, the more there is to do. So there will probably be more. Sort of." It is with mixed feelings that he watches the days pass by. To him, a balance between work and empty labor is of vital importance to his well-being. This becomes particularly palpable when the workday is over: "If you've had a lot of shit during the day, you can be tired. But you can also be tired if you've had nothing to do." Although the desk manager is a devoted Wikipedia surfer, he feels that "you can't do that the whole day." Work is not experienced as a burden or as humiliation. Work is stimulation, not necessarily with any intrinsic value, but still a better way to "kill time" than cyberslacking. In coping, this sense of work obligation is equally strong, but here the potential output is high.

4.5 Coping

Before entering more deeply into the category of soldiering, which is of most interest in this study, I must first mention coping in some detail. How can a strong sense of work obligation and high potential output lead to empty labor? The answer can be found only if we look at some of the persons that I interviewed who did not spend half or more of their working hours on empty labor but just a minor proportion of the working day. These are the interviewees whom I found accidentally.

Psychologists and management scholars have labeled the idea that empty labor can be used as a way of coping a "neutralization technique" that employees use to rationalize their "offense" (D'Abate, 2005; Sagie et al., 2003; Vivien and Thompson, 2005). Even if it is impossible for an external observer to tell the difference between a "neutralization technique" and a valid argument, I would rather submit that employees who work under stressful conditions can have good reasons for taking refuge in periods of empty labor. Among the coping employees whom I interviewed, two shared a history of long-term sick leave and burnout that they now believe they have found means of avoiding. Five of them are social workers, either working at care facilities or with social security. Among these, taking some time off is considered "an ability" known to be more productive in the long run. This is also reflected in how management can encourage the personnel to obtain their share of empty labor from time to time. As one allowance administrator points out, however, policy and practice are often decoupled from each other: "'Of course you should, of course you should take some time off,' they say. But then you're not always ready to take the consequences." Another allowance administrator even criticizes her boss for cyberloafing too much: "She uses MSN to communicate with her husband – even when you come in to her office to ask her about stuff! To me, that's beyond limits. You shouldn't be online all the time like that. You have to be present." The work pressure does not necessarily come from management imperatives; it can also, and more effectively, come from the clients or more specifically from the moral meaning of their work. The feeling of underachievement often urges them on; or as a nurse puts it: "Sometimes it feels like only the basic mission is fulfilled. To give them [the patients] food and keep them whole and clean." Coping is not really a solution to this situation, just a way of handling it. Now, the nurse has learned to "say no" from time to time, but at the cost of a constantly bad conscience.

But coping does not have to be a matter of pure survival. It can also be a way of proving to yourself that you are in control of your own time, that the long education that is needed for some of the posts has paid off, that you are privileged. An allowance administrator who worked under heavy pressure described how some minor "time perks" functioned as veritable safety valves:

I guess it gives a feeling of freedom. To know that 'yes, I can actually take that private call now or do that thing now' gives the feeling that you're in charge of your time. . . . If I weren't able to do it, I would feel trapped. I think that a little space of freedom is what makes people stand it. I can make decisions on my own and to be able to decide on your own creates a cheerful atmosphere. (Allowance administrator)

As in many cases of soldiering, less meaningful work is what coping employees avoid. Typically, this means less bureaucratic work and cleaning. A keeper at a psychiatric care center describes her situation: "There are a lot of other things as well in our job. We're supposed to write a bunch of, well . . . write-ups and fuss around. And I feel like . . . I mean, to sort hundreds of files that nobody has touched during the last 10 years and so on? That makes no sense." This statement reflects how work obligations can be unequally distributed in relation to different work tasks – the official job description is of less importance than professional and personal ethics. This might certainly be translated into psychological concepts such as "rationalization" or "neutralization," but that would imply that the employee is less rational than the organization of which she or he is a member. Particularly within the sector of social services, this seems to be open to debate.

4.6 Soldiering

The earliest mentioning of "soldiering" that I have found is in Taylor (1919: 13) who defines it as "deliberately working slowly so as to avoid doing a full day's work." How do you manage to appropriate half of your working hours without getting caught? The answer can now be provided in all its simplicity: you exploit others' ignorance of what the job entails. Among professionals, this method of "making time" has been noted before: "A lawyer will take two weeks to do what can be done in two days. A watchmaker will say 'ten days' for a job he knows will take ten minutes. This juggling with time is rarely questioned" (Mars, 1982: 50). The reason why professionals may get away with it, is, according to Mars, their "statelessness" and "status" that make them unaccountable and lift them above the control apparatuses of wage labor. But there are also other conditions facilitating radical forms of soldiering that are not exclusive to professionals.

A difference between coping and soldiering is that coping rarely occupies more than one hour a day whereas soldiering can easily free the autonomous use of more than half the working hours. Yet, the most important difference is that of work obligations. When soldiering, the employee has no ethical or identity-grounded relationship to the work activity. Trying not to lose one's job and still get away with minimal effort is a typical example of an instrumental work attitude. In Chapter 6, I will turn the focus on *why* employees engage in soldiering, and as we shall see many do it because for one reason or another, they have grown tired of their jobs and set much store by autonomy. But not even soldiering can be equated with subjectivity as such. Several structural elements are interacting with employees at this point: both organizational structures and institutional structures. For instance, the labor contract can be designed so that soldiering is an almost inevitable consequence. A particularly interesting example is a machine technician who was employed to calibrate machine tools at an industrial workshop for a few summers in order for the employer to receive a certification. The employment ended when the job was done – so he stretched it out. As he puts it:

I had work as long as there was work for me to do . . . so it was in my own interest to prolong the work as much as possible and gain as much money as possible. So a job that could have been done in four weeks was extended to six or eight weeks. Well, to sum up my profit as it were.

As with many other interviewees who were soldiering, time appropriation was not the only type of organizational misbehavior that he was engaged in. Private production corresponding to what Certeau, Anteby, and other French call *la perruque* was widespread at the workshop, especially the construction of private distilling apparatuses, and the more desirable instruments had a tendency to "disappear."[1] According to the technician, there was a "culture" that promoted soldiering and misbehavior at all levels. "What I have seen is actually men in their fifties and sixties who deliberately furnish the room to facilitate *maskning*," he says. Some of his friends who did nightshifts could "just clock in, go away, come back and clock out." Whether that is true is beside the point; what matters is that he felt that there were economic reasons and a culture that provided moral support for his soldiering. The potential output was thus considerably higher than what he actually did, and the motivation to work at the top of his ability was low.

We have now seen examples of how organizational and motivational conditions surrounding empty labor may vary. The types of empty labor raise questions that we need to take into account when studying subjectivity. If the potential output is low, as in cases of slacking and enduring, can we talk about empty labor as workplace resistance? Furthermore, how can the potential output be low to begin with? What are the organizational circumstances that allow this to happen? And how can anyone manage to work less than half of his or her working hours when the potential output is high?

In the next chapter, I address the latter question. This will be the first chapter where I address the how-questions. The following chapters are organized according to the two different scales of potential output and work obligation. I begin by treating the how-questions in

---

[1] Advice to fiddlers: According to the technician they used a very clever method for workplace pilferage that I have not seen described anywhere in the literature. Instead of just taking the instrument or material home, he hid it first at the workplace, to let it "cool off" for a while. When it had been forgotten or no one could any longer tell who had used it the last time, the risk of bringing it home was considerably lower.

relation to high potential output, i.e. coping and especially soldiering. In Chapter 6, I then treat the why-questions, i.e. why the interviewees themselves think they engage in time appropriation, still in relation to cases of empty labor with high potential output. In Chapter 7, I return to the mystery of low potential output.

As the reader will notice, in some instances it can be hard to distinguish between the different types of empty labor. A case of individual slacking such as the one described above could also be viewed as collective soldiering. Potential output is not only a matter of how much work the organization could theoretically (and profitably) perform. There may be much work to do, but a lax manager or low production norms can effectively lower the potential output for the individual employee.

5 | *How to succeed at work without really trying*

"Eighty percent of success is just showing up." This quote, attributed to Woody Allen, was recently verified by Elsbach et al. (2010) who in both qualitative and experimental studies demonstrated a positive correlation between displaying "passive face time" (i.e. the time one is passively observed at the office) and being considered "dependable" and "committed" by coworkers and managers. As they conclude, passive face time will "affect employees' status, performance evaluations, raises, promotions, and job security – even though being observed at the work site may not be linked to actual productivity" (Elsbach et al., 2010: 755). In this chapter, we learn how to make this link between face time and productivity as weak as possible. More concretely, we explore the tactical patterns of soldiering in the form of five pointers on how to succeed with radical time appropriation. While this more practical part may serve the reader in very direct ways, it will also contribute to a theoretical understanding of the organizational mechanisms that are at work behind empty labor and serve as a background for the next chapter, where I discuss the motivations behind soldiering. As stated in the methods chapter, it would be impossible to go through the exact, sometimes very technical, operations each employee employed when appropriating time. I can tell you that the telephone operator managed to fake calls and manipulate the monitoring system by some kind of tactic that involved keeping track of the managers, pushing the mute button, and pretending not to hear the clients, but I cannot say which monitoring software she dealt with, exactly how she balanced the fake calls with real calls, or which managers were "sloppy" and which were "fascists," and how she learned to tell the difference. In most cases, such details are not even necessary to answer the how-questions referred to in the introduction.

Although I will exemplify the tactics more thoroughly in some instances, revealing everything in detail would also be hard to justify ethically. As Michel Crozier points out, the effort bargain between management and workers is determined by the uncertainty in the labor process. Thus: "The risk, of course, is that by disclosing too much the know-how necessary for 'making out,' the workers give weapons to help further rationalization. This is another reason for keeping such practices at least half secret" (Crozier, 1971: 162). This is also one more argument against thick descriptions in this field of research. The purpose of critical workplace studies cannot be to provide rich data on how employees circumvent managerial control. The challenge is rather to explain and inspire organizational misbehavior while guarding the half secrecy of its exact workings in relation to a particular labor process. As the reader will notice, each suggestion is quite general in character; each separately provides an answer to the how-questions of empty labor in contexts of high potential output.

5.1 Pick the right job

If I could offer only one tip for succeeding in the appropriation of your own time, picking the right job would be it. As we have seen in the case of slacking and enduring, if you pick with precision, you may not have to do any more to enjoy long hours of empty labor. Evidently, the difficulty lies in deciding which jobs are more amenable to emptiness and which are not. Struggling with the same problem, Adams gives the advice to "[s]elect an area that is so dry that when the average person is exposed to it he'll want to drill a hole in his head to let the boredom out" (1996: 114). He suggests facilities management, database administration, and tax law as typical examples. Less interested in the substance of work, Guy Standing argues that it is the conditions of employment, whether you belong to those who still have stable full-time employment – the "salariat" – or to those in more precarious forms of labor – the "precariat" – that decides the emptiness of your job:

In many modern offices, employees turn up early in the morning in casual or sports clothes, take a shower and groom themselves over the first hour 'at work'. It is a hidden perk of the salariat. They keep clothes in the office, have mementoes from home life scattered around and in some cases allow young children to play, 'as long as they don't disturb daddy or mummy', which, of course, they do. In the afternoon, after lunch, the salariat may take a 'power nap', long regarded as a home activity. Listening to music on the iPod is not unknown to while away those hours at work. (Standing, 2011: 118)

To aim for dryness or stable employment is not a bad piece of advice, but I want to argue that there is an even more important principle for picking the right job. To get a feeling for it, you can start by skimming through the stories posted at websites such as dettommearbejde.dk and maska.nu, where anonymous slackers share their experiences. Typical occupations that are represented at these sites include business development managers, pharmacists, churchwardens, receptionists, museum guards, librarians, janitors. What do these occupations have in common? My answer would be that while it is easy for an outsider to see their organizational *function*, it is harder to tell what they actually *do*.

A concept that I will elaborate here and in Chapter 7 is the *opacity* of a certain job. By that I mean the degree to which the labor process is difficult for a layperson to understand and estimate in relation to time and effort. Sometimes the opacity may simply be the consequence of how complex the labor process really is; sometimes there may be other factors obscuring the content of a job. As Mars puts it: "Where ambiguity over the quantity of a good, its quality, or its exact category is inherent in its nature, this may not only cloak fiddling but be specially developed to do so" (Mars, 1982: 115).

The opacity of a job stands in direct relation to the expertise, education, and status associated with it. An archivist says that archival science was the best subject with which he could have complemented his degree program in liberal arts. From "no chance to get a job" he went to "a prospering labor market" and a job quite different from the often assumed "being down in the dusty archives all day long." Writing his master's thesis in another subject while at the job, he has never experienced any trouble or even the need to justify his work rate. According to him, that is because he is in good company:

There are many who have a work task as an archivist and who write their book, or their articles, or whatever during working hours that are supposed to be used up doing tasks for the company. It can be related to the job in one way, since you often consult certain sources, but you do it for your own profit, to promote your own career. And this often takes place with the implicit consent of the employer.... I mean, sometimes you *know* that no human being could work this slow. It's just impossible.... But I have never heard of anyone being accused or anything.

The archivist claims that his superiors "really aren't interested as long as nobody complains." This is a recurring theme to which I will return.

Nearly all the interviewed employees were subject to a management strategy that Andrew Friedman once termed "responsible autonomy." In his words, this allows "individual workers or groups of workers a wide measure of discretion over the direction of their work tasks and the maintenance of managerial authority by getting workers to identify with the competitive aims of the enterprise so that they will act 'responsibly' with a minimum of supervision" (Friedman, 1977: 48). Today, responsible autonomy is often combined with using clients as a control instance. But what happens when the employee does not identify with the "competitive aims" and when there are no clearly defined clients, or the client is just as oblivious as the superiors of how much to demand? This is when it might be more relevant to talk about "irresponsible autonomy," to use a term from Ackroyd and Thompson (1999: 53–74).

What is remarkably clear among the employees in this study is that the involvement of new technology, especially software, may create a nearly impenetrable opacity in the labor process. That may be one reason why most of the interviewees had jobs that involved working in front of a screen. As Figure 5.1 shows, surfing the web is by far the most popular way to engage in empty labor.[1]

When the knowledge of new technology is monopolized or shared by just a few, the possibilities for soldiering increase dramatically. A software engineer who was employed at a company and responsible for developing the internal system and the web interface explains how he managed to break free from the pressure despite a potential output that was well beyond his capacities. Since it was a "never-ending job" with no clear concept of what the finished product should be, with "the solution to one problem leading to twenty new problems," there

---

[1] This result, which represents the Finnish population, is similar to that of a US survey where 52 percent cited web surfing as the "#1 distraction at work." In the same study, number two was "socializing with co-workers" (26 percent) and number three "running errands off-premises" (8 percent) (Malachowski and Simonini, 2006). A survey from 2012 found that "the most popular time-wasting websites" were Facebook (visited by 41 percent of the respondents), LinkedIn (37 percent), Yahoo (31 percent) and Google+ (28 percent; Gouveia, 2012). Many of the interviewees attested to how easy it is to log on and out; "it's like having a whole universe just a couple of clicks away," an accounting clerk said. Also, it can also be hidden with a single click. A job involving a lot of computer use may therefore be a good option – as long as computer-monitoring programs remain as exceptional as today (cf. Shellenbarger, 2012).

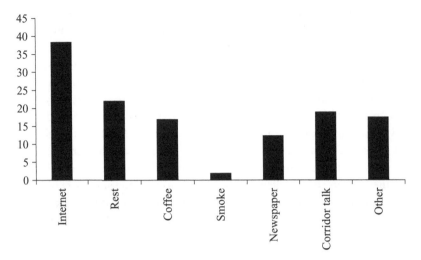

Figure 5.1 Average time (in minutes) spent on private activities per day. Finland, 2010.
1. Non-work-related internet use. 2. Rest and relaxation between tasks. 3. Coffee breaks. 4. Smoke breaks. 5. Reading the newspaper. 6. Idle talk in the corridors. 7. Other non-work activities such as just doing nothing.
Source: Taloustutkimus Oy (n = 1077).

was nothing, not even the salary, that motivated him to work full-time. The fact that they were only two in the department – both sharing a weak sense of work obligation – at a large-scale company where the other employees were strangers to them, greatly facilitated their collective soldiering:

Then it is quite easy to say 'no we haven't had time with your project yet because we are busy with these ones.' ...They know nothing about how long things should take. So you can say that you are still working on it when you are done. Because they don't know what you do. They just have to listen to what you say, and besides, they don't have time to watch you either.

Here Mars' distinction between "cyclical" and "linear" time in relation to what he calls "time fiddling" is most relevant. A pilot who spends his or her working day flying to a single destination experiences time more linearly than a bus driver who repeats the same journey ten times a day. The most extreme type of cyclical jobs is evidently Taylorized piece-work where a small operation is repeated hundreds of times during the day. What Mars proposes is that in occupations where employees perceive their tasks to be cyclical, they will "fiddle time" by slowing down the work rate, whereas with linear tasks, time is made by speeding up the rate. By this, he means that cyclical tasks must be slowed down when they are being "priced," which is an observation that dates back at least to Donald Roy's (1952, 1953, 1954) early studies of the piecework system to which I will return in the next section. Although variants of that tactic still are at play in radical soldiering, I would say that the safest way to really succeed in time appropriation is to avoid cyclical jobs altogether. No one in this study had piecework jobs, and if there were cyclical job tasks, they were few and spread over longer periods of time. Linear jobs are thus a better option, but there are probably other time dimensions that one might discern to distinguish between jobs in relation to opacity.

One that I would like to propose is that of *infinite time*, i.e. occupations where employees perceive their tasks as infinite – or to put it differently, where the potential output does not seem to have any limits, where there is no clear beginning, and no clear end. At first view, this may seem like a very bad condition for making time; on the other hand, if you are working with an archive that may be organized and reorganized over and over, what difference does it make if you work half as much as you could? In comparison with infinity, the work of a single employee makes little difference. Similarly, when projects are piled up from the beginning and you feel that you will have to prioritize, why say no to ten projects when you can say no to twenty? As the software engineer makes clear, you do not even have to say no if you play your cards well. If a project is supposed to take two weeks, you wait until the two weeks have passed and then you say: "'well, we tried, but unfortunately we will need five weeks.'" If there is an urgency, you can also play off the projects against each other: "'Sure we can do your project, but then you will have to talk with them.' . . . You can always let them fight about your time like that and say something like 'it's up to you to decide whose project is the most important.'" Everyone understands that you cannot be in two places at the same time, but less recognized is the fact that you may be in *neither* place. Similarly, one project can cover up for ignoring another. If you do not have such a cover project, why not invent one?

Of course, opacity is not the only factor to consider when picking the right job. Another, much more studied aspect that I will return to in Chapter 7 is irrational organization or "bad management." Sometimes, even if you work at the supermarket, your boss might, out of sheer ignorance, create the right conditions for plenty of empty labor without any effort on your part. How do you find such a boss? I do not know, but based on the interviews, there seems to be no sector of the labor market where they do not exist. You might find them in the public sector – or in the private sector. You might find them in industries – or at offices. You might find them in utterly hierarchical bureaucracies – or in flat, "organic" organizations. Unfortunately, unless we are in the position to jump between jobs, we are quite powerless when it comes to selecting our bosses. A good guideline, therefore, is to think more in terms of opacity.

Opacity, however, is not only related to profession. Another factor that others have emphasized and that is related to the infinity of work tasks mentioned above is the size of the company (cf. Bolchover, 2005; Parkinson, 1957; Rothlin and Werder, 2007). This is an important reason why some of the interviewees came from occupational groups that you would not expect in a study like this. One such example was a construction worker who describes his time in Norway as particularly relaxed. The bigger the building constructions were, the less he normally had to do. The contractor he worked for was not a large-scale firm, but the teams worked at three to five different building sites, which meant that they rarely saw their foreman. The proprietors were overwhelmed by the different contractors and subcontractors that were scattered over the sites. Apparently, there were too many teams to control, or even to make sure that each of them was constantly at work:

So sometimes we could be given a task like 'today you're going to build this scaffold.' Like, okay? And because we were from Sweden, the Norwegians had this idea that we were hard-working and so on. So sometimes they said: 'you better do this so that it gets done.' 'Thanks a lot,' we said and then we took a three-hour lunch break.

Juggling projects, as demonstrated, or writing a master's thesis at work with the employer turning a blind eye to it are not options available to everyone. How easily these things come is primarily a question of how opaque your job is. If you pick the right job, you can enjoy thick opacity from the beginning. But opacity is not an unchangeable constant; you can always make your job more opaque than it currently is.

5.2 Exploit the uncertainties

Despite the fact that none of the interviewees had piecework jobs in a strict sense, early industrial sociology literature on soldiering remains very relevant since it captures the basic principles of time appropriation. This is particularly the case with Roy's (1952) work on quota restriction and goldbricking. A distinction that you will still notice when talking about soldiering is that between "gravy" tasks and "stinkers." In the machine shop where Roy did his ethnographical work, gravy jobs were those that paid well, whereas stinkers were those where you had to put in a great deal of effort to get above the base-pay rate for "take home." Roy observed that soldiering could follow two different rationales, depending on which work tasks you had. With gravy jobs, you had to take it easy in order to not exceed the limit (then, $1.25 an hour) where the suspicions of the Methods Department were evoked. This was called "quota restriction." If you worked too fast, the risk was always that "they'd retime this job so quick it would make your head swim!" as one of the workers succinctly put it (Roy, 1952: 430). With stinkers, the rationale was to do as little as possible in order to save your energy and maybe provoke a retiming: "I'm not going to bust my ass on stuff like this," as another worker said (Roy, 1952: 436). This was known as "goldbricking."

Whereas the equivalence to quota restriction is very much alive today, goldbricking is probably less practiced. Once it has been established how long a certain task should take, it is hard for the individual worker to change the standard unless there is reorganization or a new manager or client involved. Stinkers are rather defined by other factors, of which more later. Gravy jobs sometimes come from nowhere, but they can also be created – particularly in effort bargains that are related to time-limited projects. Thus, although it probably is a bad job for those interested in empty labor, even a cleaning job may have some opaque segments in relation to certain tasks or projects. According to a cleaner, the most gravy jobs are those during the summer when whole buildings are "sanitized" or cleaned more thoroughly. One summer when they were cleaning a school, her manager, who was also a cleaner, had done a great bargain that allowed or rather required them to take longer breaks than they were used to and also to leave two hours early every day. I asked her how she thought that was possible on a labor market where there is so much competition:

Competition sure, but everyone knows that if someone starts tampering with it, all will follow. Do you see what I mean? They call the cleaning companies and it has to be a company in the district so they can't pick and choose too much. Then Berith says 'yes we need three months for five persons.' Well, who can check that?

In his work on the bureaucratic organization, Crozier argues that there are always "zones of uncertainty" in the labor process that workers may exploit for their own good. This observation is used both to challenge the mechanistic model of the rational organization and the human relations school. "A human being," he says, "does not have only a hand and a heart. He has also a head, which means that he is free to decide and to play his own game. This is what almost all proponents of the human relations theories, as well as their early rationalist opponents, tend to forget" (Crozier, 1971: 149). Gravy jobs, whether they occur following negotiation with the Methods Department or with cleaning customers, derive from the uncertainty inherent in every labor process. To build up opacity, you only need one task, one new project, or piece of technology of which you are the expert. It can be the simplest work – you are still the expert. A building superintendent worked this out by putting a margin on all he did:

Now it's very rare that someone actually cares, but just in case I always put a margin on everything I do. Like doing the lawn takes two hours quite exactly, but then pulling out the lawn mower also takes an hour and driving it back takes yet another one. Some things never get done. Like weeding out the grass between the paving stones, I'll probably never get that finished. But when I do it, I'm very careful!

The uncertainty in the labor process that Baldamus and Crozier discuss can be complemented by another type of uncertainty, one that I would call the uncertainty of subjectivity. Since subjectivity, as I have defined the terms in Chapter 3, is beyond identity, the subject can use identity as a disguise. When working under "responsible autonomy," the type of identity that you want to convey is precisely that of responsibility. This is a recurring theme in all types of empty labor: the identity not only of responsibility, but also of excellence. "I quickly became their favorite employee," the web designer said about the first weeks at her job. Likewise, a home-service employee summarizes his career as follows: "it's a bit like in *Office Space* when he stays home and gets promoted." The important part, however, is that no one successful in appropriating time acts like the careless protagonist of *Office Space*. Again, empty labor must never be practiced overtly. As demonstrated by Campagna, the deceit may even be regarded as a heroic aspect of the soldiering employee – or of what he calls "the squanderer":

Squanderers dress like employees, smile to customers and bosses like employees. They perform as much as it is requested of them, or, if they are able to, they falsify the books. Always smiling, always cunning. Then, when the lights of the shop are off, when the door to the manager's office is closed, they pillage all they can. They mix whiskey with water, fraud bank transactions, export and sell databases, use till money to bet on horses. They take a nap when no one is watching, they work to the rule, play arcade games on their computers, steal the stock or give it away to friends. Perfect criminals are not those who rob a million banks in plain daylight with their face uncovered, and get away with it. Perfect criminals are those who are able to hide their theft and are never found out. (Campagna, 2013: 35–36)

Erving Goffman's trite notions of back stage and front stage may here be mentioned to make the point clear: the two must be kept separate. What Goffman calls "dark secrets" – facts that are "incompatible with the image of the self that the team attempts to maintain before its audience" (Goffman, 1956: 87) – and "strategic secrets" – "intentions and capacities of a team which it conceals from its audience in order to prevent them from adapting effectively to the state of affairs the team is planning to bring about" (ibid.) – must constantly be managed in order to succeed in time appropriation.

A way of doing this is, as Campagna advises, to keep the front stage clean and tidy: "I never come late, I always keep the clothes as they should be, clean and buttoned you know, I'm always nice with the bosses. That's all that's needed really," a subway ticket collector says. Others stress the importance of "performing" well on the more visible parts of your job. A typical example is that of a copywriter at an advertising agency who learned that the text material that she produced was not what her superiors and clients were interested in. Her value, or what comments she received and whether she had to rewrite, was rather determined by how well she presented and "framed" what she had written. From being one of the women who were close to burnout at the office, she allegedly "learned the talk," which eventually allowed her to cut her work in half. "When the job is so free the boss must literally hang over your shoulder to form an opinion and say you are actually not working now," she observes. Since nobody did that (and since the use of spyware would probably have damaged the "friendly atmosphere") she could do her writing tasks rather quickly, prepare for the presentation and rely on the fact that "it was the packaging that decided how it would be received in the high quarters." The informal behavior was also key in constructing an identity of responsibility: "then, during *fika* [the coffee breaks] you could sit there and say 'well, now I have done this and that.' Things you hadn't done at all."[2]

So far, we have learned that jobs can be obscure, but also that tasks or "jobs within jobs" can be obscure or *made* obscure. A phenomenon that catches a general tendency towards obscurity is what Standing calls "uptitling" – to give a job a high-sounding epithet to conceal its precarity and, I would say, its substance.[3] Building up opacity in this and other ways while creating gravy jobs and widening the sphere of irresponsible autonomy through identity construction is crucial for laying a good foundation of long-term time appropriation. But the work does not stop there; you must also make sure not to get caught.

---

[2] For more detailed examples of how to construct identities of excellence, see Adams pedagogical account in *The Dilbert Principle*. Adams particularly stresses the importance of having a messy desk, of working on "long-range projects," of arriving at the workplace before the boss, or, if not possible, of leaving after, of coming late to meetings and of leaving early – all effective signifiers of "being busy." Furthermore, there are some useful phrases that you can use to reinforce the message in interaction with co-workers and especially with superiors, e.g. "I'm up to my ass in alligators." "I've been putting out fires all day." "I had fifteen hundred voice mail messages today. Typical." "It looks like I'll be here on the weekend *again*" (Adams, 1996: 115).

[3] As others have commented, uptitling is also part of a form of "credentialism" that ultimately springs from striving to produce a good CV with the disturbing side effect of inflation. According to Standing, the "US occupational body, characteristically giving itself the inflated title of the International Association of Administrative Professionals (having been the more modest National Secretaries Association), reported that it had over 500 job titles in its network, including 'front-office coordinator', 'electronic document specialist', 'media distribution officer' (paper boy/girl), 'recycling officer' (bin emptier) and 'sanitation consultant' (lavatory cleaner)" (Standing, 2011: 17). These are all good examples of how uptitling can generate semantic forms of opacity.

Figure 5.2 Triangle of risk and collaboration.

5.3 Manage the risks

In one of Roy's articles, he offers vivid illustrations of how workers "banked" a surplus – "a kitty" – which would later fund empty labor, and how they, in the evenings, would walk around, do nothing or go home and have someone else punch their timecards. This type of "loafing" was also practiced by Roy himself: "The last four hours I sat around and talked to various operators," Roy records in a field note, and most often "none of the bosses seemed to mind" (Roy, 1952: 433). This last observation, which Roy makes on several occasions, seems to be the most significant difference between soldiering now and then. Sitting around leisurely for hours at an open workplace is less of a possibility when working under the clock than under the piecework system. Although the job can be "linear" as defined above, you cannot do your part, drive to the destination, clean the school, write your text, and then "sit around" as it pleases you. Empty labor is not pure autonomy, it is autonomy within the sphere of heteronomy, to use the vocabulary of Gorz (1982). When work is measured in time, the actual production becomes less important than how you appear. Empty labor must therefore be camouflaged or otherwise integrated so that it does not grate on anyone in power.

It is, of course, of first importance not to get caught in the act. This is not necessarily a matter of just hiding empty labor from the knowledge of management. As Figure 5.2 illustrates, there are other sources of risk. The client is a potential squealer. "If you stand at the cash desk revealing what you do isn't work, you will provoke the customer," a cashier at a furniture retailer said. When surfing the web, she therefore had to keep an eye on where in the room the clients were so that they could not see her screen. Others attested to the importance of having the screen turned against the wall when in an open-plan office. Other colleagues were a common concern among the interviewees. As we shall see in the next section, these risk elements are also potential collaborators. Here, there are different combinations of risk and collaboration. Collaboration is not only something you do with your colleagues. There were several cases where the closest manager turned out to be an ally, whereas the risk was represented by colleagues, especially from other departments, or managers higher up in the hierarchy. Collaboration with the client also occurred among some of the social workers.

As I have already mentioned, it is always good to have a cover project if someone wonders what you have done during all those hours in front of the computer. "Inventory," "networking," "customer service," "routine check-up," "research," "multitasking," "analyzing," "evaluating," are words that may be used as a final expedient, depending on the circumstances. Even if opacity is your best friend, the cover project does not have to be sophisticated. Typical advice for taking a nap at the office (which can be found among authors in the popular literature on workplace misbehavior) is to put a pen and some paper clips on the floor and lay down beside with your feet against the door and, if possible, your head under the desk so that when someone tries to step in, you will wake up and engage in the project of picking up things from the floor (see Gibbons, 2008: 56, for example). A similar principle was followed by a care attendant who worked nights at a residential care home where his only task was to be available for a young girl and check in on her if any noise came from her bedroom. The salaries for working at night were different depending on whether you were allowed to sleep or not; those who could sleep were given their own bedrooms, but they only earned about half as much as those who had to stay awake. In this case, it had been decided that the girl needed quick assistance if anything happened, and therefore the attendant was not allowed to sleep in a separate bedroom. His solution was to pull a couch right outside her door – and sleep:

Then you lay on the couch right beside her room. And there was no danger involved. If she started to yell you would naturally wake up. I woke up once and I went in and calmed her down. That was what the job was about. I sat there and it was so quiet and everything was peaceful. That was also what the others told me. 'You can sleep if you want, it's cool,' they said, like in confidence. So I did.

Here, like in all cases of soldiering, the worker is confronted with ethical considerations to which I shall return. Not only the risk of getting caught must be managed but also the more serious risk of harming other people. This was in fact a major theme among the social workers that I interviewed. None of them seemed worried about what their manager knew since the manager was rarely at the workplace.

Leaving the workplace during working hours was another practice that required careful planning. This type of soldiering has a long history and is known by various names. Going "AWOL," originally a military term for Absence Without Official Leave, or "jacking," i.e. hanging one's jacket at the office chair and then disappear, are two examples (Edwards, 1986: 232). This procedure will look quite different depending on which workplace you are leaving. When escaping a care home, for instance, all the necessary precautions make "jacking" a quite misleading term. "It has to be without risking the safety of anyone," another care attendant said:

I'm damn careful about that. . . . Everything must be clear. That's why I also say exactly what I'm up to all the time, now I'm off, now I go to the lav. And if I go earlier, I always say that I'm on the cell phone and where I will be and how fast I can come. Because you're still responsible. If something goes to hell it's not the person who's been kind with you, letting you go, who should take the shit. You have to take your responsibility.

As we will see in the next section, the tricky part when collaborating like this is that others may have more rigid ideas of what "taking responsibility" means.

Risk is not an absolute concept. As Ulrich Beck notes in *Risk Society*, the assessment of risks involve value judgments, and a risk that one person is willing to take may be unacceptable to another (Beck, 1992: 57–59). Persons with housing loans, children, and without formal education are probably less willing to risk revealing empty labor than someone who has just quit high school. If you are willing to live with risk, or if you are planning to resign within the near future, then you are in a good position to stretch the boundaries of empty labor.

This was the case for a young woman I interviewed three months after she had left her job as a telephone operator at one of the biggest market research companies in Scandinavia. Since call centers typically are described as the most extreme organizations concerning monitoring and electronic performance measurement (cf. Sewell et al., 2012), this was by far the most unexpected interviewee in this study. "Maybe you have heard in the news about all these 'silent calls' that paranoids yell about?" she asked. "That's us. It is all those who are paid in time who are doing those calls." Using a devious tactic that I will not reveal to the reader (other than that it involved the mute button) she and some of her colleagues had found a way to outwit the system. But it was not a purely technical solution, it also involved keeping an eye on the "Nazi managers," i.e. the persons who did the monitoring, and the rather complex interaction between them:

When that person comes from that room it means that she's been on the dialer listening. So when that person sits there it means that you have to be careful, she must be on that place and so on. So you learn everything. And also who's been dating who and that whole concept. So if you know that that person has been in the smoking area with that person, then you know that she will probably go and bust some bastard for wasting time that way. So you were always following them.

Managing risks also involves having a plan B in case you get caught. If your boss catches you while on Facebook, the safest thing to do is to pretend that nothing is amiss. In Sweden, most employees have the stipulated right to take breaks, so unless you have been observed for a longer period, there is nothing to worry about. The lunch break is particularly useful since it is longer. If you are allowed to schedule it yourself and no one keeps track of when you start, you may easily double it (this was practiced by a subway ticket collector) or, if it goes unnoticed, "put it at the end" of your working day as an excuse for leaving early (as suggested by the two care attendants).

If confronted in a more aggressive way, with evidence presented against you, the most important task is not to lose your temper. Employees who are unaccustomed to simulative subordination may have trouble here. A typical example was recently offered by a pair of Euro MPs who were filmed while fraudulently claiming the daily "subsistence allowance" (€300) without having attended the parliament during the day – a well-known phenomenon among MEPs called "sign in and slope off." When confronting the two men, the journalist was slapped and heavily pushed. Naturally, the incident became world news (see Bremner, 2013; Waterfield, 2013). Similarly, a recalcitrant magistrate received a warning from the Swedish State Disciplinary Board for bending his flexible working hours too far. Instead of playing along when warned by his superiors, he had refused to adjust to the normal working hours of the court (9 a.m. to 4 p.m.) and would often turn up at 11 a.m. to the annoyance of his colleagues (TT, 2006). This type of "Voice" is not always helpful.

A more convenient attitude, which may come more naturally to less imperious individuals, is to play stupid. This was the advice of the operator: "Someone said that if it's the first time, then do it, but you can't do it twice. 'Oh, so I didn't hear because of the mute button?' I was blond when it happened so it was easy to play stupid. It is surprisingly easy to play stupid." Yet again, to risk being put in a situation where you have to play stupid is not advisable for someone who is trying to build an identity of responsibility or who wants to avoid being closely monitored in the future.[4]

The case of the operator suggests how even the most advanced panoptical control systems can be hacked from below. As David Lyon argues in the *The Electronic Eye*, it is a fine balance between "skepticism about high tech paranoia" and "realism about authoritarian potentials resulting from information technology" (Lyon, 1994: 88). Furthermore, the "authoritarian potentials" must be treated precisely as *potentials*, not as *facts* – which is what many writers in the Foucauldian tradition, including Foucault himself, tend to confuse. This is also an argument of Ackroyd and Thompson:

Of course, new information technologies are promoted as having integrative properties independent of old-style personnel. But we have to be careful not to confuse the technological potential of such devices with the extent of their

---

[4] Here it might be useful to insert a critical remark regarding some of the sources used in this book. Another well-practiced misbehavior at the call center was apparently sabotage. The operator admits to filling in the blanks incorrectly "to get rid of aggression." This could also be used as a means of soldiering; one tactic she claimed to have shared with others was to lie that a young person was 75, tell him "sorry you are not in our selection group" and "go for a smoke." "So it's just nonsense", she said about the reports that were written. "Everything that is based on telephone interviews is just bullshit and nonsense. That's something I really learned." Recently, former workers at the Swedish survey company Skop similarly estimated that ten percent of the survey results were fabricated. In their account, it was impossible to live up to the demands of the job in order not to be sent home (Olausson, 2012).

use [...] Companies, such as those running centralized call centres, do use enhanced methods of surveillance, but it does not stop employee resentment and resistance towards monitoring and enforcement of scripted behaviour. (Ackroyd and Thompson, 1999: 157)

After all, the essence of panopticism is not that of absolute surveillance but rather self-surveillance induced by the image of absolute surveillance. Another illustration of how that image is but an image comes from a home care assistant who learned that the registers that were installed in each home where they were supposed to swipe their cards upon arrival and departure could easily be programmed manually by pressing the "change time" button. "So it not only allows me to do what I want, it also looks like perfect work in the statistics."

Such "hacks" are even easier when employees must self-report how much time they spend on different tasks for which there is now a good supply of computer software and smartphone applications. As Sam Ladner notes in her interview study of how web workers record their time, "[w]orkers routinely 'hide' hours that they don't know what to do with" (Ladner, 2009: 25). This was an important part of time appropriation among her interviewees: "Another worker explicitly noted that 'dragging his feet' as a form of resistance must necessarily be accompanied by an act of concealment in time tracking. Dragging one's feet only works if one's time sheets reflect an effort to secure full billability" (Ladner, 2009: 26). Since it is widely, if only implicitly, understood that the time categories seldom match the actual time use, and that "full billability" is as ridiculously divorced from reality as it sounds, full accuracy is never expected. This may open doors for you.[5]

5 As some readers may be aware, time reporting has become so popular that even university professors may have to subordinate themselves to its "rationality" nowadays. As some readers may also be aware, it is highly improbable that this has resulted in more than an expansion of the bureaucracy of auditing (cf. Power, 1997). Daniel Miller, professor of anthropology, here offers some advice on how professors may get this type of time-consuming and often frustratingly stupid administration "off their backs": "I am, for example, expected to fill out work time sheets which specify the exact [time] spent on an EU post-doctoral student and this will very likely be audited. But what most academics do is in effect hire a new level of bureaucracy to keep the audit off their backs. So my reaction is to ask a secretary to find out how such forms 'should' be filled out, and the correct number of hours a post-doctoral student is supposed to be working, and to fill the form out based on that information,

A third web developer whom I interviewed said that he actually tries to report *the proportions* of how much time he spends on each project, but that actual time is a different story:

You don't really care about reporting the exact time that you spend on work. So as a routine, I always report full day. But it's not so much out of spite, but more out of laziness.

RP > So even then you waste time?

Well, so far no one has reacted. I like it here.

To sum up, managing risks involves more than avoiding apprehension; you must think about what you risk ethically and you must calculate the other risks in relation to your position. If you are not willing to take *any* risk, time appropriation will be an option only if you pick a job where it is customary.

5.4 Collaborate

Another good way to reduce the risks is to collaborate. As mentioned in Chapter 2, a relatively new projection of the Panopticon in critical workplace studies is what is often called "peer surveillance," i.e. the organization of teams in which employees control each other, sometimes boosted by more or less symbolic bonus programs (cf. Barker, 1993). However, as Keith Townsend (2005) demonstrates in his study of a call center, group dynamics may not always be managed from above. "Some team members have 'turned the tables' on management and use their team cohesiveness to challenge managerial prerogative," he observes. Members could also "cooperate through the sharing of information to get around the technological system and improve their working lives" (Townsend, 2005: 58). In this section, I will give some examples of how to initiate and develop such cooperation, and what pitfalls to avoid. You do not always have to collaborate in order to soldier, but it is highly recommended, not least since attractive activities such as sleeping and leaving the workplace become considerably easier if you have someone who covers for you. The larger the group, the

thereby keeping this other bureaucracy from interfering and thus destroying the actual relationships upon which their academic work depends" (Miller, 2002: 230). Of course, this tactic would have to be somewhat modified in some countries like Sweden where professors normally do not have secretaries.

less cover work is needed from each individual. A magnificent example of the potential of organized soldiering was recently offered at the Swedish mining company LKAB. Allegedly, each individual member of a group of 25 miners took turns in punching each other in and out on the time clock. Until it was revealed, the cooperation lasted for several years supposedly "costing" the company millions of dollars (Drevfjäll, 2013; TT, 2013).

In Sweden, there usually is at least one period during the working day where you can openly engage in empty labor. This period is called *fika*. In travel guides and other introductions to the Swedish culture, *fika* is often mentioned. One of them describes *fika* in the following way: "The coffee break, or what is called fika, is an institution in Sweden. Work is briefly discontinued as employees gather in the staffroom to drink coffee and perhaps eat a bun or a biscuit" (Tellström, 2005: 428). Except the supposed brevity of these coffee breaks, this is a fairly accurate description. The Nordic countries, Sweden included, have for a long time been at the top of countries with the highest coffee consumption per capita (Bloomberg, 2010). Although coffee is sometimes considered a "work drug" (cf. Botton, 2009: 266), it might be speculated that there are other reasons than work (in the sense of "productive activity") to explain why we consume so much coffee in the North. Another guidebook says: "Many Swedish companies take a *fika*, or coffee break, at 3:00, and some also take one in the morning at 9:30 or 10:00. The coffee break in Sweden is an important social gathering, a time to talk about what one is working on or doing. Management and employees sit together and drink coffee and eat cookies, sweet rolls, or cake, and not showing up is considered impolite" (Robinowitz and Carr, 2006: 148). This is also fairly accurate, but somewhat exaggerated; it is rarely considered impolite to be absent from *fika*. But why take the risk? Depending on the workplace, "*fika* talk" sometimes concerns more what one is "doing" than "what one is working on." If the *fika* is brief and work-centered, then you can use it to construct your identity of responsibility. If not, it might be a good opportunity to learn how to appropriate time.

An accounting clerk says that at her job, empty labor is not a taboo subject during *fika*. "You talk about it, or at least with the younger ones. With them you can say 'today I've surfed away the whole morning.' And you exchange tips on different websites and so on. But not with everyone in the team, just with some." The *fika* can thus be an occasion for sharing information about empty labor and what to do with it. But it can also be more of learn-by-doing, a reversed *kaizen* for slackers, sometimes without any comment whatsoever. This was an observation that the cleaner made; despite how "soft" it was from time to time, the older cleaners never talked about it openly. Since they worked in couples, time appropriation was never practiced collectively with the exception of the *fika*: "Then someone came with a bun ring and said 'time for *fika*.' And then you could sit one hour in the sun and then like 'oops, time to leave.' And then you went home." Despite these long hours of perfect idleness together, "taking it easy" remained just a "silent agreement": "It was not like you could talk with them and say 'cool! We're not working!'"

This is another tip: if new in a workplace, learn to observe the manifestations of empty labor. Some people may be less open verbally, but nevertheless willing to practice and cooperate. In the next chapter, it will become clear that not all engage in time appropriation for the same reasons, so concentrate on *how* and less on *why*. You may not even have to talk about it. The notion of "implicit agreements" was repeated by several interviewees. The software engineer who shared his duties with another person said: "It was probably more on an implicit level. Maybe you said things about it or referred to it but more because it was fun to sort of plan the tactics. You didn't say 'oh, this week I won't do anything.' But we knew what we were up to. We sort of grew weary at the same time." Although it may seem hopeless to initiate a healthy partnership (a frustration that some interviewees expressed), it is important to try to see beyond institutionalized forms of face-work – your colleagues may be just as involved in identity construction as you are. Sex, education, position (unless it is your boss) mean little when it comes to empty labor. As we will see in the next chapter, few framed their misbehavior politically. Some were outspoken communists; others voted conservatively. Therefore, try using deeper intuitions than mere prejudice when assessing the potential of others. Against common belief, I would even advise against taking age into account.

Both in social science and in general thought, there is a popular notion that those born from the early 1960s through the early 1980s, the so-called *generation-X,* and that those born from the early 1980s, the so-called *generation-Y,* care less about work than consumption (Bauman, 2004). According to the theory, they "will not settle into any of the occupations for which they are suited because none of these

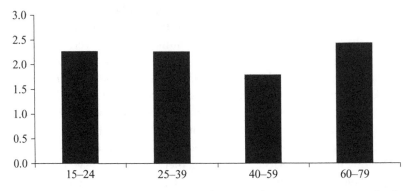

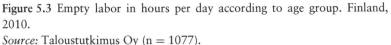

Figure 5.3 Empty labor in hours per day according to age group. Finland, 2010.
Source: Taloustutkimus Oy (n = 1077).

has 'sufficient substance'" (Gorz, 1999: 61); instead they "ask for something more than the previous generations of workers since they insist (and are encouraged) to 'just be themselves'" (Fleming, 2009: 106). The notion that older colleagues "don't get it" and that the younger you are, the less you suffer from protestant notions about "the work ethic" and "the sweat of your brow" etc., was also, as we have seen, expressed by many of the interviewees. Yet age does not seem that significant when it comes to empty labor. American survey found that employees between 20–29 years old reported 2.1 hours of empty labor per day, whereas the average for 30–39 year olds dropped to 1.9 hours and ages 40–49 appropriated 1.4 hours per day (Blue et al., 2007). However, a later study found that among those who appropriate more than 10 hours a week, the 18–25 group comes in third (15 percent) behind employees 26–35 (35 percent) and 36–45 (29 percent)" (Gouveia, 2012). As we see in Figure 5.3, age is even less of a decisive variable in the Finnish results. 2.3 hours per day seem to be the standard regardless of whether you are between 15–25 or 25–39 years old, and if you are between 60–79 years old, it even increases to 2.4 hours per day.

Whether valid or not, *opinions about* age differences in relation to empty labor should nevertheless be taken into account when you collaborate. Framed categorizations may easily develop into barriers that must somehow be bridged. Humor can be very useful here. Although the cleaner came in during a calm period, she felt that there was a great difference in how seriously she and a younger colleague regarded their work in comparison to older colleagues. One day during the first weeks at work, the two found a piano in one of the classrooms which sparked off a spontaneous singing session. When the team leader suddenly came in, the two threw out their dusters and started wiping the walls. "But she reacted differently, 'don't stop singing, it was so nice,' she said. They were down the corridor and had probably heard us all the time." After that they began living it up more provocatively:

That old lady, it was such a bitter woman. But we started joking with her. So sometimes we would ride on the cleaning trolley, you know like kids ride on the shopping trolley? We were pushing each other in the cleaning trolley and that sort of stuff. 'Stop fooling about' she said, but you could tell that she thought it was funny. Her name was Berith, and we would go 'Berith! Come on Berith!'

For others, breaking the ice was not that simple. One care assistant, one of whose duties was cleaning, said that opinions about how much to clean were very generational. Although the conflict was not resolved, his way of dealing with it was to clean halfheartedly as a way of proving his respect despite the fact that his assessments of the need to clean were different.

I am 35 and I work with two ladies, one who's 63, the other 60, and they think that cleaning is very important. And... well, I don't like when it's filthy obviously, but if I consider the floor to be clean, or acceptably clean so that you can't see the dust, I don't see the point of vacuuming. But they think that if it's on the schedule, then you should do it no matter what. They are cool to talk with, but they get really upset when I say 'I don't care a damn about cleaning.' 'What??' they say. 'What the hell was that?' And then we can have a bit of an argument. So I've done some cleaning too when in fact I feel like, well, there's no need here but what the hell... Sometimes I just do what's visible. If they come in to the laundry room for example, I wipe the top of the machines perhaps, but not the floor since it's clean. I mean, it's not like you come in and say 'wow, how dirty it is, let's forget about it,' but you do it more lightly so that someone with greater cleaning needs won't pass by and get a nervous breakdown. Remember, I'm talking about the employees.

In other words, even if you collaborate with someone, that person may have different perceptions about when and why empty labor is legitimate, which is why "symbolic wiping" of the type the cleaner and the care attendant describe can have a calming effect on some.

This does not have to be related to age. Another care attendant in her thirties said that despite what she conceived to be a relaxed attitude to empty labor, one of her colleagues was so "unmotivated" that he started to get on her nerves. "I mean, his *maskning* is not that he just checks his mails," she said. "He just sits there, never taking the initiative, just drinking coffee. And it becomes so irritating because he never compensates for it."

Time appropriation must never lead to putting a greater workload on your colleagues – this is something that nearly all interviewees wanted to stress.[6] Yet it is not hard to imagine how a principle like that may be interpreted differently when applied to a concrete situation. This is a fine example of how subjectivation, in Touraine's words, requires "an adequate interface between the world of instrumentality and that of identity" (Touraine, 2000b: 57). All types of empty labor require some adjustment to the rationality of work whatever the substance of that rationality may be (more on that in Chapter 8) and when soldiering collectively, the group must jointly decide on how far the adjustment should go. Otherwise, there is a risk that the whole project may fail.

This was the case at the workplace of a mining mechanic, where three of his colleagues eventually were fired, much to his delight. Their job was to repair the machinery when a part broke. They worked long hours and lived together in barracks when they were not on leave; in other words, they came "claustrophobically" near each other. Those who annoyed him were the ones who "just disappeared" or "stood hiding behind a gravel heap" without informing the others:

---

[6] To get a sense of how soldiering at the expense of your colleagues has been treated earlier, Charles Vaught and David Smith's (1980) story from a coal mine is very informative. After the mechanics found out that one of their colleagues – Short Ruby – had stretched out in the bucket of a scoop and gone to sleep, they decided to "hang him": "After binding him from head to foot with electrical tape, they raised the bucket of the scoop, tied a length of shooting wire to his penis, secured the other end to a roof bolt overhead and then lowered the bucket until the wire was stretched tight. The men then sat in a semi-circle before the scoop bucket and tossed small rocks at the shooting wire. Each time a rock found its mark, the men were rewarded by an 'ooh' from Short Ruby. When Short Ruby began to worry aloud about what would happen if the hydraulics bled off the scoop, allowing the bucket to drop, one of the men suggested that: 'Maybe we'll have to change your name to Long Ruby'" (in Ackroyd and Thompson, 1999: 62).

There are different ways to *maska*. You can take it easy, but still do your job. That's when it goes unnoticed. But if you're not doing your job, others will have to work much more and that's incredibly mean to those who are working.... I prefer when you are two or three at the same place. Then automatically, one will watch the plant so that everything works while the others take it easy, so to speak. And then you replace each other.

The right adjustment and collaboration were thus necessary to assure both empty labor in the future and a just distribution of the empty hours. When someone does not adjust or is accused of not adjusting to the group, workers can "go around angry at each other until it explodes":

You can quarrel about it like very intensively. Very intensively. Sometimes it turns into, well, not quite a fight, but not far from it either. But when everyone does what they're supposed to, you can actually take two or three hours where you do nothing. But you're still there.... After all, a company has to make money.

Depending on the organization, cooperation is not only preferable, but quite necessary when appropriating time. There are many ways to deal with the conflicts that may arise in such cooperation. Based on the interviews referred to above, I would advise the reader to use humor, communicate, discuss, and be ready to make compromises. As we have seen, radical soldiering does not necessarily mean that the employee is a radical. However, in the process of organizing and perhaps discussing the motives of appropriating time, you have a great opportunity to help others to reconsider the value of their work and what exactly they want to spend time on.

5.5 Redefine your work

The "stinkers" of today are not primarily defined by how little they pay in relation to effort. As we shall see, job tasks that people avoid are rather those that they consider to be meaningless. Of course, there are exceptions to this rule; exceptions that often make for good news material. For instance, *The Guardian* and several other newspapers recently reported that a Balpa/ComRes survey had found that 43 percent of pilots had unintentionally fallen asleep during flight, and that a third of these had awoken to find that their co-pilot was also asleep (Topham, 2012). This type of empty labor is not celebrated by anyone.

There is also more intentional abuse where very meaningful work tasks are shirked on very unstable grounds. One example is an American surgeon who departed in the middle of an operation on a car accident victim, leaving a crucial procedure to his medical residents (Allen, 2005). Another example is a distinguished Harvard surgeon who walked out for 35 minutes during a complicated spinal surgery to cash his paycheck (Swidey, 2004, 2010). Both surgeons were convicted – the latter also for drug abuse. Only rarely will time appropriators who deliberately have caused others harm defend their action without regret. The only example I have found is a Norwegian physician (now known as the "rock-doctor") who left the emergency ward to see a rock concert. Although they denied it, he asserted that his "French leave" was agreed upon by his colleagues (Røyseland and Vikås, 2010).

Another example of empty labor that hit the headlines was a juror playing solitaire at his laptop during the trial of Norwegian mass murderer Anders Behring-Breivik. The incident was accidently captured on film during the hearing of Mattias Gardell, professor of comparative religion, who later said that even if he was not "particularly upset," he thought it was an "ill-mannered" thing to do (Svahn, 2012). When soldiering, it is imperative to learn to feign "good manners." Good manners means doing what you are told, fully engaging in each job task regardless of how meaningless it is, reporting to management or inventing new tasks when you have done what is required. That is why the hidden transcripts that Scott discusses are so pervasive; they are the results of our search for deeper meanings than those imposed on us (see Chapter 3). Although these transcripts must remain hidden under most circumstances, it can be both helpful and inspirational to find and refine them – to redefine your work beyond good manners, for your own sake. This is not an easy task and, as we have seen, it requires ethical judgment.

In *Organizational Misbehaviour in the Workplace*, Karlsson collects different "narratives of dignity and resistance" among which I will here quote one in its entirety – the only one that is based on Karlsson's own misbehavior.

At my faculty at the university, all teachers and researchers are summoned to attend an administrative meeting. If I am unable to attend, I have to notify a manager because the meeting is obligatory, but I cannot be bothered. I do not have time for administrative meetings. I am doing my real work – I am writing a book of narratives about resistance. (Karlsson, 2012: 149)

To use the vocabulary that Karlsson himself has developed, Karlsson is here resisting the rules of management with reference to "professional rules," i.e. working standards "established outside the organisation [as] the result of formal academic education" (Kirchhoff and Karlsson, 2009: 469). Workplace resistance can also follow other rationales: "Service rules" are "informal rules or tacit agreements that evolve through an interpersonal relationship between employees and their clients" (Kirchhoff and Karlsson, 2009: 465); "collective rules" are rules constituted by "the formal and informal interactions between employees in the workplace" (Kirchhoff and Karlsson, 2009: 466). In their study, which was based on different case studies of health care enterprises, Jörg Kirchhoff and Karlsson found that service rules were particularly prevalent among home care assistants. The home care assistant interviewed in my study said that although it was not written anywhere that he should interact with his clients, he considered the social aspect much more important than both bureaucracy (which he completely ignored) and cleaning:

But that's the Swedish culture, you leave your parents in isolation and forget about them. So almost all pensioners are very, very lonely. And they can be very angry, bitter, or just totally confused, and the reason, I think, is that they are so excluded from social intercourse. So it's obvious that even if you don't do that much, they feel much better if you make some coffee and sit down to drink with them instead of doing the dishes.

What type of alternative rules did he follow? Based on the typology of Kirchhoff and Karlsson, it might be argued that since there were neither professional rules (resulting from academic education), nor collective rules (he always worked alone), he must have followed some type of service rules. But is that the only conceivable rule here?

Let us look at another example of resistance against management rules. A web developer said that the time that was demanded for a project often stood in relation to what the workers at the web department thought about it. For instance, when they were asked if they could make sanitary napkins fly over the screen each time you visited the website as part of an advertising campaign, the time demanded became unusually long: "We all froze until [the boss] said: 'That can be done, but it will take several weeks. At least.'... Technically, it was a very simple thing to do, but why would you want those damn sanitary napkins flying over the screen?" Again, it could be argued that they were here following a collective rule – the sillier the job, the longer it will take – but the question then becomes: where did this rule originate?

Although it is true that "there is no such thing as rule-free rule-breaking" (Kirchhoff and Karlsson, 2009: 457), my final advice to the reader is not to worry too much about finding interpersonal, pre-established rules (or "transcripts") to rely on when soldiering. All rules emanate from subjectivity, and you can also be a subject. If you have had a job for a year or so, you are in all likelihood the best suited person for assessing which tasks are worth caring about, and which are meaningless.

During a visit to the German town Neubrandenburg, Scott noticed that although the landscape was "flat as a pancake," allowing him to peer a mile in each direction of the roadway intersection outside the railway station, there was a strange taboo against jaywalking. Even if there was no car in sight, sixty pedestrians could sometimes stand waiting up to five minutes before the light changed. If someone dared crossing against the light, it was always to "a chorus of scolding tongues and fingers wagging in disapproval." While standing there, Scott began rehearsing a thought-provoking discourse in which the rationale of "anarchist calisthenics" is succinctly summarized:

You know, you and especially your grandparents could have used more of a spirit of lawbreaking. One day you will be called on to break a big law in the name of justice and rationality. Everything will depend on it. You have to be ready. How are you going to prepare for that day when it really matters? You have to stay 'in shape' so that when the big day comes you will be ready. What you need is 'anarchist calisthenics.' Every day or so break some trivial law that makes no sense, even if it's only jaywalking. Use your own head to judge whether a law is just or reasonable. That way, you'll keep trim; and when the big day comes, you'll be ready. (Scott, 2012: 4–5)

For the working population, time appropriation can be regarded as a central part of the anarchist calisthenics that Scott puts forward. As we have seen, "doing nothing" while at work can be a very demanding activity requiring planning, collaboration, risk calculation, and ethical consideration. What we have seen is the subject appropriating time within wage labor – the creation of autonomy within heteronomy. This is much easier in some jobs than in others, mostly depending on their inherent opacity, but there is always a certain amount of uncertainty in the job that you can learn to exploit. It is hard to give any general advice on where to find this uncertainty, but you will always have to manage the risks of getting caught and of causing harm to others. Clearly, the resistance against work is not resistance against *all* work. Which work to resist and which to perform is, on the contrary, a key issue for each interviewee involved in soldiering. It may therefore be assumed that soldiering (as represented by persons who are ready to be interviewed about their soldiering) is an ethical endeavor. In the next chapter, I will further discuss the ethics of soldiering with reference to how those engaged in this type of empty labor motivated their actions.

6 | *The time-appropriating subject*

We now know something about the methods that people employ when appropriating time. The ingenuity that people employ to avoid work gives a feeling of the energy and opposition that can be involved in the process. But is it reasonable to interpret the act of time appropriation as an expression of subjectivity in the Tourainian sense?

We may never know the exact reasons why individuals misbehave at work, but a way to approach the answer is to listen to what they think of their work and how they motivate their actions. Especially in labor process theory, motivation remains an undertheorized subject. This is very unfortunate – especially in relation to the study of workplace resistance. As Scott asserts, the focus we had in the previous chapter, i.e. on the technical and behavioral aspects of resistance, risks missing much of the point:

> It reduces the explanation of human action to the level one might use to explain how the water buffalo resists its driver to establish a tolerable pace of work or why the dog steals scraps from the table. But inasmuch as I seek to understand the resistance of thinking, social beings, I can hardly fail to ignore their consciousness – the meaning they give to their acts. (Scott, 1985: 38)

In this chapter, I use the study of time appropriation as an empirical base for further analysis of why people misbehave. What interests us here are the voices of the time-appropriating artists, the subjective meanings recognized in this specific type of organizational misbehavior – *not how, but why*. This we will do by means of elaborating on different vocabularies of motive.

The main argument in this chapter is that subjectivity has been misunderstood as an either-or-phenomenon, and that we should be more sensitive to different expressions of subjectivity including the less political ones. Touraine's emphasis on "Speech," the "Dissident," and traditional forms of social movement tends to ignore covert types of resistance that take place on an everyday basis. If the subject is defined as the will to become an actor and this will is primarily manifested in the resistance against different power centers, such ignorance will lead to an unwarranted focus on the tip of the iceberg. Scott's notion of "the hidden transcript" goes beyond such focus, yet in most studies of passive resistance, there is a tendency to attach a single "Voice" to the action. As described in Chapter 3, the same tendency can be found in many of the early accounts of workplace resistance. Lupton's idea that "'go-slow practices' happen when working conditions are not as good as they might be, in which case going slow becomes a protest" (in Dubois, 1979: 7), represents the impoverished type of analysis of soldiering which captures only *one* aspect of why people soldier; it is far from the full spectrum of motivations. Whereas labor process scholars tend to stress working *conditions*, others have interpreted worker recalcitrance as a reaction against wage labor *as such*. As Sprouse contends in his study on sabotage: "several people explained that they felt trapped by meaningless work, while others made it clear they didn't like working for other people. These conflicts might be commonplace but they are also the most basic reasons for sabotage" (Sprouse, 1992: 7).

Earlier, there was a period when workplace resistance was largely ignored. Now, "the controversies of the sociology of work are not about the existence of 'resistance' or other forms of informal behaviors but about the meaning of these," Stewart asserts (2008: 47, my translation). As I have already argued, the debate on the meaning of organizational misbehaviors has engendered a multitude of studies of more or less trivial transgressions where the scholars' abilities in interpretation appear considerably more radical than the transgressions *per se*. This research has been subject to much critique in later years, especially in the field of critical management studies, where the impotence of organizational misbehavior concerning the established power structures of the firm is a typical concern. Saving this issue for Chapter 8, I will focus only on the subjective meaning of soldiering here. Touraine's concept of the subject does point out an important difference from the concept of the actor: the subject is *the attempt* to become an actor. It may not necessarily succeed, as I have already mentioned; the subject and the actor can sometimes be deceitfully decoupled, but it is

Table 6.1 *Motive vocabularies of time appropriation according to different levels of analysis*

	Adjustment	Withdrawal	Direct dissent	Framed dissent
Ethical dimension (Scott, 1991)	Adjustment	Survival	Office politics	Infrapolitics
Form of discontent (Morrill et al., 2003; Snow and Benford, 1992)	Passive resignation	Active resignation	Personal indignation	Meta-narrative related indignation
Perceived target (Hollander and Einwohner, 2004; Scott, 1985)	None	The job	Penultimate links	The system
Perceived deprivation (Brewer and Silver, 2000; Runciman, 1966)	None	Absolute and individual	Relative and ego-centered	Relative and group-centered
Intended degree of output restriction (Ackroyd and Thompson, 1999)	None	Imperceptibility	Disruption	Sabotage

important to keep the two concepts apart. To study only actors would entail an empiricist focus on that which is. The subject tells us something about the strivings and yearnings that negate that which is, and albeit counterfactually, how the individual would prefer things to be.

As described in the Appendix, I have distilled what I found to be the most prominent motive vocabularies from the narratives constructed/extracted/generated in the interviews. Table 6.1 depicts different interviewee motivations behind a phenomenon that has traditionally been treated as "oppositional." This typology does not necessarily have to be understood as a static categorization of what motives time-appropriating employees "really" have etc. Kondo's (1990) contention that employees may "consent, cope, and resist at different levels of consciousness at a single point in time" (in Collinson and

Ackroyd, 2005: 321) encourages us to see beyond the either-or discourse and discern the subject from different angles. We have an act of resistance; now we must probe its target. Is it a reaction against a particular change, or is it more general in nature? Does it signify a wish to transcend the existing power structures, or is it just a symptom of the employee's disenchanted wish to advance in these very structures? What are the direct benefits, and is there a motivation beyond these? Is it linked to a meta-narrative or rather conceived as a personal matter? The answer to these questions may vary, sometimes incoherently, and there is no need to refer to levels of consciousness to explain why. As David Collinson puts it: "Resistance frequently contains elements of consent and consent often incorporates aspects of resistance" (in Karlsson, 2012: 19). The uncompromising type of resistance that takes place in the open could never be realized in the sphere of labor, short of the abolition of its power structures or the quick dismissal of the employee. Workplace resistance is always of the intriguing guerilla type, and people who engage in it may have their very own reasons.

What I want to suggest is that if the subject, as Touraine suggests, is the will to act and resist power structures, including the power structure most central to modern life (work), this *will* is far from homogeneous. For example, when appropriating time, it may be the will to be an actor in your own life, the will to be an actor at the workplace, or in society. Time appropriation emanates from a variety of motives. Some time appropriators identify wholeheartedly with these, and others appear to have very little allegiance to them. That is why I suggest that subjectivity is layered. Another way of putting it may be to talk about different dimensions of subjectivity, or simply different ways of motivating resistance.

The typology summarized in Table 6.1, conveys four motive vocabularies behind the practice of time appropriation: *adjustment, withdrawal, direct dissent,* and *framed dissent.* These vocabularies will be further elaborated in relation to five levels of analysis that others have discerned in the study of resistance in and outside the workplace. The *ethical dimension* refers to the type of interests employees have in reappropriating company time for themselves. The *form of discontent* is decided by whether the employees show signs of indignation or of resignation and whether they contextualize their discontent or not. This dimension is closely linked to the *perceived adversary*, i.e. whether the employee regards the source of their discontent as a structural or an individual phenomenon, or if they simply conceive of it as an aspect of the job. The *perceived deprivation* refers to whether the employees speak of their frustration in absolute or relative terms and whether they describe it as a shared experience or not. The *intended degree of output restriction* is the level at which one can analyze the external goals of the act of time appropriation, i.e. what possible changes the employees wish that their actions will result in. In the next sections, I will present examples of what these dimensions entail, describe how they differ from each other, and explain why they are relevant when discerning the respective vocabularies.

6.1 Adjustment

A point that I will just mention briefly but develop more thoroughly in the next chapter is that, as we have already seen exemplified, empty labor does not have to emanate from *any* type of subjectivity at work. When the potential output is too low to fill a whole working day, empty labor is simply the effect of adjustment. Here an act of resistance would rather involve demanding more meaningful work tasks or the right to leave once the work is done. Whereas slacking, as defined in Chapter 4, may border on collective soldiering, enduring is but the resignation to the current state of affairs. Here, we see how professional rules can conflict with the organization of labor and how the employee learns to resign in the face of organizational power. Diverging from the more generalizing emphasis on the omnipresence of oppositional subjects in Certeau (1984) and Scott (1989), it should be stressed that we only have *the option* to "become subjects" as Touraine puts it. Compliance and subordination are also viable options, or to quote Michael Gardiner: "Subjecthood is not simply given to us; we must *create ourselves* as subjects, as purposive, responsible and self-reliant entities. If we do not make this existential 'leap', we become passive and conformist, and hence subject to external powers" (Gardiner, 2000: 156).

Nevertheless, this passive form of resignation reveals a fundamental distrust of the supposed possibility of making changes via communication with management. Those enduring empty labor are trapped in situations where the simulation has become so integrated in their daily work that speaking truth would mean nothing less than organizational suicide. Comparing their dissatisfaction with the more active withdrawal from labor suggests how deep differences in work obligations can be.

6.2 Withdrawal

As Mars comments regarding fiddling, "[p]risoners serving long sentences are advised by colleagues to 'do your time and don't let your time do you'; fiddling allows many workers to control their jobs rather than be controlled by them" (Mars, 1982: 206). The urge to control time, or rather to infuse it with meaning (however thin it may be), is also what motivates many to engage in soldiering. Unlike adjustment, withdrawal can be described as a form of resignation that emanates from the employee's wish to control, but also to avoid work. Here, empty labor is actively created by the employee, normally because work is perceived as such a burden that it cannot be endured for a whole working day. The distaste for work varied heavily among withdrawing employees in this study, but in contrast to the next two motive vocabularies, withdrawing employees attribute their dissatisfaction exclusively to the job itself – not to its organization, as in direct and framed types of subjectivity. No overt political framing, personal indignation, or revenge narratives are in the vocabulary of withdrawal. The common narrative is rather the need to create what Certeau (1984: 23) would call a "utopian space" of free time in a milieu that is otherwise characterized by routine and coercion. The cleaner I talked to is a good example. She said she enjoyed working with her team and even liked her boss. The problem was the actual work:

There was no point in working hard, that would only give you more to clean somewhere else.... Of course, you don't want to clean more than necessary. Cleaning means scrubbing toilets. You don't want to do that, it's very simple. There's no chance in the world that I would clean more than I had to.

As described in the previous chapter, her boss, who was more than double her age, had no problem with taking long breaks for *fika* or a smoke in the sun. She would also let the team go home a couple of hours early from time to time. But they expressed pride in the job that the interviewee could not identify with. "You couldn't say 'who cares about work?' When they actually were working they were so serious, always appearing busy with their big machines going *vroom, vroom, vroom.*" While not willing to keep up with this, the interviewee and one of her colleagues were soldiering more than what was already collectively practiced.

As we have seen, the withdrawal may also be partial in the sense that it concerns only certain job tasks. To return to the term "time waste," a recent survey asked employees what they thought were the biggest time wasters. "Having to attend too many meetings" came out number one and was listed by 47 percent of the respondents. That was followed by "dealing with office politics" (43 percent), "fixing other peoples' mistakes" (37 percent), and "coping with annoying coworkers" (36 percent). Only 18 percent listed the internet as a time-waster despite the time that goes into it (see the previous chapter); it was not far from "dealing with bosses," which was listed by 14 percent (Gouveia, 2012). Much of what managers describe as "work," is thus regarded as time waste by employees – it is not "real work." Administration and excessive cleaning were other "supplementary tasks" that annoyed employees as seen in the previous chapter. These are not minor tasks in present-day organizations – in Sweden, it has been estimated that near half of the working hours are devoted to administration in the police, the school system, and the medical service (see Bark, 2008; Ivarsson Westerberg, 2004). When the administration concerns less meaningful work, it is no wonder that activities such as Facebooking what you had for breakfast, YouTubing Japanese television shows, or twittering how much money you are losing on internet poker gain priority in your schedule. In fact, it could be argued that access to "the universe" of the internet – "just a couple of clicks away" – makes meaningless work even more intolerable. As an allowance administrator put it:

It's like immediate gratification. You just click along and it's inexhaustible. I think it's great fun to Google things. For instance, I Googled you and found you at the university and a picture. And at my job there are always people you can Google who tell you where they live . . . you know. I can put much time on that. Trying to find people.

RP > But you like your job – you said you would continue working even if you won on the lottery?

But that's because I know how boring it is to sit home alone. It's the social aspect. It's not the job in itself, it's more about having workmates, I think.

In this sense, soldiering can be a way simply of re-introducing "'popular' techniques of other times and other places into the industrial space (that is, into the Present order)" as Certeau (1984: 26) puts it. For others, withdrawal goes deeper, resembling – at least in the narrative reconstruction – the "Great Refusal" that Marcuse once proposed as the only viable resistance in the face of one-dimensional society. A less political vision on the same theme was formulated in the later writings of Horkheimer, where he advocates the idea of "retreat" from the world in which, as Joan Alway (1995: 60) puts it, "the moralist without belief in divine providence or in the revolutionary agency of the proletariat is left with only longing as a form of resistance." This melancholy was also shared by Adorno, who asserted that "[t]he best mode of conduct, in face of all this, still seems an uncommitted, suspended one: to lead a private life, as far as the social order and one's own needs will tolerate nothing else, but not to attach weight to it as to something still socially substantial and individually appropriate" (Adorno, 2005 [1951]: 39). Although they surely did not have workplace time appropriation in mind, they describe a purely negative reaction that also is adaptive since it is not aimed at making any change except for creating a sphere of autonomy within the established order of power. This sums up the essence of the motive of withdrawal. The frustration of the employees it is not formulated in relation to an ideal or a sense of being personally wronged as in the motive vocabularies below (cf. Brewer and Silver, 2000; Runciman, 1966), but as a fact of life that simply has to be managed in the best possible way. The case of a ticket collector illustrates this pessimistic form of resignation:

It's a stupid job and society would definitely be better off without it. But I could say that about just about every job that I've had. So I try to get along. I've this room where I can watch movies, read, surf, and still get an income. It's what we all do here, it's the whole point of being here.... At least I don't cause any harm. It's not like I spread advertising or neglect any sick people.

The ticket collector's apology exemplifies how time appropriation can be stretched between radical narratives and the narrative of personal failure. The job as a ticket collector is "stupid" and yet better than others in the sense that it does not "cause any harm." Hence, it is the last refuge for someone who feels she or he has failed (or has no ambition) to succeed on the labor market. The joke of a young electrician also illustrates the narrative of personal failure: "If I'm still a building electrician when I'm sixty, then please shoot me." The narrative of personal failure highlights how neither management nor organization is singled out as culprits for the dissatisfaction, but the job itself. Another example of this sense of meaninglessness was expressed by a warehouse employee who made this reflection on his contribution to the world:

The goods often are of such poor quality that you find them broken already when you open the cartons. One thing that really opened my eyes was when a guy working there, who wasn't an environmentalist or anything, said: 'think about it, one day, in just a couple of years or so, everything you see here will be on the garbage mountain.' It doesn't take long. Just five or ten years, and all will be part of the garbage heap. And we're talking about areas big as football fields . . . of commodities, all commodities.

In this particular case, the sense of meaninglessness somehow infused the whole workday. According to the interviewee, he was not the only one depressed by his job. I interviewed him during spring, and he had just made the observation that although the warmth was coming back, which is a dramatic occasion when you have endured the Swedish winter, some of his colleagues preferred staying indoors with their lunchboxes. "I asked one if he wanted to go out. He said 'no, it makes it so hard to go back in.'" According to the interviewee, this reaction is perfectly understandable:

You don't see any daylight for months except during weekends. You don't eat and become tired and low. It's the monotony and the understimulation and the fact that the job is completely meaningless. Each time you've cut a carton open there is a new one. And each time you've filled a shelf they empty it. And then a new carton comes some days later. Well, now it's time to fill the shelf again. Eventually you start recognizing the cartons. 15 000 articles and you recognize each carton. . . . I've been here for seven years now. Seven summers. It's like a nightmare.

No matter how well-organized and just both management and society were, this experience of *the job itself* would not change. As another interviewee suggests, explaining time appropriation as a consequence of the job itself without personal or political indignation does not have to emanate out of lack of "sociological imagination" to use Mills'

(2000 [1959]: 8) term for understanding seeming "personal troubles of milieu" as "public issues of social structure." Despite (or perhaps because of) her being active in both parliamentary and extraparliamentary politics, she does not regard time appropriation as political action: "To me it's a purely egoistic action aimed at creating a space for the individual, you know. So I can't say that it's political action or workplace struggle." As we shall see, others ascribe opposite meanings to the very same behavior.

A final remark concerning withdrawal should be made in relation to Albert Hirschman's deliberately reductive action theory presented in *Exit, Voice and Loyalty*. Without some modification, his theory would be hard to apply to the phenomenon of time appropriation. In labor economics and management studies literature, Hirschman's concept of exit usually is equated with the employee's decision to quit a job, whereas the concept of voice is the ability to communicate complaints (usually through a trade union; see Dowding et al., 2000 for a review). Yet Hirschman himself did note that management tends to "strip the members-customers of the weapons which they can wield, be they exit or voice, and to convert, as it were, what should be a feedback into a safety valve" (Hirschman, 1970: 124). Time appropriation might be regarded as such a safety valve – a valve in which we find a multitude of voices. Clearly, exit does not have to be formal – we can dissociate ourselves from an organization while still being official members of it. High unemployment, economic dependency, children to feed are situational factors that may cause employees to grasp at this solution. Withdrawal here represents this informal type of exit that is chosen instead of formal exit. Direct dissent, on the other hand, should be regarded as an informal exit that is chosen instead of venting formal voice.

6.3 Direct dissent

Unlike withdrawal, direct dissent originates in feelings of indignation rather than resignation. Mars describes the variety of reasons for engaging in fiddling in the following way: "And while fiddling is seen by some employers as an incentive, almost a part of wages, and therefore tacitly welcomed and even encouraged, some undoubtedly occurs because of resentment... it is a way of hitting out at the boss, the company, the system or the state" (Mars, 1982: 32). This analysis, as applied to what Mars calls "time-fiddling," might be regarded as a summary of this chapter, albeit I believe that there are several distinctions to be made here. One such is the difference between hitting out at the boss or the company on the one hand, and the system or the state on the other hand. Direct dissent is not aimed at abstract concepts such as the system or the state, but at what I will here call the *penultimate links* of larger structures. According to Frances Piven and Richard Cloward (1977), people's experience of structural oppression is always mediated by these links which might, nevertheless, appear as structurally detached phenomena:

[P]eople experience deprivation and oppression within a concrete setting, not as the end product of large and abstract processes, and it is the concrete experience that molds their discontent into specific grievances against specific targets. Workers experience the factory, the speeding rhythm of the assembly line, the foremen, the spies, the guards, the owner, and the paycheck. They do not experience monopoly capitalism.... In other words, it is the daily experience of people that shapes their grievances, establishes the measure of their demands, and points out the targets of their anger. (Piven and Cloward, 1977: 20–21)

Narratives of direct dissent, i.e. a dissent that does not talk of transcendental changes of larger structures but of such penultimate links as those mentioned in this quote, demonstrate how indignation does not have to be (and perhaps only in exceptional cases is) framed by political meta-narratives (cf. Snow and Benford, 1992). As for time appropriation, it is typically described in terms of a payback rationale. The telephone operator sums up the logic in these words: "This company steals money from us and what we do here is charity. So if they steal from us, we can steal from them." The stealing alluded to is not the capitalist exploitation in any universal sense, but the fact that the administration at her company frequently miscalculated how much she had worked, which she experienced as a personal insult. This was also the reason she engaged in more definite forms of sabotage: "Like if you know that that team leader must have a certain response rate in each category, and you don't like that leader, then you just say 'this is nonresponse, this is nonresponse,' so that they will hear from higher quarters."

The most common source of indignation among the interviewees (including the slacking and coping type of time appropriators) was to have a bad boss. Even the slacking web designer eventually grew tired of her boss despite the fact that "everything was allowed" at the department:

He did literally nothing. I told you about the e-mails. He just deleted them. He was also fired for doing nothing. He was just rowdy and disgusting. At MSN, he could suddenly write 'cock.' And if you didn't reply, he just wrote: 'answer, cunt.' That's why I hated it, he was so disgusting.

Sexist, sadist, authoritarian, and unintelligent bosses recur in many narratives. Other penultimate links provoking dissent include:
    Stupid colleagues:

Those donkeys. Those who are mindlessly hard-working, and with low intelligence quotient if you know what I mean. Those who are just taking orders and happy to obey, almost ridiculously, vulgarly stupid. These people are given positions such as 'assistant desk manager,' you know, just meaningless names, invented to make them feel even more important. (Sales clerk)

Unethical companies:

We all hate the company. Once, Johan [the team leader] had brought this yellow kiwi, and he was so angry: 'they think they can play God,' he went on. And he's pretty much the same when it comes to [the medical company where they work]. We all know who those on top are. They earn money on sickness, not on health. What they want is to remove the symptoms, that's it. (Laboratory assistant)

And homosocial cultures:

I could see what was happening with the other women [at the advertising agency]. I mean, they had a very serious gender equality plan, there were no sexist jokes, no widespread sexism, but there was this negligence. Women had to struggle much harder. And then there was this 'us-bosses-between,' this laddishness and all that. It was simply harder for women to get somewhere. And there were many young women who wanted to get there and who knew their stuff. Many had this 'good-girl-complex,' but it just turned against them. They just worked, worked, and worked until they totally burned out. (Copywriter)

The conception that men held advantages in the particular organization and were unaffected by the pressure that women experienced was conveyed by three interviewees. It did not appear to be part of a patriarchal structure, however, but more as individual concerns and in one case as a quite essentialist idea of how men and women "are": "I think that men generally are more relaxed than women. They don't take it as hard. I feel like women sometimes want to show off a bit more." Quantitative studies of empty labor are so far incompatible concerning sex differences in empty labor. Two studies report little or no difference between men and women (Gouveia, 2012; Jost, 2005) whereas the Finnish statistics showed that men generally had 32 minutes more per day of empty labor. Whether such variation would reflect a difference in attitude or an unequal occupational distribution in which men get less demanding jobs is an open question. While not measuring empty labor in actual time, Kelly Garrett and James Danziger found that men and women use the internet for personal communication to the same extent, but that men use it more for personal leisure interests (Garrett and Danziger, 2008: 291).

Unlike withdrawal, the motivational structure of direct dissent contains an urge toward sabotage. Time appropriation can therefore constitute part of a "secret revenge," a form of sabotage that entails significant alleviations in the work intensity, and yet puts little at personal risk for the employee (cf. Morrill et al., 2003). Here, the meaning attached to the practice of time appropriation is ambiguous. In Fleming's words, "it does not belong to the organization at all, but the initiative, creativity, and discretion of the workers themselves as they endeavor to be 'cool' in a decisively 'uncool' environment" (Fleming, 2009: 89). Yet, as Fleming develops his argument, the motive vocabulary of this type can also serve an ideological purpose in giving the employee a self-conceited sense of "I work here, but I'm cool" (cf. Liu, 2004: 299).

Since the sources of dissent are not put into narratives of oppressive universality, the vocabulary of direct dissent still expresses less resignation than any of the other vocabularies. Hope exists, and it is not beyond this world. The revenge can be taken here and now; if that is not enough the possibility of formal exit always exists. The telephone operator who eventually quit her job confirms her belief in the existence of a better world outside the workplace: "I would never like to return to that company again. The stupidity and abusiveness was just amazing." Making her old workplace a singularity in this way, it is considered an *exceptional* disgrace. As we shall see, this is a decisive difference from the vocabulary of framed dissent.

6.4 Framed dissent

Campagna's analysis of "the squanderer" includes a curious contrast with what he calls "the punk." Unlike punks, Campagna writes, squanderers "do not enter [the world of work] with the badge of rebellion stapled to their lips. Punks feel obliged to show their disgust and disagreement, at the cost of losing an opportunity to silently steal from the storeroom and the till" (Campagna, 2013: 35). Beside the fact that this ideal type of the punk is somewhat disconnected from reality (cf. Hannerz, 2013), a problem with Campagna's analysis is his assumption that those who manage their lives as invisible "parasites" are predominantly "disbelievers." They are not "immoral" in the sense that they strive to violate certain societal norms, but rather "amoral" in the sense that they are outside the scope of all morality, Campagna argues. As the examples of withdrawal and direct dissent make clear, there are good grounds for attributing such an elusive "Voice" to employees actively appropriating time. There are, however, those who inconspicuously engage in the very same misbehavior with more political motives.

In his extensive work on the history of workplace sabotage, Geoff Brown (1977) describes how the Glasgow dockers by the end of the nineteenth century were deprived of the force of strike as a consequence of mass-employment of so-called blacklegs. The dock workers retorted by the practice of "ca'canny," "foot-dragging," "working to rule" and other classical forms of output restriction, arguing that they kept their efficiency at the level of the blacklegs. This activism turned out to be a successful tool of negotiation, and the incidence would later have an immense impact on Pouget (1913 [1898]) and the French anarcho-syndicalist movement. Brown (1977: 15) observes that ca'canny thus became political whereas "it was previously only practiced 'unconsciously' and instinctively by the workers."

This political dimension of time appropriation lingers on even if it has ceased to be part of the unionist arsenal. One thing that separates the vocabulary of direct dissent from that of framed dissent is in what type of hidden transcript it is rooted. Scott makes a difference between transcripts that are formed to "answer daily insults to dignity" and those formed to "confront elaborate ideologies that justify inequality, bondage, monarchy, caste and so on" (Scott, 1991: 117–18). The latter type may require some type of "counterideology" or "negation" that goes beyond fragmentary practices of resistance. The Soviet worker adage "they pretend to pay us and we pretend to work" exemplifies how hidden transcripts can provide ethical fundament for time appropriation while not being directed against any penultimate link in particular, but the system as such. Another example can be taken from Mars' ethnography, where a docker motivates his fiddling by saying: "It's all insured and nobody's heard of an insurance company going broke. In any case, they've made millions out of this port and it's us who do the work" (Mars, 1982: 106). Time appropriation within such a narrative framework is not only motivated in reaction to a low salary, a certain boss, or the corporation, but against a perverted system. As one of the web developers contends: "We're not being paid for being effective. Sometimes I feel effectiveness should rather be avoided."

It is important to point out that for those interviewed in this study, the framing of narratives was but an extra dimension in their vocabulary of motive. In framed dissent, we see a cumulative aspect of time appropriation concerning the dimensions of aim, perceived enemy, negation, and ethics. As for the aim of time appropriation, framed dissent does not exclude that the employee may enjoy the autonomy and personal payback that in other vocabularies reign supreme:

It's like killing two birds with one stone. You both avoid selling yourself entirely, and still get paid for watching movies. It's a kind of struggle that pays directly and therefore [time appropriation] is in fact better than union matters and the like that lead nowhere. Here it's instant and therefore I think it's much more of a thorn in the side to capitalism. (Security officer)

To pick up the thread of unionism, another aspect of time appropriation that objectively might speak against its political value is the fact that like most oppositional workplace actions including sabotage, pilferage, and identity struggles, it cannot be completely overt unless it is collectively endorsed as a symbolic act – which it rarely is. Individual employees are nearly always replaceable and no employee in this study has even mentioned Hirschman's "voice" as a useful option. An increasing part of the labor force is today experiencing *precariousness* (Bourdieu, 1998; Standing, 2011), and this kind of vulnerability is exactly the condition that separates politics from what Scott (1991) calls *infrapolitics*: due to differences in power, the latter has to be covert in order to exist at all. Despite this fact, a widespread notion of workplace resistance is that it should be formally organized and overt in order to qualify as "resistance," whereas "misbehavior" represents more individual and spontaneous forms of oppositional practice (cf. Collinson and Ackroyd, 2005). Time appropriation in this study is with very few exceptions informal, yet the aspect of *peer collaboration* dramatically changes when dissent is framed. While time appropriation can be informal in the sense that it is not known to the employer or outside the organization, it may be more or less explicit among the employees. The vocabulary of framed dissent makes a point out of keeping the infrapolitics as explicit as possible among colleagues:

What we do is simply to level some of the class inequalities. It doesn't matter if it's public or private, the injustice is the same. People from the lower classes usually understand that... You should talk about it so that it becomes a normality. It's like gatecrashing [in the subway], I'm open about that too. If someone questions it, I take the discussion. Workplace struggle shouldn't simply be something you do. It's good to create a collective consciousness of that it's ok. It's the same thing with file-sharing. (Care assistant)

The class-identifying effect of time appropriation may in fact be experienced as more valuable than the damaging effect it might have on the profitability of the company. Although not formally organized, it may even turn into open opposition in some situations:

Sometimes we are all caught in the act. Like one time, I think we were forty persons who just stood looking through the window. We barely have any windows on the floor so we never see anything. It was spring and everyone just stood there longing to get away. It was as if we were in a madhouse. We were locked up in there.

Then the foreman came and lined up, he too. 'Well, I think it's time to make an effort now, let's roll up the sleeves. Cause this doesn't look too good, does it?' 'Oh, don't worry. Come here you,' the others said. We didn't care a damn about him. Some slinked away obediently. Others didn't give a damn. (Factory worker)

As this episode indicates, a condition for explicitly rebellious time appropriation is that it involves more than one individual. Yet it should be noticed that the colleagues could perfectly well have been driven by direct dissent. Although the factory worker made reference to political narratives such as "global capitalism" and the "society of competition," his colleagues may have been staring out the window for different reasons, as he puts it himself, "longing to get away," to pro-voke the foreman, or maybe just to get a short break from work.

The results presented in this chapter differ radically from what other researchers have found when studying the reasons for why people engage in empty labor. Since there is so little of this research, it might be worth mentioning some of their results. In Caroline D'Abate's stud-ies, there is no mentioning of employees expressing dissatisfaction with their jobs, their bosses, or society at large. Rather people seem to appro-priate time "because the phone, computer, e-mail, or Internet is readily available," "because time constraints and the time demands created by home life, leisure interests, a long commute, or long hours make it nec-essary," or because "business hours are the only times they can reach these people or accomplish their tasks" (D'Abate, 2005: 1022) etc. In a quantitative study, whose scientific merits are highly debatable,[1] D'Abate and Erik Eddy similarly found that "engagement in personal business on the job is not related to self-reported measures of per-formance, efficiency, job satisfaction, organizational commitment, or intentions to stay, only to procrastination" (D'Abate and Eddy, 2007: 361; this was written already in the abstract and is the main "finding" of the study). Unfortunately these studies are written from the man-agerial perspective that empty labor represents a cost that should be reduced and controlled, and that it is an irrational type of behavior which the employee must somehow "rationalize and construct mean-ings to explain" (D'Abate, 2005: 1014). For instance, Lim Vivien and Teo Thompson argue that cyberloafing is often "neutralized" by work-ers employing a technique that she calls "the metaphor of the ledger" meaning that "they rationalize that they are entitled to indulge in deviant behaviors because of their past good behaviors, which have led to the accrual of credits that they can 'cash in'" (Vivien and Thomp-son, 2005: 681). Only the assumption that cyberloafing is a "deviant behavior" seems very strange given its prevalence. Also, one might question why such a rationale should signify a "rationalization" – there are many instances when employees are entitled to take back what their employers have stolen from them. Indeed, in most cases, it

---

[1] D'Abate and Eddy did a web survey based on a snowball sampling with no more than 115 respondents. Although interesting as a sample, the ambition to generalize the results from such a survey is very hard to understand (cf. Healey, 2013: 129–31 for the essentials of probability sampling).

seems more irrational that they should continue toiling nonstop like obedient slaves. Basic reflections like that are, however, taboo in this genre of research. Rather, it emanates from ideological worries about how "organizations need to manage their human capital to compete" and how "the potential cost to organizations of [empty labor] is substantial" (D'Abate and Eddy, 2007: 380). The reason why the results in this study concerning the motives of time-appropriating individuals differ from those presented by management scholars should therefore not only be deduced to differences in sampling. There are ideological differences in the research approach to empty labor, as to all forms of organizational misbehavior, that still make the worn epithet "critical" meaningful when referring to different schools of research (cf. Ackroyd and Thompson, 1999: 1; Karlsson, 2012: 15).

The most empathic remark that I have found in the management literature is that empty labor may enable "individuals to balance and cross the boundaries between life realms" (D'Abate, 2005: 1013). This notion is also shared by many critical scholars. Fundamentally, they argue, work is good, but when there is too much work, when it is either intensified or polluting home life, employees may react by appropriating time in order to "balance" work, home, and leisure. The only legitimate reaction then, is against the *conditions of work*, never against *work itself*, against the lack of meaning, or against the fact that you have to subordinate yourself to a boss and instrumentalize your creativity for a wage. However, it might reasonably be asked whether a person soldiering away two hours a day is not actually "rationalizing" a bit when saying that this is part of creating a "work-life balance." The impression from the interviews referred to here is not that all employees identify with their jobs and are just appropriating time to "cope" with the realities of work. Their (mis)behavior may be more than a pure "reaction" to organizational changes, it may be grounded in a *decision* to "cheat the system" and even to change it.

It is at this point that the meanings of different types of workplace misbehavior tend to converge. In a typology of different types of misbehavior, Karlsson defines "private business" during working hours as "anything you consciously are, do and think at work that you are not supposed to be, do and think, and that is directed outwards from the hierarchy" (Karlsson, 2012: 193). Although this is a good description of what the *action* of soldiering means (and fits well into Karlsson's typology), soldiering can certainly be defined as a type of "resistance" as well (defined by Karlsson as "anything you consciously are, do and think at work that you are not supposed to be, do and think and which is directed upwards through the organizational hierarchy" (Karlsson, 2012: 185)). Whether it is fiddling, sabotage, or soldiering, it always goes upwards – both in terms of consequences and intentions. What you do will reduce the profits of the company you work for; you know this, and therefore you would not misbehave in the same way if it were your own company. As Karlsson defines resistance, soldiering cannot but be considered one of its expressions. In this sense, it is also an act in which *the subject* must be involved – there must be a *will* to act differently, to resist the power structure called "wage labor" which, officially at least, demands full commitment and relentless work. As we have seen, however, this will may look very different despite its resulting in the same type of misbehavior.

My goal in this chapter has not been to present the layers of subjectivity, but those found among the time-appropriating interviewees. If you isolate the motive vocabularies from the fact that they are coupled with advanced forms of time appropriation, they appear merely as different forms of resentment. The point here, however, is that they cannot be reduced to that type of inconsequential "subjectivity" to which some studies of workplace resistance sometimes refer. Whether employees are able to think critically about the work they do is only interesting in relation to the hyperbolic claims that deny them this ability (see Chapter 2). Here, the resentment is coupled with a rather advanced form of workplace misbehavior. The will is more than mere thought. More organized types of resistance in the form of non-assimilated social movements and trade unions are probably anchored in different types of subjectivity, perhaps less afflicted by the desperation and resignation that time appropriation after all must emanate from as long as it is not collectively organized as a means to provoke structural change.

It should be noted that the typology is not hierarchical in the sense that framed dissent can be regarded as more "developed" than withdrawal. On the contrary, the resignation and hopelessness expressed among withdrawing interviewees struck me as more original than the other two. As Touraine notes, "subjectivation no longer takes the form of the defence of workers or citizens; it is initially manifested at the level of individual lived experience, of the anxiety that is born of one of the increasingly contradictory experiences to which I have referred so often" (Touraine, 2000b: 59). Withdrawal might be regarded as the result of such an initial experience, of experiencing both the meaninglessness of one's work, the coercion to stick to it, and no counter-movement – for a liberation from wage slavery – as far as the eye can see.

If the subject is the individual's will to be an actor – and it can be assumed that some forms of empty labor can be expressions of such subjectivity – the question remains whether time appropriation is a viable way of succeeding with something more than escaping certain job tasks. Touraine repeatedly points out that his concept of the subject, unlike the "personalist vision," describes "an *empty* Subject which has no content other than its attempt to reconstruct the unity of labour and culture as it resists the pressures of both the market and communities" (Touraine, 2000b: 83). The possibility thus remains that subject and actor are decoupled in the sense that the motives in direct and framed dissent never result in more than the mere withdrawal. Before returning to this question in Chapter 8, I will complicate things a bit further by looking at how empty labor results from adjustment to an already wasteful economy.

7 | *The organization of idleness*

Among scholarly studies of empty labor, only one mentions that it may result from low workload. Asking why middle management employees engage in "personal business" on the job, D'Abate (2005: 1022) found that one of the most frequent answers was "to reduce boredom on the job and/or fill downtime." Despite more than half of the participants claiming this reason, D'Abate does not pursue it. When the first interviewee told me how little she had to do and that her type of *maskning* actually was involuntary, I was prepared to do the same thing, to keep it out of the analysis and to concentrate on what I here call soldiering and coping. In the current sociology of work, the employee who does not have enough work to simply does not fit in. What I call "enduring" and "slacking" (see Chapter 4) are anomalies in a discipline whose meta-narratives are still "globalization" and "intensification."

With the exception of some articles, which through various statistical exercises have discussed Parkinson's Law (of which more later), slacking and enduring are not parts of the social science literature. This would not have been a problem if it were not for the fact that, at least in Sweden, most people who have worked during summer, when their colleagues take their vacation, *know* about the phenomenon. Likewise, it would not have been a problem if it were not a dear topic in popular culture and much discussed in mass media. Again, the examples of "media scandals" mentioned in the introduction are not only examples of how "unethical" employees can be but also of how one can perform one's function in the organization while spending half of one's working hours surfing the internet. The second feature would probably become more salient if the "offenders," rather than their bosses, were being interviewed about their empty labor.

One case where this did happen was in Germany, 2012, when a civil servant wrote a farewell message to his colleagues on his retirement day: "Since 1998," he wrote, "I was present but not really there. So I'm going to be well prepared for retirement – Adieu." The e-mail was

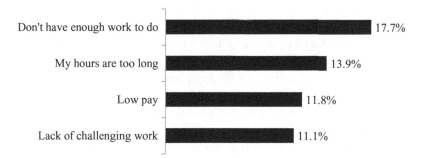

Figure 7.1 Percentage of survey respondents listing the four top reasons for "time waste." US, 2007.
Source: Blue, 2007.

leaked to the Westfalen-Post newspaper and quickly became world news. The man had worked in a municipal state surveyor's office since 1974, and in the e-mail he shared some critical remarks on the history of the organization. The municipal authorities had constructed overlapping and parallel structures and even employed another engineer to do the same job, which left him with nothing to do. "Of course, I well benefited from the freedom that came by to me," he wrote, even boasting that he had earned €745,000 for doing nothing. The mayor of Menden commented that he felt "a good dose of rage," apparently believing that the problem could have been solved if only the employee had communicated his situation (Waterfield, 2012). Afterwards, Menden also sent out a press release regretting that the employee never informed his superiors about the problem. In a less known interview with the German newspaper *Bild*, the former employee then revealed himself, name and picture, saying that he was not as "cold" as media had depicted him. "There never was any frustration on my part, and I would have written the e-mail even today. I have always offered my services, but it's not my problem if they don't want them," he said (Engelberg and Wegener, 2012).

Figure 7.1 shows the result from an American survey where it was found that employees spend an average of 1.7 hours of empty labor a day.[1] The unique feature of this survey is that respondents were asked

---

[1] Unfortunately, Salary.com has not surveyed these reasons for "time waste" again. In a study from 2012, it was found that most respondents listed "not challenged enough" as one of their reasons (35 percent), whereas "long hours"

to list the reasons for "wasting time" and offered the option "don't have enough work to do." This option turned out to be the most popular one, listed by almost a fifth of the respondents, followed by "my hours are too long" and "low pay" (which may both be regarded as typical examples of direct dissent), and the very similar "lack of challenging work," which was listed by slightly more than a tenth of the respondents. To refer to the typology of different motives in the previous chapter, adjustment to an already wasteful organization thus seems to be the most important motive underlying empty labor.

In this chapter, I start by looking at those who, like the German civil servant, *enjoy* living their life in organized idleness. Also I discuss the flows and differences between collective soldiering, slacking, and enduring. I will also discuss the most puzzling mystery, why some employees *are forced* to empty labor, and provide a provisional answer based on the interviews.

7.1 Cultures of fun

Arlie Hochschild's bold thesis, that for more privileged workers work is increasingly becoming home whereas home is becoming work, has been supported by numerous good examples supporting the second part, how home becomes work. The "electronic leash" of information technology, the ideal always to be available "if something comes up," the taking home work from the office, the deskilling of housework, are all concrete and well-founded examples of how home has become subordinated to the dictates of work. But is there really a reverse movement in her account? Does she provide any examples of how "home" (i.e. leisure) interferes with work in the same way? Not really. The strongest argument for work becoming home is that nearly half of the employees at the company she surveyed said they felt more "at home" and relaxed at work than at home (Hochschild, 1997: 82). She also gives other examples of how workers experienced more emotional support at work (from colleagues) than at home (Hochschild, 1997: 81), how Fridays during summers were "dress down" days, how there were free Cokes for the white-collar workers at the headquarters (Hochschild,

got 34 percent, "no incentive" 32 percent, "unsatisfied" 30 percent, and "bored" 23 percent. Of course, both "not challenged enough" and "bored" come close to not having enough work to do (see Gouveia, 2012).

1997: 85) and how the workers were engaged in corporate culture programs and indulged in "commitment ceremonies" (Hochschild, 1997:
89). Although standing in great contrast to the spirit of Taylorism,
these are at most examples of how the *feeling* of being at home can be
managed, but hardly evidence of "reversing worlds."

Empty labor is a real example of "home at work" – especially when
it is organized from above. The closest I got to an employee whose
empty labor was combined with organizational "culture of fun" ambi-
tions (cf. Fleming, 2005a) was yet another web developer who actually said that he felt "very at home" at work. Working at a small
consulting agency, all his colleagues (about thirteen men and two
women), including the CEO, were also his friends and it was not
unusual to engage in "friend activities" during working hours. Collective cooking sessions for lunch, "Friday beer," a "well-being commit-
tee," yearly "conference/vacation trips abroad" were some collective
activities that the interviewee seemed to appreciate without cynicism.
Unlike the shameless, not to say dull, management strategies described
by Fleming (2005a, 2009) of making employees apprehend their work
as "fun" with the explicit aim of enhancing productivity, this firm also
allowed *unproductive* fun. It was not only a case of how "nonwork
dimensions are *symbolically* drawn into the sphere of work" (Fleming, 2005a: 300, my emphasis), the symbolism is here complemented
by something real. Most importantly, the official working hours were
seven hours a day (with full pay), with the overarching motto "as long
as the work gets done." Despite the small-scale size of the company,
the notorious day-and-night-working-hours within the creative industries was an unknown phenomenon to this programmer. When they
approached the deadline of a project, the work became more intense,
but they rarely worked overtime.

This was the working day of the web developer the first time I
interviewed him:

First I came an hour late, I should have started at 9, we have flextime, of
course, but I came in at 10, because I slept till 9 so . . . since we have flextime
I can catch up later but there is no one who checks whether I actually do it.
Then, yes what did I do? I fixed a couple of bugs and so on. Then we had
lunch. We eat lunch at 11.30. At 2 p.m. I was going somewhere else, to the
editorial office of [a big newspaper] to help them with a thing. When we were
done with lunch the clock was around 12.30 so then I sat waiting till 2. I

was there a couple of hours until 4 and then I thought there's no idea to go back to the office so I quit at 4. So yes, I guess I began late and quit early.

As a perfect example of what Mars calls "hawk" occupations, the web developer works under conditions that are completely different from, say, those in a call center: "He can turn the idea of 'office time' on its head: office time is time the hawk chooses to allot to the office. It is one of a number of options a person of initiative, *hired* for initiative, is expected to have. The justifying phrase is 'I am employed for the *quality* of my work, not the amount of time I put in'" (Mars, 1982: 50). Since they can work from home and often visit their clients, the time spent at the office is not used as a means of control. The interviewee said that he tries to avoid working from home since "nothing gets done there" and since he prefers spending his days with his friends at the office.

At the office there was also the opportunity of engaging in more advanced forms of slacking: "We have Nintendo Wii installed in our cafeteria, but that was hot last summer, now people have grown tired of it. Now we're more into Guitar Hero where you can compete with each other." The CEO likes to participate in the video games, but he is usually too busy. I asked him if there were any limits to this type of activity or whether they could play all day long: "Well, one time some guys actually were told by one of our bosses, the assistant manager. He thought that 'shit, we have so much to do, you can't play now.' But he didn't know that those who were playing actually had very little to do. So I guess he was just stressed out."

Although he enjoyed the freedom at work, he did not want to abuse it, he said. Empty labor was okay, but only in the right doses:

You can sit and surf the whole day, but usually it gets quite boring. In those cases I still think it's up to the firm to provide you with tasks. So it isn't *maskning*, it is more like not having enough to do. I at least think of *maskning* as you yourself seeing to it that you do other things than what you're supposed to.

The interviewee himself thus expressed a sense of this being a different type of empty labor than the individual misbehavior that we usually associate with "time waste." Although he enjoyed the relaxed atmosphere and the activities he filled the empty hours with – blogging, photo editing, and the whole palette of social media – an equally important reason for him working so little was that no more was required of him. He did not dissent from the spirit and hierarchy of the firm, and the effort bargain was more taking place between the consultant and the client rather than between the employee and the employer. This financing of empty labor would have been worth exploring more if the interview material did allow for it. The case of the web designer, the florist, the web developer (see Chapter 4), and some instances of where the employer "turns a blind eye" to it (cf. the archivist, the cleaner, the accounting clerk) suggest that a prerequisite for *real* cultures of "fun," i.e. when empty labor is promoted as fertile soil for "creativity" (a term through which production norms are but faintly suggested), is that there are abundant wealthy clients who are willing to pay not only for the product itself but also for the aura of the company. This becomes even clearer when taking into account the monopolist position of a company like Google – perhaps the company most associated with "fun" cultures. The Google Zurich office, which has attracted much media attention with its slide between the floors, the games room, the "chill out" aquarium, the hammocks, and the easy access to free food and masseurs (Wakefield, 2008), is a typical example of the conspicuous waste that Veblen (2008 [1899]: 25) observed in the leisure class – waste that signals superiority and refinement and that ultimately relies on the exploitation of the consumer and the abundance of capital.

7.2 Collective soldiering, management misbehavior, or hidden rewards?

Returning to the issue of potential output and Baldamus' effort bargain, including frequent imbalances resulting in "overbooking" and "underbooking" (Baldamus, 1961: 94), we have so far established that the potential output is not entirely determined by how well workers cheat management; it can be low despite the worker wanting more tasks. One reason can be that the employer is cheating the client; another reason can be that the manager is cheating the employer with the backup of the whole department. The situation of the web designer described in Chapter 4 is a good example. That the potential output in her situation was deemed low was not because there were not enough tasks where her design expertise was needed, but because her boss effectively reduced the potential projects to a minimum. When the manager is involved and cheats other departments or his superiors, low potential output – for the individual employee – can also be the consequence of managerial misbehavior.

As Ackroyd and Thompson notes: "One of the reasons why managers have so many problems with misbehaviour is that they are frequently implicated themselves. Managers may be the agents of capital or part of the line of command in public sector organizations, but they are also individuals with their own goals and needs" (Ackroyd and Thompson, 1999: 80). As Karlsson notes, however, "[m]uch of the resistance literature has neglected management misbehaviour, mainly studying management control versus worker resistance" (Karlsson, 2012: 17). Since resistance, also in Karlsson's account, is rightfully conceived of as directed upwards within the power hierarchy, it is easy to assume that those in power – managers – cannot resist. But unless they rule the whole firm, managers are also subordinates to someone else. Although it may be harder for the obedient yes-man who has spent considerable energy on advancing in the hierarchy, even managers can become subjects. Also, they have more resources and chances to succeed.

The most elaborate example of managerial misbehavior that I gathered from the interviews came from a laboratory assistant who related how her department, including the boss, developed a fantastic "team spirit" and engaged in the collective forms of empty labor including having a book club with long discussions during working hours. They worked at a massive laboratory that was part of an even bigger factory, and they all had academic degrees (she was a molecular biologist). Despite their knowledge, good salaries, and white coats, the job was very monotonous, she claimed. It mainly consisted of taking water samples each morning from the taps in the factory to make sure nothing was wrong with it. This usually took two hours, thus leaving abundant time for socializing. Despite the company being a flagship for the Swedish industry, there was a sense in the group that something was wrong not only with the company and its products but with the whole industry (a typical example of framed dissent). For "security reasons," the workplace was under heavy electronic surveillance. Employees had to punch in on a time clock when they entered the laboratory, when going for lunch etc. They also had to swipe their cards when walking between the different departments, which meant that the HR department knew (or thought they knew) exactly where they

were in the factory complex. If they went where they were not supposed to, or if their lunch were unacceptably prolonged, they would
therefore have to explain to the HR-managers. Needless to say, this
rarely happened. What took place at the department was still a black
box for the HR-department, and the surveillance system could easily be
manipulated through cooperation. Even going on long lunches could
be managed by drawing each others' cards in series, and sometimes the
boss would gather the cards, send everyone home, punch them out at
the end of the day and meet the employees at the parking lot the next
morning to return the cards.

Occasionally, approximately once every three weeks and normally
during mornings, they had to deal with the spectacle of "management
by walking around." Since, in order to enter the laboratories and pass
between them, one had to swipe a card and press a code, employees
usually were allowed some time for preparation. There also seems to
have been some degree of cooperation among the laboratory managers:

Johan [the boss] is like best friends with the other lab bosses so sometimes
they call each other and then you hear 'they are coming!' Then it's just
straight to the lab, away with the *fika* stuff, run down, on with the white
coats, hats, eye protectors, masks, gloves. Then we have a division of labor
where Anna receives the bottles, I watch the oven, and Sara reads the bacteria
cultures and fills out the blanks. And Johan is so funny. He is so tired of
them and being our boss he usually pretends to do the dangerous stuff all
concentrated by the microscope. And when they say 'hi Johan,' he can go
'Shhh! I'm working.' And then they probably think 'oh, they're so busy here
they don't even have time to talk.' So they stay around five minutes and then
it's like 'the coast is clear.'

The assistant said that she did not believe her boss helped the others
to shirk out of mere kindness; he did not want to work himself and he
also knew that the salary was "not so good considering the education."
Based on Mars' typology of work and its different forms of rewards,
you might say that the boss personally increased the total rewards of
the job (cf. Mars, 1982: 7–11). When we (including old-school industrial sociologists like Baldamus) think of the rewards of work, we tend
to consider only formal rewards like wages, commissions, overtime
pay and employment security. Frequently, informal rewards, such as
perks, tips, extra work, and more extralegal ones like pilferage, over-
charged expenses, overloading, underdropping, and different types of

empty labor matter to the individual employee just as much. Instances in which empty labor is institutionalized, involving both workers and management, may be regarded as slacking, collective soldiering, managerial misbehavior, or just as hidden rewards depending from which perspective it is approached. Whether it actually is a reward or not depends, however, on how the employee experiences empty labor.

7.3 Boreout

We now turn to "enduring" employees, i.e. to those who have little to do despite a strong sense of work obligation. This group has so far been virtually ignored in the sociology of work. The most sophisticated analyses of the phenomenon are rather to be found in the popular literature referred to in the introduction and especially in a book called *The Living Dead: Switched Off, Zoned Out* by Bolchover. Bolchover has a long job experience in the British insurance business and has worked for several companies. In *The Living Dead*, he writes about empty labor – a well-known phenomenon to him, but more of a curse than a reward:

During the years 1997 to 2003, I was employed to do a full-time job. If I was to be given now all the work I had to do for my employers during those six years, and I worked hard using all my ability, I would be able to complete all of it very comfortably in about six months, working Monday to Friday, 9 to 5.

One month of work for every year of employment. Sounds about right. (Bolchover, 2005: 22)

Although Bolchover changed jobs several times to find a more challenging job, he experienced the same type of organized idleness at all his jobs. For two years he was forgotten by one of the companies and did not even have to show up at the workplace. He spent his time doing the type of activities that you normally do during empty labor, and he also wrote a management book that received good reviews and was reprinted. Yet he longed for a challenging job in which what he had learned when taking his MBA would become useful. What for some might be regarded as the ideal job made him increasingly depressed over the years. His responsibilities, which at one of the firms included persuading Russian companies to insure their assets, could easily have been expanded, but no one cared and he was not given more work even when he asked for it. After some years of idleness he decided to communicate the situation to his retiring boss:

It was a great speech, full of logic and common sense, but my boss's glazed eyes made him look like an Italian at a cricket match rather than someone who was going to give serious thought to finding a role which would benefit both me and the company. He was in a far away land, somewhere near Marbella, and I had failed miserably to divert his attention away from his sun-drenched villa. (Bolchover, 2005: 27)

After this failed "speech act," Bolchover went to a new firm only to discover that the workload there was even lower. The "endless spells of nothingness" (Bolchover, 2005: 24) eventually made him leave the whole trade for more productive activities. He repeatedly points out that he "never took a day off dishonestly" (Bolchover, 2005: 108). Although he enjoyed the "sneaking respect" he sensed from friends believing that he had "cheated the system," such subjectivity was in fact not at work in his case: "I wasn't cheating the system," he writes. "The system was cheating itself" (Bolchover, 2005: 23).

Bolchover's story is, of course, exceptional in its absurdity, but the statistics represented in Figure 7.1 suggest that there probably are other employees who struggle with the same problem. The negative stress that Bolchover describes has also been analyzed from a somewhat different perspective by Philippe Rothlin and Peter Werder, who with the book *Boreout!* attracted considerable attention in the world press. They define "boreout" as a state in which "employees are understretched, unmotivated and immeasurably bored" (Rothlin and Werder, 2007: 4). According to them, all forms of empty labor (even those where the employee is the agent initiating and reproducing it) eventually develops into boreout: "a long period of doing next to nothing at work amounts to endless and horrifying tedium. Merely pretending to be busy becomes wearisome with time and, above all, it is unsatisfying. There is no challenge, no recognition" (ibid.). This is entirely in accordance with Bolchover's experience of empty labor which is why he argues that we should unearth what he describes as "the last taboo":

After all, quite apart from the huge corporate and economic effects of this large-scale inactivity, the whole experience surely also has a destructive effect on the individual concerned. I should know, because I've been there. To be honest, you can actually feel pretty much as dead as it is possible to feel while you are still breathing. Does that sound a bit over-dramatic to you? You're lucky then. You've obviously never been a member of the Living Dead brigade. (Bolchover, 2005: 7)

"The more superfluous a job of work is, the worse it becomes, the more it degenerates into ideology," Adorno once said (in Adorno and Horkheimer, 2010 [1956]: 45). Boreout is the experience of this oppressive ideology without the individual initiative to escape from it. A mystery to which I shall return in the next chapter is how it can be so difficult to avoid empty labor if you are motivated to work more – how the potential output for the individual worker can be so low. In the next section, I discuss how the enduring interviewees in this study experienced their situation.

7.4 Explaining enduring

Martin Nicolaus once wrote: "as less and less people are forced to produce more and more, more and more people are forced to produce less and less" (Nicolaus, 1970: 203). The rising "surplus class" that he had in mind consumed more than it produced, a class whose labor became increasingly unproductive as the general productivity of labor advanced, but whose role in the capitalist economy was essential to remedy the threat of overproduction. Nicolaus' analysis was significantly complicated by the vagueness of the Marxist distinction between productive and unproductive jobs that he endorsed, yet he used the concept of the surplus class to explain the constant increase of the middle classes. If we want to study those who really are forced to produce nothing, those whose labor is not necessarily unproductive, but quite empty, the linkage to class structure is not that straightforward.

According to Rothlin and Werder, boreout is an office diagnosis that is far from applicable to the whole working life: "Workers in agriculture and industry do not suffer from boreout because measurable results are demanded and the boreout strategies will not work" (Rothlin and Werder, 2007: 85). At another page they say: "It arises in professions where people are under stress during peak periods, but for the greater part of their time do not know what they are supposed to be doing, other than reading magazines and surfing the internet" (Rothlin and Werder, 2007: 80). Regardless of the fact that they present very little empirical support for their generalizations, it seems reasonable to assume occupational patterns in both empty labor and boreout. According to the most recent survey from Salary.com, the more educated you are, the more "wasteful" you will probably be. Among high school graduates, 59 percent reported having empty labor on a daily basis whereas the percentage among those with doctorate degrees was 67 and those with master's and bachelor's degrees fell in between (Gouveia, 2012).

Another notion, which also is repeated by the inventor of Parkinson's Law – "work expands so as to fill the time available for its completion" (Parkinson, 1957: 3) – is that the more money you earn, the less you actually do. According to Parkinson, this is because managers have a structural interest in gathering subordinates in order to secure their own position. The more work they delegate to assistant managers, the less for themselves. Since no interviewee mentioned this strategy, I could not possibly comment, but the outcome seems to be applicable to Bolchover's succinct description of his own career:

- Small company (PWS) – No Title – Quite Hard work – Crap money.
- Bigger company (Minet) – Divisional Director – Less work – More money.
- Even bigger company (Humungous) – Assistant Vice-President (practically up there with Dick Cheney) – Even less work and including 11 months of doing literally no work – Even more money.
- Another very big company (Gargantuan) – Director – Very little work, apart from writing a book – Still more money (Bolchover, 2005: 31).

Bolchover's career mirrors the result of another study according to which cyberslacking is significantly more frequent among high status employees: "In particular, those who are highly paid, managers and professionals, better educated, and employees with greater workplace autonomy spend substantially more time online for personal purposes during work than those below them in the workplace hierarchy" (Garrett and Danziger, 2008: 291). The case of a former director general whom I managed to interview also supports the thesis that the higher up you are, the emptier labor becomes. She had been abruptly dismissed from her post and thrown to what in Sweden is called "the elephants' graveyard." Here, former chief executives of civil service departments are stowed away with full salaries in wait for further

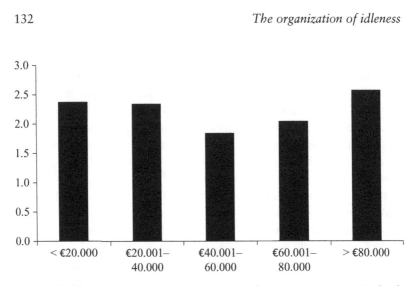

Figure 7.2 Empty labor in hours per day according to gross income. Finland, 2010.
Source: Taloustutkimus Oy (n = 1077)

instructions (which may never come). When I met her she earned the equivalent of $21.000 a month and she had just been on a two-hour workout. Despite the media turbulence that preceded her discharge, there was no trace of shame or regret in this rare case of enduring: "you go from shock to reaction. And the reaction was: well wait, what have I delivered? And then you realize that it's not you who have the problem. Someone else owns the problem." This woman, wearing both Prada glasses and a Rolex watch, was the only person I interviewed who was openly, not to say publicly, engaged in empty labor. Yet she did not regard it as labor at all, it was just one of many perks to which she had the legal and moral right.

However, if we disregard the more spectacular cases of empty labor, the relation to income is less clear. According to the results from the Finnish survey presented in Figure 7.2, those earning between €40.001 and 60.000 have considerably less empty labor than those earning less or more. It is hard to tell what this might indicate; my suggestion would be that although deskilled labor is more prevalent in the same industries that the working class traditionally has been associated with, there is no direct relation between income and opacity.

This brings us to the question of low potential output. To begin with, it should be stressed that even in cases of enduring, there has to be some personal consideration of which job tasks are worth performing and which are not. An "assistant store manager" (this was the Swedish title they gave him for working as receptionist, janitor, and seller) at a storehouse said that he appreciates empty labor only when he feels "under the weather" or in small doses, at maximum, half an hour: "Some days you just stand there waiting for a customer that will give you something to do, then you almost go out to rake them in. When someone calls, you don't want them to hang up because you want something to do." The workers are told that during downtime they are supposed to clean, remove trash, and keep the storehouse in order. The only problem is that some days there is nothing more to do: "If you have cleaned everything during the morning, you will have several hours in the afternoon during which there is nothing to do." As the interviewee was aware, "nothing" really meant "nothing worth doing" – an evaluation that varied among the employees. They always worked in couples, and the colleague with whom he worked at the moment of the interview, apparently judged the nothingness differently.

The colleague who I am with now thinks it's very boring not having anything to do, so she often runs away cleaning, and polishing and pottering about. But I'm a bit reluctant to that. It's so incredibly meaningless when you think of it. To polish for the sake of polishing. I mean, when it already looks fine? It doesn't have to be clinically clean, if there's some dust on the floor it's not that . . . I mean, we swab once a week so there is no need to do it several times.

We recognize this line of reasoning from those soldiering and cutting down on particularly meaningless extras, which tended to be related to cleaning and administration. The only difference is that enduring employees have a stronger sense of work obligation – they want to work, but even they must consider the meaning of a certain task. According to the worker, the managers are well aware of the existence of empty labor and to some degree they accept it – "it's okay to surf the internet during fifteen minutes or so" – but they did not seem to understand the full extent of it. There was a bonus program that generated quite large sums in relation to the salary, probably designed to spur the inventiveness of the employees, but that did not help much and nor did the blocking of certain web pages: "I can't go working slowly only to fill out the hours. In that case, I rather feel that it's up to the management to put more work on us."

This type of "involuntary *maskning*," as the employee himself termed it, was particularly annoying since it made him feel dull. This was a feeling that all enduring interviewees shared. As mentioned in Chapter 4, empty labor could have a mind-numbing effect on some that made it harder for them to actually engage in work when the opportunity presented itself. Rothlin and Werder (2007: 39–46) call this the "boreout paradox," which develops in different stages. At the outset of your career, you worry about the stress and challenge that is mostly associated with work. You then get a job, and quickly you realize that it is far from as stressful as is always claimed. You learn to keep it as it is and to send out the appropriate messages to ward off more job tasks. Eventually, the dreadful boredom poisons not only your time at work but your whole life, according to Rothlin and Werder. The paradox is that you maintain this situation out of sheer listlessness. Since it is generally assumed that lots of empty labor characterizes a good job and you never know what they might give you instead, you are content with what you have.

Rothlin and Werder might have a point, but their explanation of why people endure empty labor also individualizes the phenomenon more than necessary. Sometimes the labor process makes idleness quite unavoidable. A typical example that has been discussed by others is the process worker who is paid to watch over automated production processes (cf. Gorz, 1989, 2003). This and other surveillance jobs are technically not cases of empty labor – here, workers are paid pretty much for staying awake, and they would either have to sleep or leave the workplace for it to qualify as empty labor. Nevertheless, I should mention that I talked with a former process worker who recalled that the job depressed him and that he gained much weight while he was there. "I was so damn bored that the only thing I could do in the end was to eat. Microwaved pizza, Russian pastry. Had I stayed longer I would have got this huge stomach. That's how it was with everyone there."

More related to empty labor, though, we have already seen how consultancy or short-time employment or projects, in which a certain job must be done but the time limit can be expanded, work as incentives for empty labor. Here, there are economic interests in prolonging working hours as long as possible. This became even clearer when

I interviewed a bank clerk who was responsible for a project that did not take more than half an hour or sometimes fifteen minutes a day. He also expressed the sense of how "relatively burdensome it becomes if you have lots of empty working hours and you suddenly get something to do. The real normality of work is suddenly felt in a completely different way than if you have a constant and even amount of tasks to do, because then non-work has been normalized." But that was not the only reason that he hesitated to communicate the problem to the managers.

He had worked on a newly instituted project for nearly a year when I interviewed him, during the first summer, at full-time. His main task was to send interested customers to the financial advisors and then report the results:

which was a good setup, except that we only had like three or four customers a day at most. . . . I had maybe half an hour of effective work during a seven-hour working day. So there was extremely much downtime.

RP > Interesting!

No, it was mostly boring.

The bank clerk confirms the process of boreout described by Rothlin and Werder: "To begin with it was very nice to not have to do anything, but when you've had it for a week you start growing tired of it. Then you might just as well do something instead of being bored." In his case the miscalculation seemed to be rooted in a lack of technical knowledge among his superiors: "Something I realized was that they were very bad at Excel. So stuff that took long time for them, I could do in no time." His bosses who had initiated the project were located at another office and therefore he asked the local manager about more things to do. "But I suppose he really didn't have time to come up with things either. He was more like 'yeah, we'll come up with something,' and then you sent him an e-mail the next day, like 'have you found anything for me to do?' and then he said 'yeah, I'll fix it till tomorrow afternoon.'"

This is a clear example of how communication does not necessarily result in a solution. Apparently, there was not enough work for him to partake fully. Yet, seeing how occupied his colleagues seemed to be made him feel guilty. He withdrew to a corner of the office where no one could see what he was doing – "mostly not to get caught in an embarrassing situation since I felt a bit like exploiting the others who did extremely much while I was doing extremely little and still getting the same salary." When he had read every column of Herman Lindqvist (a Swedish historian) back to 1998 he sensed he had hit the bottom. During a meeting concerning the prolongation of his contract he told the managers about his enforced idleness. Did he get more to do? No. At the time of the interview, he was employed for only three hours a day, mostly for labor legislative reasons that do not allow working days shorter than three hours, he explained. He had managed to initiate a couple of new projects, but he still worked little more than half an hour a day.

In *The Theory of the Leisure Class*, Veblen describes how during the nineteenth century, upcoming middle-class men would let wives and servants engage in "honorific" idleness to hide the shameful fact that they had to work. Today, work has become the new badge of honor. As Jonathan Gershuny puts it, "the dominant class now works for money. On the principle of emulation, those wishing to demonstrate superordinate social position, might thus *not* be expected to exhibit idleness – but conspicuous industry" (Gershuny, 2009: 42). Hence, from the 1980s and onwards, in the UK, the US, Canada, and Australia, the total amount of paid *and* unpaid work has steadily increased (Gershuny, 2011; see also Schor, 1991 for the US). With this shift in moral standards, it comes as no surprise that it is now idleness that must be concealed by acting busy. In this chapter, I have discussed how involuntary types of idleness occur.

The notion expressed by the mayor of Menden that low potential output is a matter of the employee not communicating downtime to the responsible managers mainly serves to individualize empty labor and reduce it to either soldiering or coping (see also D'Abate, 2005; Rothlin and Werder, 2007; Vivien and Thompson, 2005). Rothlin and Werder are quite explicit on this point: "individual responsibility plays a key role" and "it is the individual employee who must act," they say (Rothlin and Werder, 2007: 102). Yet they acknowledge that the company "has a duty to treat its employees well and to help those who cannot, or can only partially, appreciate their individual responsibilities" (Rothlin and Werder, 2007: 103).

I would rather stress that there are factors that go beyond the particular employer-employee relationship explaining why empty labor sometimes is endured. Opacity (including measurability) seems to play a key role in both enduring and slacking, i.e. opacity that is not actively created by the worker, but inherent in the job. Habituation also seems to be an important factor, regardless of whether the employee has a strong or weak sense of work obligation. In some instances, the problem of enduring could probably be removed if the employee communicated the situation to his or her manager. But one could also turn the problem on its head and argue that the endurer should rather try developing a lower sense of work obligation. Something that struck me when interviewing those whose empty labor could be categorized as enduring, was their inability to engage in alternative activities during the empty hours. They seemed to be suffering from a lack of personal initiative. And by that I do not mean initiative in creating meaningless work tasks just for the sake of it, but initiative in developing meaningful activities or "work" – regardless of whether such work would serve the company or not.

Rothlin and Werder worry about the opposite: "what if the work doesn't interest these employees at all? Just getting the more of the same will not make them happy" (Rothlin and Werder, 2007: 109). Managers must therefore "take care of other factors that help give work meaning," they argue (Rothlin and Werder, 2007: 115). But why "give meaning" to something that does not interest the employee? The notion that we can construct meaning in every type of activity, no matter how absurd, is key to understanding why we tend to question the *organization* of work rather than its *substance*. Confusing the different types of empty labor, Rothlin and Werder do not present a solid solution to the "problem" of empty labor. In cases of soldiering and slacking, developing different techniques for generating commitment might be worth the effort from a managerial point of view. But if we take the worker's point of view and concentrate on enduring, realizing that there are other, more meaningful activities in life than work seems to be a more pressing issue.

Another factor explaining the mystery of enduring is the inherent inefficiency of the capitalist employment contract. Since we are paid not for what we produce but for our time, time takes on a symbolic quality that obscures "work" as a productive activity. Spending as much time in the office as the boss, working weekends, and answering work-related e-mails late in the evening become signs of commitment. When the opacity of the labor process is so intense that these signs constitute the only guidance management has for assessing the performance of employees, they may easily lapse into a type of empty labor that at first appears agreeable but gradually becomes boring. The better the employee is at constructing an identity of excellence and the longer the charade goes on, the more difficult it becomes to get more work or to tell it as it is. Communication means taking enormous risks. The disappointment of one's boss may cost the entire job, and there is no guarantee that there actually is more work to do. There is always a risk that your job will be reduced to a part-time contract or even made redundant.

In the next chapter, I return to the question of workplace resistance and subjectivity. As we have seen, the individual motives behind a certain type of workplace misbehavior may vary widely. How employees define or perceive empty labor, whether it is a way of resisting and what they say they are resisting, complicates the whole conception of subjectivity. We now know that the same can be said about the concept of resistance (as dissociated from its subjective aspects). If resistance, as defined by Karlsson, is "anything you consciously are, do and think at work that you are not supposed to be, do and think and which is directed upwards through the organizational hierarchy," then we must recognize that its meaning derives from highly multifaceted concepts. No employer would openly advocate inefficiency or "time waste," yet many would find it frustrating if their employees constantly asked for more things to do. What you are not supposed to be, do and think is thus not a universal, and it may not always be about following the formal rules. Also, what goes upwards through the hierarchical organization can be highly ambiguous when the closest manager organizes the misbehavior. Was it resistance to slack along like the molecular biologist and the web developer (see Chapter 4), or would it have been more oppositional to demand more work from their managers? Even if the overall morality of an organization is to reduce empty labor as much as possible, there may be entire departments where other norms dominate. If maximal rationality in terms of efficiency, i.e. the highest possible output with the least possible input, is not such a dominating rationale of capitalist production as we tend to assume, in what sense can we regard time appropriation as empty labor?

8 | *Resistance incorporated?*

The subject-denying tendencies in work sociology referred to in Chapter 2 have now been refuted in this and many other studies. Employees resist work in all imaginable ways. Here, I have described resistance relating to the temporal dimension of labor – ways to appropriate time. But can empty labor really be called "resistance"? Does it make any difference in the long run? These are two questions that now dominate the debate on organizational misbehavior. We know that employees misbehave, but is it more than misbehavior, more than triviality? Is power really being challenged more than symbolically, and if so, can the struggle, even potentially, lead to structural change? These questions are highly relevant to the study of empty labor. As we have seen, people may appropriate time for a variety of reasons. Few of them are subjects in any collective sense; when appropriating time they are mostly attempting to become actors in their own lives. For some, empty labor has never been a matter of subjectivity, but rather the adjustment to an already wasteful organization. Are all these forms of empty labor resistance, and if not, are they just anomalies or incorporated parts of some type of rationality? The question of the possible incorporation of empty labor, which I have only alluded to earlier, will here be discussed in relation to the types of empty labor that I have discussed in previous chapters.

Jocelyn Hollander and Rachel Einwohner (2004: 544) have proposed a valuable typology for distinguishing between different types of resistance. Their first subjective dimension is the one I have so far been elaborating: whether or not the act is intended as resistance by the actor. This is the dimension stressed by Touraine and especially by Scott. But one could also ask whether the act is *recognized* as resistance by the target (e.g. managers and employers) or by an external observer. This brings us to the interpersonal dimension of resistance. For instance, if resistance is recognized as such only by the actor, one might talk about "attempted resistance," i.e. resistance that never results in any significant change. If the resistance is recognized as such only by the target or by the observer, one might talk about "target-defined" or "externally defined" resistance, respectively. In addition to Hollander and Einwohner's model, one could also ask whether the act of resistance is conceived of as *a threat* by the target. For instance, there may be formal rules restricting the practice of empty labor, thus formally making it an act of misbehavior, when in fact the management knows that it poses no real threat against the enterprise.

In recent years, the interpersonal dimension of workplace resistance has overshadowed the subjective issues discussed in Chapters 2 and 3. Rather than the denial of subjectivity at the workplace (against which there is now too much evidence), many scholars are turning back to the functionalist roots of the field of organizational behavior (see Vardi and Weitz, 2004: 9–12). The functionalist incorporation argument can be summarized with the following sentence: the particular act of resistance is in fact no resistance at all; it is incorporated into the rationality of the firm/work society/capitalism, and more than that, it reproduces the very system it is targeted against. In this sense, the Tourainian subject is split and separated into two halves: the attempt (1) to become an actor, (2) to become decoupled from each other. We still experience ourselves as subjects, but we are not actors in the sense that we actually challenge established power structures.

Unfortunately, the incorporation argument tends to come with extreme generalizations. For instance, we could easily say that people refusing to "sell out" and who therefore "appropriate time" under circumstances of low potential output (i.e. someone slacking) probably fool themselves somewhat, but does that mean that all types of empty labor are deceitful apparatuses of consent? Instead of reproducing the abstractions that the incorporation argument often relies on, I will here attempt to concretize the discussion. As the reader probably has already noticed, it seems plausible to assume that empty labor sometimes is incorporated, but to make the argument more tangible we need to ask ourselves: which type of empty labor and which type of incorporation?

I will argue that there are three incorporation arguments that are of particular relevance to empty labor. Each of them emanates from a certain type of rationality. In *Reason's Neglect*, Barbara Townley (2008) lists different types of rationality that reoccur in organization theory. She differentiates among *disembedded, embodied,* and *embedded* rationalities. The disembedded rationality is perhaps most associated with neo-classical economics, but it is also present in Weber's concept of the bureaucracy. Paving the way for later accounts of the modern worker as an appendage to the machine (see Chapter 2), Weber's critique was that in the bureaucracy, "rational calculation . . . reduces every worker to a cog in this machine and, seeing himself in this light, he will merely ask how to transform himself from a little into a somewhat bigger cog" (Weber, 1978 [1922]: lix). The disembedded rationality seems to operate independently of individuals and social institutions; almost as an external force it reduces us to cogs whether we want it or not. The second part of the quote, however, also summarizes an embodied notion of rationality, i.e. a rationality that incorporates the body, the emotions, and the "irrational" subconscious of the worker (see Townley, 2008: 159ff). This type of rationality might not be rational in an economic or even in a social sense; its fundamental function is to produce workers who in one way or another accept that which is and thereby reproduce the dominating power structures. What few organization theorists seem to have realized is that Weber also worked with embedded notions of rationality. Weber's theory of the bureaucracy was not a description of how organizations in general work; he presented different "types of economic organizations" (cf. Weber, 1978 [1922]: 74–75) in which other organization types were more *embedded*, i.e. following socially formed types of rationalities. Before industrial sociology was even formulated, he described how workers were not only shaped by the anonymous rationality of, for instance, "maximal efficiency" but also shaped it by manipulating the piecework system, for example (see Swedberg, 2003: 92). Production as a consequence of the struggle between management and workers that follow certain patterns is a typical example of an embedded rationality.

In this chapter, I discuss three incorporation arguments in relation to empty labor; each emanates from one of type of rationality. *Profitable incorporation* is based on the disembedded notion of rationality, or more precisely the idea that organizational phenomena that may appear utterly irrational are in fact furthering productivity in the long run. *Mental incorporation* emerges from an embodied notion of rationality in which organizational forms of resistance (such as time appropriation) are but mental safety valves that protect power from more severe opposition. *Simulative incorporation* is based on an embedded notion of rationality according to which capitalism has entered a stage where the simulation of education, production, resistance, and other key institutions of industrial capitalism outstrips the substantive value of these institutions. Simulating work then becomes absorbed by the overarching rationale of simulation.

I will argue that all three incorporation arguments must be considered in the explanation of empty labor, but that we must pay more attention to which type of empty labor they address, i.e. treat them as empirical issues while refraining from using them as tautological abstractions. I realize that my empirical material does not allow me to either refute or verify these arguments entirely – in fact, each of them require much more data than any single study can acquire. In this chapter, my ambition is rather to illustrate the analytical use of the typologies developed in the previous chapter and to open up for new approaches to empty labor.

8.1 Profitable incorporation

In their more thoughtful moments, mainstream management theorists sometimes point out how empty labor may be beneficial both for the individual and the organization. Apart from worrying about losses in productivity and the "costs" empty labor entails (for the employer), D'Abate also says that it may enable "individuals to balance and cross the boundaries between life realms" (D'Abate, 2005: 1013) and consequently, that "personal activities may not always entail negative organizational implications" (D'Abate, 2005: 1027).[1] In like manner, Garrett and Danziger also seem concerned to conclude their study of cyberslacking on a "positive" note:

For example, if parents are able to quickly and easily check on their kids or to manage a household need efficiently from their workplace computer, they might be less distracted and require less time away from work tasks. And just as very short naps have been demonstrated to revive mental activity, perhaps short virtual breaks for a quick hand of solitaire, a note to a friend, an exploration of the online deal of the day, or a check on a sports score might refresh and invigorate many individuals' work and productivity. (Garrett and Danziger, 2008: 291)

---

[1] The exact same argument has also been presented by Ivarsson and Larsson (2012), although they also acknowledge that in some instances, empty labor may be more of a resistance act.

The notion that empty labor lets employees "revive mental energy" is a common one; in the media discourse you may also hear that cyberslacking activities increase productivity since they are part of networking and public relations. Such generalizations, however, build on the assumption that all employees, even when it appears otherwise, really are dutiful workers with nothing but long-term productivity before their eyes. In other words, they reduce all forms of empty labor into coping.

But not even if we concentrate on coping is it clear how empty labor can be profitable for the company. Although it does not prove anything, most of the interviewees said they used social media at work, but no one said they did it for the sake of building work-related networks. If anyone did, it would have been hard to estimate whether the economic value of the network covered the cost (in terms of "company money") of empty labor. Similarly, empty labor as a way of balancing a requiring job with a functional family life sounds like a convincing explanation of at least some expressions of empty labor, and the notion that empty labor creates a space for ticking off home-related commitments was also expressed by some interviewees. However, none of them claimed that this was their main reason for appropriating time. Since women for various reasons are more burdened by domestic issues than men, it could also be expected that if balancing family and job were the central reason for time appropriation, this would be reflected in women engaging more in empty labor than men. But as described in Chapter 6, none of the surveys of empty labor indicate this – if anything, it seems that men generally appropriate more time than women.

Among coping employees in this study, building networks and keeping the work-family balance were overshadowed by another concern: to stay healthy. Although they were working at different social welfare offices, the stories of two social workers were almost identical in how they described the rationale of empty labor.

We know that people who work too much or who are not handling it get sick and that is much, much worse for a workplace. If you can keep someone instead of employing a substitute you will profit from it. We know that, we don't even have to talk about it. We know that's how it is. There's no suspicion about anyone not working enough. When we go for *fika*, in the morning and in the afternoon, we are very careful about having everyone there. And you also try to get the others with you at five p.m. Then, the working day is over. It's not okay to work late.

This woman had a manager position and could very well be suspected for depicting the situation in flattering terms, yet the same ideas about getting everyone to come at *fika*, about going home in time and about no one caring whether you are cyberslacking or not, were also mentioned by another social worker who worked closer to the clients. "Several from my department have been on long-term sick leave and so have I, and since it is a very slim organization the problem is rather that we get sick because of too much stress," she says. To work too much is thus perceived of as a greater threat against productivity than empty labor. The latter interviewee also said that there was a dimension of recreation to the time spent on empty labor: "When you just sit down taking it easy you start reflecting and then you can get new perspectives on your job as well." The question then becomes whether this is an essential aspect of coping or a way of "rationalizing." Do you really need two hours a day to recreate in this way or are there other aspects to why people with high sense of work obligation appropriate time? "And then about getting on well with the team and to be lax and have fun with them, the employer can sense that. If we get on we will stay at the workplace, so I can always find arguments for why it is good to take it easy and get paid," the social worker said.

The idea that happy workers are more productive workers is well grounded in the literature and in the general view of empty labor. In the latest Salary.com survey, 71 percent of the respondents said they believe that empty labor was "beneficial" for productivity: "By being able to check Facebook, Twitter and have periods of brief downtime throughout the workday, those surveyed said they believe employees will actually be more productive than if restrictions are placed on them," it says in the report (Gouveia, 2012). The theory has also been confirmed in an interesting piece of comparative ethnography by Townsend (2004). Townsend compared two aquatic centers where the managerial attitude to empty labor differed radically. At "LittlePools" the employer actively encouraged the employees to take time off during rainy days when there were few clients. At "Conglomerate Leisure, on the other hand, the board was never satisfied with either management or workers, and a repeated dictum was "if you've got time to lean you've got time to clean" (Townsend, 2004: 54). As many of my interviewees also witnessed, the idea was that cleaning should fill all periods of downtime.

Townsend observed that the employees at LittlePools developed what I have earlier referred to as "responsible autonomy," i.e. a sense of when it was "okay" (from the employer's perspective) to appropriate time and when it was not: "A culture developed where employees recognized that there was an acceptable time and level for underworking" (Townsend, 2004: 51). When the center was crowded and there was much to do, employees could risk their health and safety for the organization, whereas during downtime they withdrew without pretense (which must be regarded as quite exceptional). Managers and employees at Conglomerate Leisure were rather engaged in "irresponsible autonomy." They soldiered as much as possible – managers could go for lunch for three hours and workers would do as little as possible. Theft and skimming were also widespread practices, and the sums were considerable. According to Townsend, the results indicated that "a formal and bureaucratic structure contributed to the development of a culture of resistance" (Townsend, 2004: 57), whereas allowing empty labor was more beneficial for the overall productivity of the firm.

This is the essence of what I call *profitable incorporation*, the idea that behaviors that may appear "dysfunctional" are in fact functional – "on the whole" – and that a more tolerant attitude (Theory Y) towards (what appears to be) misbehaviors will somehow benefit the firm. Again, this theory requires much more data than what I have been able to collect here, and probably more than what Townsend collected as well. A salesperson said that when she and a friend openly sat in the clothes store talking about this and that and clearly not doing their job, the comments they got were: "Good Heavens, you seem to have so much fun here. It's so great to be here, you can see how much you enjoy it." But then she also reflected that "maybe there were other people there who didn't find it funny at all and who went out and were angry, I wouldn't know that."

This captures the difficulty of studying profitable incorporation. How can we measure the gains and losses of a "relaxed atmosphere" in the clothes store? How can we measure the economic value of networking during working hours? Since everyone realizes that the effects of social networking are highly contextual, you would have to compare the same individual, doing the same job while networking, and not networking, which is an impossible task. In other words, these notions rely on counterfactuals that do not provide evidence and often tend to be a bit rash. For instance, would it *really* be less productive if the employees of LittlePools obsessively cleaned the pool instead of reading books? How are we to know? As we shall see, the same conundrum reappears in all incorporation arguments.

8.2 Mental incorporation

Let us now return to the cases of soldiering motivated by framed dissent, i.e. based on political narratives addressing larger structures than the individual firm. Given that empty labor sometimes emerges from low potential output despite the worker, sometimes due to ignorant managers, sometimes due to mere wastefulness; given that allowing a certain amount of empty labor can be more profitable for the firm than forbidding it altogether – is it really reasonable to treat any type of empty labor as resistance in any substantial sense? Take the case of a casual laborer who always did his best to soldier at all his jobs. For him, soldiering was a way of stealing back from what society had stolen from him. The story he told me began early, already in childhood when he was confronted by political issues relating to his family:

My mother has been on health insurance since like I was born. Because of a back injury they say now. Earlier they thought it was something psychological, that she was depressed. She had a lot of other symptoms suggesting it. But then it turned out that all those symptoms came from the back injury. So she still lives on her sickness pension, seven thousand a month [i.e. barely enough to pay the rent of an apartment in Stockholm].

With his father lacking a stable income as well, this man clearly had a lot of anger that motivated his soldiering. But in what way could soldiering be said to oppose the injustices that had come upon his life? Was it anything other than an individual relief, a sense of fooling the system while stealing nothing but scraps?

Whereas the subject-denying theories discussed in Chapter 2 are becoming increasingly undermined by different resistance studies, the pessimist trend in critical workplace studies today is to regard resistance as adjustment. This is how Maier summarizes the argument:

It's useless to try to change the system, or oppose it, since this only reinforces it; challenge makes its existence all the more entrenched. Of course, you can indulge in anarchist jokes, such as setting up a special 'call-in-sick day' or adopting the slogan 'Steal from your job since your job steals from you.'

That's always fun, but rebellion was the gambit of the sixties protesters, and we know what became of them: they're your bosses now. (Maier, 2006: 134)

While not as categorical as today, this argument has been around for a long while in industrial sociology and labor process theory in particular. Tom Lupton (1963) early stressed how fiddles and soldiering can give workers relative satisfactions that decrease the potential of greater harm to the industry. Laurie Taylor and Paul Walton (1971) captured this disarming aspect in their concept of "utilitarian sabotage": some time-saving but unauthorized operations can reduce frustration and thus enhance the efficiency of the labor process. This kind of sabotage does not necessarily entail any political consciousness but rather the will to endure labor in its existing form. The most elaborate example of this argument was presented by Burawoy in *Manufacturing Consent*. Burawoy's fieldwork at Allied Corporation (which by chance turned out to be on the same shop floor that Roy earlier had studied) focused precisely on why "workers work as hard as they do." Rejecting the two standard explanations (that they work hard because of material rewards or because of lifelong socialization and internalized beliefs from external institutions such as the family, school, and mass media), his investigation brought him paradoxically to analyze "the game of making out" which he describes in the following way:

The game of making out provides a framework for evaluating the productive activities and the social relations that arise out of the organization of work. We can look upon making out, therefore, as comprising a sequence of stages – of encounters between machine operators and the social or non-social objects that regulate the conditions of work. The rules of the game are experienced as a set of externally imposed relationships. The art of making out is to manipulate those relationships with the purpose of advancing as quickly as possible from one stage to the next. (Burawoy, 1979: 51)

Once you have made out in this way, you can enjoy some empty labor as earlier described by Roy. This and other games concerned with deceiving the piecework system, constitute, according to Burawoy, a psychological safety valve for worker aggression. The relative satisfactions are several, e.g. the reduction of fatigue, the loss of time consciousness, the social rewards of making out and avoidance of the stigma of failing to make out, etc. The game also solves Ditton's dilemma of boredom, i.e. the fact that no psychological investment, too much withdrawal, tends to lead to intense boredom (Ditton, 1977: 61). With games, time passes quickly. Burawoy does not question the authenticity of these reliefs; there are real gains for the workers to be made in the effort bargain. But the problem with such zealous effort bargaining is that the effort bargain as such never gets called into question. Real, or "ideological struggle," according to Burawoy, should not be "over the shape of the effort bargain, but over the very notion of reward for effort" (1979: 177). Workers may secure some of their class bound interests while making out, but their *radical needs* – those that transcend class society – will remain unsatisfied and even inhibited by deceptive feelings of "beating the system." Since the mechanization of necessary labor under monopoly capitalism supersedes the intensification of the labor process as the most important means of creating surplus value, the fundamental oppression never is recognized. Capitalists can afford the economic losses due to workers making out a couple of hours and yet succeed in their main object, namely to secure and obscure surplus value. Thus Burawoy radically changes the notions of control and resistance of labor process theory: "Coercion, of course, always lies at the back of *any* employment relationship, but the erection of a game provides the conditions in which the organization of active cooperation and consent prevails" (1979: 83).

Since the piecework system is no longer as widespread in Western working life, the game of making out looks quite different today. As we have seen in Chapter 5, simulation is still the general rule, but its principles are more contextual today. Yet it is true that simulation always implies consent to a certain extent. To be openly oppositional, to organize or engage in collective action would be counterproductive for anyone who wants to avoid scrutiny. According to a customs officer, most of his colleagues were "probably quite content with relaxing at work, to be able to do the same stuff as at home and still get paid." As soon as someone took it a step further, however, there were dire consequences: "But there was this old man who was fired the other day because he refused to search a car that was passing the gate. They came to his office and asked why and he said: 'you do your job and I do mine.' But he was like me, mostly watching movies during the nights."

Successful time appropriation cannot be openly rebellious. As demonstrated in Chapter 5, it relies on knowledge about what you cannot do and what you can get away with. Its essence is not the questioning or shunning of work, but of simulating it. It is not against or outside the system, but inside. Therefore its practitioner must master its rules entirely, and yet secretly scorn them. As many have noted, this type of misbehavior requires *cynicism*. The analysis of cynicism has become so prevalent (particularly among critical management scholars) that one might even speak about a new genre within organizational misbehavior; a genre that might be called *cynics writing cynically about others' cynicism*. In this genre, to which I myself have contributed, the issue is not which economic consequences a certain resistance entails, but whether employees can free their minds from being absorbed by the ideology of work (Paulsen, 2010: 21ff), thus relating back to the traditional issue in critical theory of the imprint of false consciousness (see Chapter 2). Scholars writing in this genre care less about how different games are erected and reproduced, and more about how organization cultures can foster harmless types of rebelliousness and how the employee deceives himself by engaging in so called "Švejkian transgressions," i.e. "subtle forms of subversion that are invariably 'invisible' to his superiors (and often to his peers too)" (Fleming and Sewell, 2002: 859). An early example is Kunda's (1992) study of an information technology firm in which he observed how the free flow of irony and cynicism undermined the critical capacity to evaluate and reject managerial dictates morally. If we already have a moral distance to our workplace environment, cynicism can have the unfortunate consequence that we simply do not care. The argument is that the striving towards an autonomous self, a consciousness that distances itself from action, becomes ideological in the sense that it comforts us with the idea of an uncorrupted Cartesian ego that is illusory. The notion that "[c]apitalism persists, not despite, but *because* of this mode of critical awareness" (Cederström and Fleming, 2012: 29) brings us back to the Foucauldian discourse that preceded the sudden interest in resistance, but now with a functionalist twist that makes *all types* of workplace resistance appear vain.[2] As Fleming and Spicer put it, "we feel the

---

[2] Willmott early mentioned the type of absorption that the sin of assuming a real self entailed: "Moreover, by playing the role at a psychological distance from what is deemed to be the 'real self' . . . the individual feels little existential responsibility for its consequences. However, this dramaturgical 'game play' is not without its costs. For the individual is inescapably constituted in the process of playing the role, and often in ways that escape his or her conscious monitoring . . . The 'real' self is a construction of the enacted self; it does not exist independently of the moment of its constitution" (Willmott, 1993: 537).

real question is, What kinds of resistance *could not* be incorporated in these managerial ideas concerning identity at work?" (Fleming and Spicer, 2008: 304). In Contu's words, workplace resistance constitutes "inherent transgressions of the liberal capitalist relations in which they are observed" exemplifying why the "mutual embrace between power and resistance is deadly" (Contu, 2008: 367). What she calls "decaf resistance" should, if we take her account seriously, rather be called "opium resistance." Resistance is the new opium of the masses, it is a way of "having our cake and eating it too," or as she reflexively puts it: a way of maintaining "our (as in our academic personae) subtle illusion, that yes, the 'workplace' (including our own) is not a silent place" (Contu, 2008: 370).[3]

The image is both frightful and compelling: design agencies where "bourgeois bohemians" (Fleming, 2009: 85) feel they live outside capitalism because they wear Che Guevara t-shirts and reject formal hierarchies, yet in practice are fully assimilated in their actual work. Theoretically, this self-deception could also be at work in cases of time appropriation and perhaps mostly so among slacking employees. Since self-deception is quite hard to study without extensive biographical data and a readiness of the observer to make interpretations that reject the subjective account, I cannot say that I have encountered that among my interviewees. But it would, of course, be easy to say that the laboratory employees who collaborated in their time

---

[3] The same argument also occurs in studies where more tangible forms of misbehaviors are studied. Ladner, for instance, noted that the time-appropriating employees in her study questioned only certain aspects of their job: "While workers frequently engaged in misbehaviour by fudging time sheets, they ultimately did not question the legitimacy of management's right to sell all of their labour directly to a client," (Ladner, 2009: 33). One could question how they could possibly question this fundamental of the employment relationship and still expect to keep their jobs.

Whenever a liberalization of the workplace takes place one can also argue that it signifies the co-optation of the employee. In their study on the normalization of the workplace nap, Baxter and Kroll-Smith argue that the nap has moved from "its secret place in the catacombs" to become more open and tolerated (often with naively functionalist ideas of its benefits for productivity). Their cynical analysis is that this is in fact a way of regulating the nap: "Several strategies are used to govern this once fugitive act: from strict supervisory control and sanctions against those who deviate from procedures; to expansive, trust-based regimes where employees internalize napping norms consistent with intense work schedules and transgressions are handled by peer pressure" (Baxter and Kroll-Smith, 2005: 46).

appropriation were in fact fooling themselves; that, instead of resisting work *within* the institution of wage labor, they should militantly engage in "The Refusal of Work" (Fleming, 2009: 155). It would also be easy to be cynical about the web developer who enjoyed playing computer games and having Friday Beer at the office at the end of the week. But although he expressed a number of suspicious opinions – such as "we don't have any direct hierarchy here" and "you can say anything to anyone, so the atmosphere is very good" – I find it hard to see how he could have held those opinions other than *relatively*, i.e. in relation to what today's working life looks like, rather than to, say, Solanas' "automated society" in which no one works "more than two or three hours a week" (Solanas, 1967: 5).

Furthermore, the equation of organizational misbehavior with cynicism and ideas about being authentic and above the general level of consciousness seems questionable, to say the least. As demonstrated in Chapter 6, not all motivated their soldiering in relation to political meta-narratives. Some (the copywriter, the ticket collector) explicitly said that they were not resisting anything in particular but just trying to withdraw from work. Others, such as the casual laborer just mentioned, did see a political dimension in the practice of time appropriation but were also practicing more traditional forms of activism (he was, for instance, involved in the riots during the EU summit in Gothenburg 2001). Even if the misbehavior is motivated by framed dissent there is nothing saying that the individual would be content with large amounts of empty labor. In the case of the copywriter, empty labor was actually used to engage in other forms of resistance (she used some of her time to write a blog and print leaflets among other things).

Although mental incorporation may take place in some cases of empty labor and other types of organizational misbehavior, the argument thus suffers from being too general and categorical. Before it reappeared in a new theoretical guise, Burawoy was heavily criticized for his one-sided structuralist approach, his lack of dialectics, and the assumption that consent is created in the labor process regardless of external relations (e.g. Clawson and Fantasia, 1983; Edwards, 1986; Gartman, 1983; Roscigno and Hodson, 2004; Thompson, 1983). On the question of dialectics, Dan Clawson and Richard Fantasia comment: "Over and over again, Burawoy takes some feature of the workplace which had generally been identified as evidence of workers' progressive potential, and argues that it actually serves to reinforce the system. He does not seem to understand that a phenomenon can do both things at the same time, that something can be itself and its opposite" (1983: 676).[4]

The same could also be said about today's cynical critique of cynicism. As Paul Willis (1981) early noted in *Learning to Labor*, cynical youths can be easier to integrate into work society than naïve believers in the system (who are likely to become disappointed and make noise). Cynicism means fewer expectations, and if you feel that you have "fooled the system," the acceptance of visible humiliations may even grow. As we have seen, some instances of empty labor certainly can have a "calming" effect that one could call "consent" to the "fundamental" repression of work. If we look at instances of coping (see Chapter 4), there is no need of Žižekian filters of interpretation to observe these workings. The allowance administrator who says that a small dose of empty labor "gives a feeling of freedom," or as she also puts it, a "feeling that you're in charge of your time," appears very conscious of it being a *feeling of* something, rather than real freedom, where you actually *are* in charge of your time. Among those with a low sense of work obligation, it might also be argued that the motive vocabularies of withdrawal and direct dissent (see Chapter 6) are permeated with deceitful contentment in being able to get away from work or soldier as a secret revenge on the company. However, it is hard to see why full submission would lead to more oppositional actions. Also, the cynical critics of cynicism have remarkable little to say about what such oppositional action would entail.

---

[4] In their critique of Burawoy, Clawson and Fantasia also question the notion of profitable incorporation. Whether "waste" is "externalized" through raised prices must be contextualized; if the firm is in a monopoly position (which Burawoy seems to take for granted) such mechanisms may be at work, but this demands careful investigation. Using Burawoy's own data, Clawson and Fantasia (1983: 675) calculated that the difference between "making out" and producing at the standard rate was a pay differential of 20 percent. If that would entail 20 percent higher prices, the firm would either have to be in a monopoly position or have competitors who share the same "making out" costs. But if the costs were harmless, why would so much energy and resources be spent on reducing this type of slack in the manufacturing industries? To produce excitement in the worker and thereby fooling him or her into believing that they are fooling the system?

Resistance as a "real act that suspends the constellation of power relations" (Contu, 2008: 367), as an "act of terrifying and unadulterated freedom" (Contu, 2008: 376) would have to involve nothing less than social revolution. Thus, in Contu's (2008: 374) own words: "a Real act of resistance is an impossible act" – at least within the frames of capitalist society. This would be easier to digest if the structural changes that normally belong to the critique of work – unconditional basic income, expansion of the commons, reduction of working hours in proportion to productivity gains – were advocated or even mentioned. Real resistance, according to Fleming, is the refusal of work; "the only approach that provides the only viable avenue of political strategy in the context of the universalizing social factory and the cunning new spirit of capitalism: *freedom from work*" (2009: 164). Yet one senses that his "freedom of work" is quite different from what earlier critics of work have suggested. It is quite understandable for Antonio Gramsci (1988: 94) to say that "the trade union, by virtue of its bureaucratic form, tends to prevent class war from ever breaking out" and provide arguments why the factory council represents a superior type of collective organization. But in line with the most famous cynic criticizing cynicism, Slavoj Žižek, concrete propositions for alternative action or political reforms are rarely given (for more nuanced analyses, however, see Fleming and Spicer, 2003, 2007).

What these pure negations reveal could be a far more deceitful cynicism than the cynicism they address. In Žižek's reformulation of the ideology concept, cynicism plays a key role. According to Žižek, it is not ideology in the form of "false consciousness" that is the issue; dissent may be very present, but this dissent has, according to the theory, *in itself* turned into ideology: "today, we only imagine that we do not 'really believe' in our ideology – in spite of this imaginary distance, we continue to practise it" (Žižek, 2009: 3). What we see is the expansion of "enlightened false consciousness: one knows the falsehood very well, one is well aware of a particular interest hidden behind an ideological universality, but still one does not renounce it" (Žižek, 1989: 26). This not so empirical analysis, which apparently strikes a chord with left-wing academics, has been somewhat overplayed. What Žižek describes is just *one* ideological relation between political consciousness and practice. It is not hard to imagine someone *both* believing in the ideology and practicing it. One could even imagine someone believing something while in practice acting against it. The mining mechanic from Chapter 5 is a typical example. Believing that "a company has to make money," that you should "do your job," and so on, he was nonetheless engaged in extensive time appropriation. A more serious shortcoming of Žižek's conceptualization is the substitution of *power* for *ideology*. By taking power out of the equation, by neglecting that most of us *are forced to work to receive an income*, work can thus be reduced to pure ideology: we know that it is false, yet we keep turning up at the office every morning. Peter Sloterdijk, who before Žižek presented his *Critique of Cynical Reason*, makes the connection between cynicism and work explicitly: "Psychologically, present-day cynics can be understood as borderline melancholics, who can keep their symptoms of depression under control and can remain more or less able to work. Indeed, this is the essential point in modern cynicism: the ability of its bearers to work – in spite of anything that might happen, and especially, after anything that might happen" (Sloterdijk, 2001 [1983]: 5).

But what cynical functionalists seem to have forgotten about Sloterdijk's analysis (although he occasionally gets mentioned) is the distinction between "cynical reason" – the "enlightened false consciousness" (Sloterdijk, 2001 [1983]: 217) – and "kynical irony" – in which the cynical understanding is enacted by satire and resistance. Whereas the cynic keeps turning up at the office, imagining that the knowledge of how meaningless it is will somehow protect him, the kynic takes action. Kynicism is not a theory, Sloterdijk says, it is "*a form of dealing with knowledge,* a form of relativization, ironic treatment, application, and sublation... partly a spiritual art of survival, partly intellectual resistance, partly satire, partly 'critique'" (Sloterdijk, 2001 [1983]: 292). Although he does not use the term himself, kynicism thus seems to come close to what I have referred to as "misbehavior" – the disrespectful, cheeky, sometimes elaborate, sometimes unsubtle type of resistance that cares more about *action* than *being*. Cynicism is respectable, it is intellectual, and most of all, it is "theory": "in Marxism and especially in psychoanalysis it has even put on suit and tie so as to completely assume an air of bourgeois respectability. It has given up its life as satire, in order to win its position in books as 'theory'" (Sloterdijk, 2001 [1983]: 16). As Sloterdijk points out, one of the most ironic consequences of this quest for "respectability" (not to say scientific legitimacy) is critical theory's tendency to move towards "bourgeois functionalism":

Its emphasis is not on the dialectic of liberation but rather on the mechanisms of universal mystification. If every consciousness is precisely as false as corresponds to its position in the process of production and domination, it necessarily remains captive to its own falsity, as long as the process is taking place. And that the process is in full motion is constantly emphasized by Marxism. Here the hidden functionalism in Marxian theory goes into effect. For this functionalism, there is to the present day no sharper formulation than the famous phrase 'necessarily false consciousness.' From this viewpoint, false consciousness is reined into its place in the system of objective delusions. False being is a function of the process. (Sloterdijk, 2001 [1983]: 38–39)

Whereas Žižek and others inspired by him have been more keen on applying Sloterdijk's critique to everyday negations of "non-intellectuals," they have ignored the central thesis of Sloterdijk, namely that it is *in theory* that cynicism thrives – a cynical analysis that one might easily apply to the cynical organization studies (meta-meta), in which not only workplace cynicism but all types of workplace misbehavior are interpreted as mental safety valves that prevent workers from burning down the office.

Since I do not wish to contribute to an infinite regress of cynicisms of cynicisms of cynicisms etc., I should point out that the purely intellectual type of cynicism that Sloterdijk criticizes is crucial to a particular form of empty labor, namely enduring. The boreout's *modus operandi* is inactivity. In slacking, coping, and soldiering, there is a will to enlarge the sphere of empty labor. Even among withdrawing employees (i.e. soldiering without overtones of indignation), there can be great creativity and ingenuity in avoiding work (see Chapter 5). But the boreout adjusts. The boreout knows that something is wrong but remains in *mauvais foi*. Unlike slackers who use jobs with low potential output to their own advantage, the boreout is stuck in the role of the wage earner who has to get instructions on what to do and who ascribes less value to "private activity" (i.e. non-work-related activities emanating from one's own will) than to following externally imposed instructions. Except for the rare instances where enduring is formally acknowledged in the organization, the cynicism of the boreout is revealed in his resignation before the institutionalized simulation of work – the same simulation that is behind the boredom that he continues to reproduce.

In the remainder of this chapter, I will turn to this simulation and discuss what it means for our understanding of resistance. I have discussed how disembedded and embodied notions of rationality could be used to explain empty labor and what difficulties and contradictions these explanations are associated with. In the next section I will proceed to a more embedded notion of rationality: can simulation in itself be the dominating rationale in parts of modern working life? If so, how should we understand empty labor under such conditions? If work is decoupled from production, what are we resisting when avoiding work?

8.3 Simulative incorporation

As we have seen, especially in Chapter 5, to be successful in soldiering you have to exploit the opacity of your job – you have to *simulate* work rather than work. The "righteous" reader with Calvinist inclinations (who has done a good job reaching this page) may find such strategies a moral outrage. But in work society, the simulation of work is far from restricted to empty labor. In Sweden, it has for a long time been institutionalized by the state as a way of occupying the unemployed with something that is not quite work but imitates its structure. In the most extreme cases of so-called guarantee of activity programs, the Swedish State has forced and is still forcing the long-term unemployed to waste their time repainting perfectly new chairs, genealogizing their own family tree, playing ping-pong, or just sitting around – under the pretense that this will somehow "activate" them (see Bagge, 2005; Weman, 2011). Keeping the balance between meaninglessness and the public subsidization of "real work" has always been the controversial question concerning these programs. Similar organizations for persons with disabilities have excelled even more in occupying people with imitations of wage labor that, despite integrative pretensions, tend to have both marginalizing and stigmatizing effects (see Holmqvist, 2005; Rådahl, 1990).

Not only individuals invent work to hide their inactivity. Albeit with significantly less creativity, the state does it too. Right-wing commentators tend to believe that these "adult kindergartens" can survive only in the public sector. For apparent reasons, I contest that verdict. The unique feature of State simulation is that it is shameless, out in the open, without any economic rationale, based on the same fear from which the English poorhouses once emerged, the fear of "masterless people, people out of control – not surveilled, not monitored, not subjected to any regular, sanctions-fortified routine" (Bauman, 2004: 18). This fear also affects the simulation of private companies, but to a much lesser degree. Their simulation should rather be understood in the context of what Alvesson (2008) calls "the triumph of emptiness."

According to Alvesson, higher education, professions, and organizations are pushing each other in building castles in the air with no more fundament than increasingly empty euphemisms. The chain of emptiness is well known: when the university becomes a storehouse for surplus labor force, there is an inflation of academic degrees that forces people into higher education for jobs that, despite the continual process of deskilling (cf. Thompson et al., 2001), earlier did not require any degree. This triggers a race towards professionalization and an obsession for titles covering up the lack of substance – verbal creativity becomes a way to hide the actual labor process. Not all industries are as affected; most of this takes place in the "symbolic sphere," but this sphere is also expanding:

Increasingly more private firms are moving in the symbolic sphere: here, branding and managing expectations etc. matter more than delivering technically advanced products and services.... Generally, there is an expansion of businesses offering beautifying services to corporations ('corporate beauty industry'). An aesthetic and neat surface – architecture, space, letter paper design, corporate uniforms, good looking colleagues and so on – is becoming ever more important. (Alvesson, 2008: 147, my translation)

This explains some instances of enduring empty labor. The "shop window arrangements" require workforce, and sometimes the workforce itself is part of the arrangement. The florist's story in Chapter 4, for instance, cannot be attributed to neither bad management nor a weak sense of work obligation. Since the flower shop was part of a bigger department store, she was not really needed as a cashier. As she and two others who worked as salespersons said, they had to be there just for it to look good – "if you enter a flower shop, you expect that someone will ask 'hi, can I help you?'" In her case, this became rather awkward since, on the other hand, "it looks so bad if you just stand there.... It's different if you're at an office where no one knows what you do. But if I sat on the counter dangling my legs they'd say 'what the hell are you doing?' 'Nothing, just chilling?' That would never work." Whenever someone entered she tried to look busy, well aware

that "there is a limit to how many times you can water a flower."
Her being there was, in other words, mostly an aesthetic arrangement.
Her services were not needed.

Much of Alvesson's analysis reconnects with new institutionalism in
organizational theory, but Alvesson also has a historical analysis. The
garbage can decisions (Cohen et al., 1972), the oftentimes ludicrous
imitations known as "isomorphisms" (DiMaggio and Powell, 1983),
the decoupling between legitimating myths and ceremonies on the one
hand, and the operative activity on the other (Meyer and Rowan,
1977), in short *the organization of hypocrisy* (Brunsson, 2002 [1989])
may always have been part of organizational life, but under present
conditions there is good breeding ground for it to intensify, Alvesson
argues. Employees experiencing the decoupling between words and
action in their organization can be expected to adapt the same strategy
for their own purpose. Not only are there moral reasons concerning
mutuality, they may have to decouple just to keep their heads above
water. Those employed on a project (cf. the machine technician in
Chapter 4) may have economic reasons to report a slower work pace
than the actual one; the bank clerk in the previous chapter illustrates
how your job in cases of enduring can be dependent upon your ability
to simulate. Here we see how the capitalist organization of wage labor
sometimes gives remunerative incentives for the proliferation of empty
labor. Thus, the opacity of the labor process and the potential output
are not the only structural factors determining the extent of empty
labor. Regardless of the employee's sense of work obligation, we see
that there are situations in which it would be strange if there were no
simulation going on.

In *The Audit Society: Rituals of Verification*, Michael Power
describes how greater demands on accountability and transparency
have forced both industrial and service providing organizations into
an "audit explosion." Today, auditing is not only a phenomenon in
the world of finance, there are audits for medicine, technology, teaching, the environment – checking and scrutinizing organizations and
individuals has become a big industry in itself. The rule of auditing
is at the core of new public management and the shift from the welfare state to the "regulatory state" (Power, 1997: 52), and it has a
long history in industrial production and noticeably in total quality
management (Power, 1997: 58). Power argues that auditing is never
a neutral act of verification; it may affect the actual performance, but

beyond any doubt it will also affect *how* organizations and individuals work. The audit process can be decoupled in the sense that "auditable images of performance" (Power, 1997: 95) are created with little or no relation to the real organizational processes. It can also colonize the organization so that "the imposition of audit and related measures of auditable performance leads to the opposite of what was intended, i.e. creates forms of dysfunction for the audited service itself" (Power, 1997: 98).

Power considers these two reactions as failures of the auditing system, but according to Miller's notion of "economic virtualism" they should rather be regarded as rules than deviations. Miller's basic observation is that economic models (and theories) have ceased to be measured against the world; today, it is the world that is being measured against the model. This produces changes in the economy both on macro and micro levels. As already mentioned, Miller discovers that he is himself part of the auditing system when filling out work time sheets specifying how much time he spends on a visiting post-doctoral student. His reaction, like so many others', is to ask a secretary what the numbers should be and to fill the form for him – thus a typical example of decoupling. In contrast to Michel Callon's theory of performativity, Miller argues that "in capitalist society also, what lies within the frame is not the market system as an actual practice, but on the contrary a ritualized expression of an ideology of the market... The confusion is that this ritual and ideological system in the case of capitalism is actually called the market" (Miller, 2002: 224). The "ideology of the market" does not simply correspond to "the market," according to Miller. While we are forced to adapt to a certain extent, constructing rituals that will look good when measured, there is always something beyond the virtual: local and embedded institutions of economic action that have to decouple external pressure in order not to become colonized. As Roine Johansson (1992) and others have demonstrated, such decoupling may be necessary even for the functioning of a formally rational organization like the bureaucracy.

I will add two points to Miller's analysis of economic virtualism. The first concerns how easy and widespread the manipulation of an audit can be. The motto of many organizations, "better a solid mystification than a bleak clarification!" (Alvesson, 2008: 166, my translation) can also be adapted by individuals, and their decoupling can take place for purely egoistic reasons without any thoughts about the functioning

of the "real market."⁵ The more privileged your position, the less
developed the auditing system will probably be. In his study of cheats
at work, Mars found that management consultants had little trouble
inventing "extra days" if they wanted to: "If a job takes five days but
the customer appears well satisfied, an extra 'invisible day' (or days)
can be charged under such heads as 'consulting with colleagues,' for
'explorations,' for 'liaison,' for 'research,' or 'report writing' – all of
which are less visible than days spent on a site" (Mars, 1982: 51).
If stuck in an office, you have to be more creative, but even under
prison-like conditions there is always a way to manipulate the audit
system to some extent.

Second, the inefficiencies of a certain auditing system are often well
known, even among its advocates. Very few academic scholars actually
believe that good numbers in the "publish or perish" system separate
the good researcher from the bad. If they are not already practicing
it, most know how easy it is to cite each other and "trade articles"
by writing up each other's names as co-authors etc. (cf. Scott, 2012:
114). Likewise, it is recognized that writing reports, filling in time
sheets, or just clocking in and out does not have to entail any work
at all – yet sometimes the monitoring system is no more advanced
than that. Again, the most fascinating aspect of some of the media
scandals referred to in the introduction, where the degree of cyberslacking of public authorities has been revealed, is that no one must
have noticed the enormous "slack" until some monitoring software
reacted. As Crozier says in his study of the bureaucracy: "Man has
never been able to search for the *optimum* solution. He has always
had to be content with solutions merely *satisfactory* in regard to a
few particularistic criteria of which he was aware" (Crozier, 1971:
159). But what he and the institutionalists seem to neglect is that the
"particularistic criteria" of which managers are aware can be at work
and yet *be known* to be outlandish. This sense, that they really do
not know *anything* about the work being done, explains the growing
popularity of monitoring software. At the time of writing, 30 percent of US employees have Facebook and Twitter blocked at work

⁵ In the world of finance, there is even a branch called "creative accounting" that
specializes in how to go around the system. As Power contends: "Creative
accounting practitioners have always known that profits can be 'what you like'
and that for every financial accounting rule there is a way to frustrate the
purpose of the rule while appearing to comply with it" (Power, 1997: 94).

(Gouveia, 2012), and computer-monitoring programs for employees working from home are beginning to spread among US employers (10 percent of employers are currently using them). In a *Wall Street Journal* article, one employer related how a monitoring program led her to discover that one of her employees was using most of her work-day studying for a master's degree (Shellenbarger, 2012). One could ask: if the criteria in terms of output are not being met, why the need for monitoring software? Would it not be easy to see which employees are not meeting the requirements of the job by looking at what they produce? Even if auditing and externally imposed rules generate a virtual wall around the "actual" economy or labor process, it remains *virtual* in the sense that while we know it is there, we also know it is not real. This is why management must constantly develop new quality guarantees and monitoring systems – they know that they are not "in the know."

For an organization to be truly hypocritical, however, the decoupling cannot be overt even when everyone knows about it. Instead, rituals are constructed, rituals in which the simulation of efficiency and professionalism are enacted. As the copywriter puts it:

I knew that no matter how much time I put on writing the text, I would have to rewrite it five more times. [In the beginning] I wrote without really knowing the jargon for selling it to the boss, but once I learned it I didn't have to work for four hours to improve the text in any subjective meaning. By then I could just say 'I thought like this and that' and that was what finally got it accepted regardless of how intelligent it was. So there was no point in doing more research or thinking about how to improve the text. It was just a matter of acting.

Under these circumstances, empty labor cannot be a way of "fooling the system" since it is part of the system. This was also something that some of the interviewees seemed to have understood. The sense of *the unreal*, that something is fundamentally wrong, was even shared by slacking interviewees despite their relative satisfaction. One of the web-developers said that he always felt that something was not right with his job; especially when he was a teenager and earned almost twice as much as his mother who by then had worked in child care for more than 20 years: "I mean, I can't say I feel that I'm worth more money than she is. She has toiled a lot harder than I have, and even made a bigger social contribution you could say. I make flash banners that will just irritate people."

Like the copywriter, he still learned to play along. Even if it is just "a matter of acting" or does not feel quite as right or meaningful as you would like, the most worrying aspect of simulation is that its effects are very real. Others have to treat it as if it were real, it results in formal or informal rules, it gives you a salary, perhaps even social esteem, and in some cases, it can become so real that you cannot get out of it.

Jean Baudrillard has famously driven this argument to extremes. Not only has Saussure's signifier been decoupled from the signified, Baudrillard argues, the distinction between exchange-value and use-value of modern political economy has equally imploded. Long before the "financialization" of the economy became the popular concept that it is today, Baudrillard described how the "the monetary sign" escapes "into infinite speculation, beyond all reference to a real of production, or even to a gold-standard" (Baudrillard, 1993 [1976]: 7). Similarly, work is decoupled from production. This is the essence of what Baudrillard calls "the death of labour." Labor still exists, but it has lost every contact with the basic needs (which according to Baudrillard also have dispersed) to which the concept of use-value refers. Instead, its main purpose is its own reproduction:

It remains, however, more necessary than ever to reproduce labour as a social ritual [*affectation*], as a reflex, as morality, as consensus, as regulation, as the reality principle. The reality principle *of the code*, that is: an immense *ritual of the signs of labour* extends over society in general – since it *reproduces* itself, it matters little whether or not it *produces*. (Baudrillard, 1993 [1976]: 11)

This "code" of reproduction concerns all institutions related to labor – even the strike is incorporated: "Corresponding to the absurd circularity of a system where one labours only to produce more labour is the demand for strikes for strikes' sake" (Baudrillard, 1993 [1976]: 28). The point of these reproductions is to hide the new power shift in which capital no longer buys labor from workers. What shines through mainstream political debates is that labor really is *a gift* from capital to the people – a gift that the people can receive only if they are clever enough to vote for a government that will guarantee great rewards to capital for giving labor to the world. That is why wages are not paid for what we actually produce, wages are given for subjecting ourselves to the simulation of work: "Wages are the mark of this poisonous gift, the sign which epitomizes the whole code. They sanction this unilateral gift of labour, or rather *wages symbolically buy back the domination exercised by capital through the gift of labour*" (Baudrillard, 1993 [1976]: 41).[6]

If labor is already simulation, what then does simulating labor *within* this simulation signify? Consider one of Burawoy's (1992) later ethnographies conducted in the Lenin Steel Works of communist Hungary. In the chapter "Painting Socialism," Burawoy describes how, one day, workers are given orders to prepare for the visit of the prime minister. The relatively (in comparison to Burawoy's earlier work in the Chicago machine shop) slow production rate is halted, and all efforts are suddenly aimed at *cleaning the steel mill* (which for natural reasons is quite dirty). In the ensuing turmoil, Burawoy is assigned to paint the "slag drawer" yellow and green, but all he can find is a black brush. Rather than doing nothing, he starts painting a shovel in black:

I had hardly begun this critical task when Stegermajer came storming over, with his hand behind his back and his hard hat bobbing, his head bowed for combat. 'What the hell are you doing?' 'Painting the shovels black,' I replied as innocently as I could. But he was not amused, so I quickly added, 'Haven't you got any more brushes so I can help the others?' No, there weren't any. 'So I can't help build socialism?' I continued, somewhat riskily. My mates cracked up, amused at the thought of their 'kefir furnaceman' [a nickname Burawoy was given] building socialism. Even Stegermajer caved

---

[6] No one has probably emphasized domination as the ruling principle of work society as audaciously as Baudrillard, but much of his critique dates back to *One-Dimensional Man* by Marcuse. Marcuse also formulated an explicit critique of Weber on this point. In his essay *Industrialization and Capitalism in the work of Max Weber* (1969), Weber's disembedded notion of purposive rationality is heavily criticized on the grounds that it equates "reason" with capitalist reason, thus raising a historical and biased form of rationality to the ranks of objectivity and maximal efficiency. This was a critique shared by the entire first generation of the Frankfurt School, according to Jay: "the Institut rejected Weber's contention that capitalism was the highest form of socio-economic rationality. As Marxists they repudiated the notion that an unplanned economy without socialized means of production could be anything but irrational" (Jay, 1973: 121). Rather than "instrumental reason," Marcuse would use the term "rationality of domination" in his writings, and one of his most important contributions to critical theory was to challenge the idea that technology (here understood in its widest sense) was a neutral tool bare of ideological content. Although this was one of the most fundamental critiques of early critical theory, it was completely rejected by Habermas.

in when Józsi interceded, 'Misi, Misi, you don't understand anything. You
are not *building* socialism, you are *painting* socialism. And *black* at that.'
(Burawoy and Lukács, 1992: 125)

Burawoy argues that whereas the capitalist enterprise depends on profitability – a rationality that is painted "*out*" – authoritarian socialism
"*calls on us to cover up* injustice and irrationality and to paint a vision
of equality and efficiency" (Burawoy and Lukács, 1992: 129). But is
the preparation for the visit of the prime minister really that different
from how empty labor is constantly being covered up in our economy?
Is not the incident described above very similar to how the lab staff
had to engage in the charade of "doing science" when our counterpart
to "the Red Barons" put on the show of "management by walking
around?" If we really live under "Monopoly Capitalism" as both Burawoy and Braverman want to underline, would it be that far-fetched
to say that empty labor – in all forms – is indeed a way of *painting
capitalism*?

In this chapter I have discussed three ways that empty labor can be
incorporated in the production system. Profitable incorporation builds
on the disembedded notion of rationality stressing the inherent efficiency of the modern workplace. Even apparent anomalies to this
thesis, such as empty labor, are in fact contributing to the maximal
efficiency, the argument goes – during periods of empty labor, employees get a chance to recreate, to fulfill some of their private duties, and
to get the rest necessary for working productively during their active
working hours. Mental incorporation is derived from an embodied
notion of rationality according to which the system depends upon people directly or indirectly accepting it as it is. Even when empty labor
emerges from a low sense of work obligation, it ties you close to that
which is. The feeling that you have fooled the system, or that you have
"seen it through," mitigates the despair required for a more radical
reaction. Simulative incorporation builds on the notion that economic
rationality is embedded in a society where simulation is becoming the
overarching rationale. To simulate work within such a society merely
signifies another outgrowth of an already simulative economy.

Even if none of these arguments refutes that the prevalence of empty
labor indicates a rather neglected type of workplace resistance, they
provide valuable perspectives on empty labor beyond its subjective

dimensions. Sometimes, especially in cases of coping, empty labor may well be beneficial to productivity in the long run, especially in cases where there is a risk that employees may face burnout. Sometimes, in cases of soldiering and slacking, there is the risk that employees may feel that their job, at least in relative terms, is not that bad after all. If we want to avoid the totalizing aspect of Baudrillard's analysis, we could also say that *sometimes* the global concepts of "labor" and "production" may be decoupled from each other. Analogously, the political and operational processes in an organization may also be decoupled. On an individual level, the satisfaction of auditing systems and the actual work may equally be decoupled. If these decouplings coincide and time-appropriating employees think that their particular decoupling is a way of resisting some aspect of work society, we could also say that *sometimes* the subject probably is decoupled from the actor. This is what all three types of incorporation arguments say: although we may think that we are resisting work, we are actually strengthening its position as the dominating institution of our time.

My main objection against functionalists refuting all types of resistance as "in fact" incorporated is that they seem a little over-impressed by their own theories. HRM scholars repeating the brilliant theory that small doses of empty labor may be good for productivity seem to ignore that this theory is already in practice by coping employees. Cynical functionalists feverishly arguing that cynicism does not put you "on top of the system" seem to ignore that very few, if any, actually believe that their cynicism equals autonomy. I would also say that few scholars understand the extent to which labor is becoming simulation better than the interviewees of this study. "We are digging holes just to fill them up again," the warehouse employee contends. For him "the domination exercised by capital through the gift of labor" is more than a theoretical notion – it is the daily experience of how work steals from life. Under such circumstances, empty labor cannot be a way of "fooling the system" since it is part of the system. Empty labor is not freedom; it may be a relative freedom, but it remains *labor*.

This does not mean that soldiering, as an act of resistance, is particularly deceitful. The hidden transcript is never a "realm of freedom," Scott (1991: 5) points out; it is always conditioned by factors beyond individual control. This is also something that Touraine says about the subject:

The Subject is never its own master; nor is it the master of its environment. It always forms alliances with the devil against the powers that be, with the eroticism that overturns social codes, and with its own superhuman or divine self-image . . . the Subject cobbles together fragile and limited combinations of instrumental action and cultural identity by taking things from both the world of commodities and the space of communities. (Touraine, 2000b: 62)

What Touraine calls the "the world of instrumentality" and "the world of identity" are areas that must be dealt with when appropriating time (as seen in Chapter 5); they might be changed and manipulated, but as long as the resistance is individual, only marginally. This also counts for the macro simulations of Baudrillard. In *The Gulf War Did Not Take Place*, Baudrillard (1995) argues that the Gulf War was not in fact a war – mainly for the reason that the US-led coalition was fighting a virtual war with technological advantages that made the Iraqi army look like nothing but a joke in comparison. Yet in terms of subjectivity, the resistance to power centers is not defined by the chances of winning the battle. The subject is the will to become an actor no matter how small the social changes are. Even if the misbehavior the individual employee can engage in is infinitesimal in relation to what "capital" can do, in each individual life the difference between no empty labor and two hours of empty labor a day can make the difference between "hysterical misery" and "common unhappiness." This obviously depends on the specific context; as Mike Noon and Paul Blyton (2007: 273) put it: "a particular piece of behaviour associated with a survival strategy might be considered a form of consent in one situation but a form of resistance in another, because of the different circumstances that surround it." The extremely elastic concept of "work" confuses the discussion since the diverse realities it denotes are so different from each other.

Notwithstanding the actual consequences, it is important to understand the intrinsic value of the will to resist. Even if it is just a vague will to get away, the pettiest acts of withdrawal remind us of the coercion of labor and the longing for something else. Few believe that the modern workplace is crowded by the cheerful robots of Mills (cf. Chapter 2); today, intellectual pessimism thrives in functionalism. Yet every type of reminder that we are not robots should be endorsed. Commenting on the German utopian Ernst Bloch, Sloterdijk says: "no one can be talked into believing in the 'spirit of utopia' or a 'principle of hope' who can discover no experiences in himself that give these expressions meaning" (Sloterdijk, 2001 [1983]: 125). The official transcript – that we are merely trying to survive the endless "rationalizations" of production and that the system is so effective we nearly cannot bear it – currently serves both parties. Managers and executives can pride themselves on how wisely they have structured the system; the rest can use it as a virtual wall to cover up the real. Hidden transcripts, on the other hand, are of no benefit to any master. They are the result of subordinates understanding their relative powerlessness and seeking ways to covertly negate that which is. Hence "one wonders what sort of psychological law lies behind the safety-valve theory," Scott writes. "Why is it that a ritual modeling of revolt should necessarily diminish the likelihood of actual revolt? Why couldn't it just as easily serve as a dress rehearsal or a provocation for actual defiance?" (Scott, 1991: 178). As Scott convincingly demonstrates, history is full of examples supporting the latter hypothesis.

9 | Conclusion

I began this book by referring to the feeling that work absorbs life, that it structures our time, thoughts, and emotions, and that there is little we can do to resist it. Needless to say, the feeling may be well grounded: there are workaholics who cannot stay away from work, who dream about it, who want to please their superiors etc. The precarization of the labor market, the weakening of the labor movement, and the continual development of new managerial techniques put the worker in a very vulnerable position in which complete submission appears to be the logical reaction. But in social science and especially critical theory, there are also less empirically grounded precepts that make us assume that we are but slaves under the reign of work. Since early industrialism, it has been assumed that the worker is but an appendage of the machine, hopelessly powerless under its control. When industrial production proportionally decreased in the Western world, the notion of false consciousness became central in critical theory. Again, there were and still are very good reasons for assuming that power can influence us ideologically and make us believe in things that are against our best interests, but the problem with the concept of false consciousness is that anyone can be accused of it and that it is impossible to refute completely. An even sorrier version is to say that there is no "right" consciousness, that power-based ideologies (or discourses) are all there is and that it is because of them that we become "subjects."

In order to study empty labor without the a priori assumption that every action at work is either ideology or part of a discourse, I have referred to a quite opposite concept of "the subject" defined as the will to become an actor, constituted in the very "resistance to power centres" (Touraine, 1995: 167). The subject in this sense has mostly been studied in relation to different social movements, but less in relation to individual expressions of resistance at work. Work is often assumed to be the hub of power in modern society, the institution in which instrumental rationality reigns supreme and resistance is effectively eliminated. The overarching motive for studying empty labor was to problematize that picture somewhat and to see if we might learn anything new about the subject by looking at how it operates under the more trying conditions that most labor represents.

If everything had followed the dim expectations I had, this would have become a very boring study. I was sure that empty labor was the result of some type of worker resistance. I never thought that there could be a limit to the potential output at any job and that people without any motive to withdraw from work could be so enmeshed in empty labor. When looking at the tactics that employees who actively appropriate time employ, it is easy to see why enduring and slacking can take place. The most decisive factor seems to be how opaque the labor process is, i.e. how easy it is for others to estimate how long your work tasks could take. The opacity can be manipulated: just as management makes continual efforts to decrease it, the worker can exploit the uncertainties that remain to increase it. But the opacity can also be there from the beginning, and sometimes whether you like it or not. There is a dynamic here that should not be downplayed: what may begin as soldiering, or maybe even as coping, can eventually turn into slacking when the relatively low level of effort is static and acquiring new work tasks becomes painful. Once you are in that situation, the boredom of spending so much time simulating work can turn the whole project into enduring, or perhaps even into boreout. How smoothly that process runs varies, however, between jobs, and there may be singular circumstances at one workplace that increase the opacity of a job that at another workplace would be more transparent.

The analysis of time appropriation as an act of resistance turned out to be much more complicated than I had assumed. Evidently, the worker who is just a cog in the machine, or induced with all sorts of false beliefs that make him or her work mindlessly without the slightest sign of dissent, is at least not the sole type of worker. The subject can be active at the workplace as well, but since open opposition at work will most likely lead to your dismissal as long as you are alone, work resistance differs a lot from civil disobedience. The most obvious difference is probably also the most important one: at work, you cannot resist openly. If for some reason you disagree with something, the legitimate means to handle your frustration is to consult the manager or engage the union. To "exit" while simulating that you are still doing your job is indeed not as constructive as voicing your concerns.

Appropriating time is considered the egoistic option, and sometimes it is. Some of the interviewees did it precisely for personal reasons without any other motivation than that they could not stand working the allotted hours. Others expressed different types of revenge narratives, whereas yet another group motivated their time appropriation in political terms. These different ways of engaging in a certain form of activism could be further elaborated. They are probably not unique to time appropriation; also, when there is a clear cause there may be degrees to which activists embrace it. A study of more trivial instances of empty labor, focusing on coping, would probably find even more nuances than I was able to discern.

If we only consider the subjective part of the resistance in time appropriation, it would therefore be misleading to talk about "the subject" as a homogeneous entity that we all become part of when engaging in this particular type of resistance. When we consider the more objective part of resistance, how others conceive of it and how it affects the "target," the resistance of time appropriation becomes even more ambiguous. Only the fact that we can talk about the potential output of a certain job challenges the rationale that we often ascribe to wage labor, namely that of maximal efficiency and exploitation of the available resources. If there is no such rationale, what exactly are we resisting when appropriating time? Here, I would like to stress the contextual factors that complicate every general comment on workplace resistance.

As mentioned in the introduction, I have tried to escape the all-embracing semantics of the work concept by adopting a pragmatic approach that lets the interviewees decide what they regard as "work" and "non-work." This pragmatism creates problems if we want to compare or say something general about work and its negation. The differences are not only discernible in what you produce or in which services you provide, there are also considerable differences in opacity, surveillance, production norms, and efficiency that make it hard to speculate about the general consequences of time appropriation. This is especially true for empty labor occasioned by the employee's attempt to cope with a stressful work situation; it could very well work as a buffer that guarantees greater efficiency than if the employee mindlessly went on working towards burnout. At the upper echelons of work society, where the service actually is valued for the knowledge rather than for the time employees put into it, we could also imagine that some may fool themselves when thinking that they fool "the system" by only working half of their working hours. If we assume that simulation or "facework" is becoming the meta-rationale of our culture, including the sphere of labor, then the simulation that makes empty labor possible could also be regarded as adjustment, i.e. the opposite of resistance.

Since the empirical material I have is not sufficient to either reject or approve of either incorporation argument, my discussion of them must remain speculative. A combination of field observations and interviews would have made it easier to assess the relation between the subjective and interpersonal aspects of resistance. Yet, the functionalist tinge of the incorporation arguments, that what appears to be a dysfunction in fact reproduces capitalism or the power structure of the firm, makes them almost immune to fundamental revision. Paying more attention to which type of empty labor workers are engaged in and how they motivate a weak sense of work obligation (if they have it) can help us nuance the incorporation arguments and create a much-needed sensitivity for the importance of context. There are variations in the extent to which the "time waste" can be economically incorporated by the firm, to which employees use time appropriation as a mental safety valve, and to which simulation precedes substance that allow us to differentiate between cases where the incorporation arguments are more or less relevant.

The same type of contextualizations should be made in the whole field of organizational misbehavior vis-à-vis the incorporation arguments. For instance, cynicism is beyond any doubt incorporated when sociologists criticize the organizations where they work. In my own experience, such cynicism is almost obligatory – the academic sociologist who does not harbor a sound amount of contempt for the chancellor is a dubious person. Undoubtedly, the same cynicism in a military organization, in the police, or in a monastery would be regarded differently. Ethnographies that lack comparative reflections on profession, trade, and class can be produced in endless numbers without any cumulative progress, leaving it open for functionalist analyses to reject the whole field of organizational misbehavior.

Most literature on workplace resistance suffers from severe academization. Before the popularity of organizational misbehavior backfired, Mumby (2005: 39) wrote: "Hopefully this is not a simple pendulum swing that results in the privileging of resistance over control. Instead, it perhaps signals a concerted effort to explore resistance as a

constitutive element in the complex dynamics of routine organizing."
Interestingly, in these scholarly accounts of resistance, it remains an
"element" – just as alive as a corpse ready to be dissected by Science.
With this book, I have provided yet another study that provides examples of how resistance is part of "the complex dynamics of routine
organizing," or differently put, that the subject is at work even in the
sphere of labor. But I also want to confess that the worry that my interviewees struggled with – what is the point of this? – also came over me
during the years I worked with this book. To celebrate the existence of
organizational misbehavior in studies like this one, or in jargon-packed
conference papers and articles, can be meaningful for your own career,
but if it is part of a *critical* study, i.e. with an emancipatory ambition,
it appears rather meaningless.

Here I agree with the critics: there is little point in providing more
of these terribly "thick" descriptions of how people break the most
trivial rules in all too specific organizational settings. As Touraine
asserts, sociologists have a moral responsibility that goes beyond writing articles for one's subtribe: "If sociology does not take the side of
the subject against society, it is fated to be an ideological instrument
promoting social integration and socialization" (in Gorz, 1999: 141).
The study of workplace resistance is rapidly gaining in respectability,
rapidly becoming the private pleasure of "fat-cat sociology" Nickson
(cf. Nicolaus, 1968). This is a worrisome development. The mass production of academic papers treating workplace misbehavior reveals
that there is something fascinating about this subject. Although the
"petty acts" of workplace resistance make little difference on a structural level, and although they provide little information about how to
proceed to organized action, they are nevertheless small signs of life
inspiring and teaching us about the everyday negations of work. The
academic study of workplace misbehavior is of very marginal value as
long as it stays within the walls of academia. What I am suggesting is
not only to address, but also to actively stimulate the public to resist
work. There are a few examples of how to do this. Both Pouget (1913
[1898]) and Sprouse (1992) belong to the relatively established genre
in which workplace sabotage is analyzed and embraced in accessible
style. I have also mentioned a more recent example, namely Karlsson
(2012) who translates a selection of the numerous examples of organizational misbehavior provided by academic scholars into entertaining
stories intelligible to everyone.

Having said that, I believe that the study of empty labor also raises some questions that should be further studied in the sociology of work. Besides those that I have already mentioned, the first concerns *the concept of work*. As Karlsson (1986) points out in one of his earlier works, throughout history the work concept has periodically expanded and diminished between comprising almost every human activity and being more exclusive. Beyond any doubt, we now live in a time in which the work concept is in an expansive phase. It is indeed one of the strangest linguistic marvels of our time that the activities of the call-center operator, the warehouse employee, and the machine technician respectively are collected under the mega-category called "work." When Aristotle wrote that "all paid jobs absorb and degrade the mind" (in Beder, 2001: 9), he had a very concrete activity in mind. Work was activity in the sphere of the necessity, the requisite for our reproduction, a dirty business that belonged to slaves and women, the opposite of philosophy which had itself as its only goal. Now, as Karel Kosík (1979: 183) has noted, even philosophy has become "work." Several interviewees noted the difficulty of conceptually differentiating between work and non-work. The archivist, the copywriter, the allowance administrators were all paid for reading and writing. What were the activities they engaged in during empty labor? Mostly reading and writing. Today, sitting still, watching nearly automated production processes can be work. As we have seen, work can be pure simulation – like acting, with the only difference that no one knows that you are acting. Work can be emotional, aesthetic, athletic, immaterial, industrial, creative, secure, or precarious; it can result in health care, public transport, web pages, clean floors, filled-in blanks, dissertations, bombs, and grenades. Which type of work are our politicians talking about when they proclaim the necessity of creating jobs? If we want to regard most of what we do as work, perhaps we could develop a greater sensitivity to the heterogeneity of the concept. Subcategories like empty labor and the ones just mentioned help us to do so, but we are still in need of conceptual tools.

This brings us to my second point. In Sweden, class-consciousness is becoming increasingly dual in the sense that we (politicians, journalists, and even social scientists) often are content with distinguishing those who have jobs from those who are "left outside" the labor market (cf. Davidsson, 2010). In this rhetorical dualism, wage labor can come across as being a rather pleasant community where people realize their inner selves while guaranteeing the wealth of nations, whereas unemployment is inactivity, isolation, and parasitism. The phenomenon of empty labor challenges this dualism on several points, but it also helps us broaden our understanding of *the social strata of wage labor*. Income and employment conditions are not the only factors to take into account when studying the stratification of working life. Empty labor may be equally important for our well-being. On this issue, there is a real gap in most time use research: while susceptible to work-related activities taking place during spare time, it cares little about private activities at work (other than metaphorically at the most, cf. Hochschild, 1997). The research that comes closest to this divider is the one on work intensity mentioned in the introduction, but its measures are far from exact enough to discern any patterns in how empty labor is distributed professionally, hierarchically, not to mention qualitatively (for example, according to the types of empty labor that I have analyzed). The tendency is rather to merge the multitude of activities belonging to wage labor into the mega-category of "work" and to speak of average values on "work intensification" with little or no attention to which type of work we are studying (Green and McIntosh, 2001; Green, 2001, 2004). Instead of adding to our understanding of the strata of wage labor, the research on work intensity has rather obscured it. A way of circumventing this would be to measure intensity in empty labor, or more precisely in time spent on different activities at work, instead of the subjective estimates that intensity studies now rely upon.

Thirdly, an additional dimension that would further a stratified understanding of work would be to research the conception of *the meaning of work*. Sociologists often write about meaning, but the "meaning" they care about mostly has to do with our understanding of things – "meaning" as in "denotation" or "interpretation." I am here referring to the existential, purposive aspect of the meaning concept – "meaning" as in "the meaning of life" or "a meaningless job" (cf. Dreyfus and Kelly, 2011). This is not an entirely new point, and there have been some attempts to empirically approach this aspect of work (see especially MOW International Research Team, 1987). However, too often, it is completely neglected. In the recent anthology *Are Bad Jobs Inevitable?* (Warhurst et al., 2012), there is an abundance of parameters to define what constitutes a "bad job," e.g. wages, job security, health risks, work intensity, voice, job control, social relations at work, opportunities for learning and advancement, working time arrangements such as length of hours, unsocial/shift hours etc. As the reader can see, none of these parameters address the meaning of the job or even its substance (the productive activity that the worker is being paid for); they all refer to *conditions* of work. Many of the interviewees in this study would score pretty high on the job-quality scale according to these parameters; their wages were above average, they had secure full-time employment, there were no major risks involved in their work, they worked during normal office hours, and so on. The problem with their work was of a different kind: it lacked meaning.

Empty labor is just one way to approach the meaning of work. Every researcher knows how it feels when the job prevents us from doing research; every researcher has experienced meaningless work. As working life scholars, we have the possibility to elaborate cognitive frames that make us more sensitive to meaningless work, and to suggest ways to resist it. There are scientific, emancipatory, and egoistic reasons for going in this direction. A deeper awareness of the meaning of work may have the effect that refusing meaningless work becomes more legitimate. The restricted type of autonomy that empty labor represents could thus gradually be transformed into autonomy beyond the heteronomous frames of wage labor.

Appendix: Methodological notes

The empirical material that I refer to comes from many sources. By mere chance, I managed to get my hands on the dataset of a recent Finnish survey of empty labor with a great battery of questions. I also collected a decent compilation of reported cases of empty labor from newspaper stories, internet forums, and other academic studies. But most of the stories come from interviews I did with people who spend large proportions of their working days on empty labor. The methodological considerations in this appendix deal mainly with these interviews.

All studies of organizational misbehaviors stretching beyond the trivial share certain methodological challenges. The most obvious one is how to find people involved in a particular misbehavior ready to talk about what they do. Older studies of organizational misbehavior have mainly employed the standard ethnographical methods that involve picking a workplace, doing fieldwork, and hoping for the best (cf. Burawoy, 1979; Ditton, 1977; Roy, 1952). Scholars who are interested in pursuing the study of empty labor may want to think twice before opting for such an approach. Today, with new means of networking and announcing, there are more efficient ways of reaching employees who are involved in secretive behaviors of particular kinds. In this appendix, I will discuss some of these ways, and also the liabilities of being left in the hands of interviewees.

Firstly, I describe the selection process and particularly how I was able to find employees ready to talk about their experience of empty labor and who these employees were. Secondly, I explain why I decided to do an interview study instead of an ethnography. Thirdly, I address some epistemological issues concerning the interview process. And fourthly, I discuss the interview procedure and the analytical strategies.

A1 The interviewees

The existence of empty labor may be regarded as a "public secret" (Simmel, 1906) in the sense that although everyone has been engaged in it (more or less of course), under most social circumstances it must be denied. This problem is well known among students of organizational misbehavior. As James C. Scott puts it, "[r]esistance has self-interest in not showing itself" (Scott, 1991: xxi). The major challenge of this study has been how to find employees with the right experience who are ready to talk about it. Before committing fully to this project, I did around ten interviews starting in 2007 with respondents whom I had met before (through friends) but who were not my own close friends. Based on their suggestions, these interviews led to a couple of new respondents in a "chain referral sampling" (also known as "snowballing"; see Lopes et al., 1996).

I only had one criterion for the selection: I wanted respondents who had spent or were spending *half or more* of their working hours on empty labor. Most suggestions, however, were of the more modest kind. The reason I targeted such an extreme group was that I wanted to add something to the standard explanations of empty labor. For instance, shorter "breaks" (another term that can be bent pretty far) often tend to be regarded as beneficial for productivity (cf. D'Abate, 2005; Gouveia, 2012; Scott, 1998: 235). Another popular notion is the blurring of boundaries between work and leisure (Allvin et al., 2011; Baxter and Kroll-Smith, 2005; Fleming, 2005a). The "electronic leash" (i.e. information and communication technology combined with norms of constant accessibility) makes knowledge workers in particular susceptible to falling into the habit of working while not at work. Accordingly, one could expect employees to compensate this loss of time by running private errands on the internet while at work. The point with extreme case samplings is that they can enable you to unleash the analysis from ingrained notions of this type and thus make your interviews more illuminating (see Patton, 2002: 230–34). While not disregarding the standard explanations of empty labor, I reasoned that it would be harder to argue that breaks during half of the working hours, regardless of occupation, actually promoted productivity or merely compensated for homework.

I did some advertising on various forums, but the results were very meager (all in all, four new interviews). The real breakthrough came rather late when I was able to put an advertisement at the activist website maska.nu (a free translation might be "wastetime.now"). Maska.nu is a well-guarded website (it took me a long time to figure out who was behind it) that posts political texts, often relating to burning issues on the labor market, in which work society is questioned and appropriating time is promoted as a way of resisting it. It also has a suggestion section where people anonymously share their experiences of empty labor and exchange advice on how to get away with it. Since this website, at least at the time, had many visitors, the advertisement garnered good response.

Then, another thing happened: suddenly my e-mail address was the only one appearing on the website, and within a couple of weeks a journalist called me to ask whether I wanted to give an interview on my research. At that time, the newspaper articles on time waste mentioned in the introduction had just begun circulating, and they needed someone (representing "science") to comment upon them. I explained that my research project was only in its preliminary phase and that nothing had been published so far, but we agreed to do an interview on why my research project was motivated and what empty labor might signify more generally. In the interview, which was published in *Sydsvenskan* (one of the daily newspapers in Sweden), I was somehow allowed to deliver my personal opinion on whether empty labor is "good or bad" and say what I still believe is quite obvious, namely that empty labor does not have to be the result of laziness and that it can be a legitimate reaction against meaningless work. Within two months, I had given two interviews on national television, three radio interviews, and four newspaper interviews. Although the effect should not be exaggerated, the media appearances were most successful in attracting new interviewees.

In sum, the interview subjects include twenty women and twenty-three men. Most were office employees with academic degrees, working in isolation (although not totally separated from others), mainly in the private sector and of young age (ranging between 22 and 51). In nine interviews, it turned out that the workers probably did not "waste" half of their working hours but were engaged in milder forms of empty labor. Although not analyzed in detail, these interviews became valuable for a fuller understanding of the varieties of empty labor, especially of what I call "coping" (see Chapter 4). Fourteen interviewees had service jobs (e.g. one store cashier, one cleaner, three social workers), five belonged to the industrial sector (e.g. one ware-house employee, two mechanics, one factory worker), and the rest had typical office jobs in either the private or the public sector (e.g. three web developers, one accounting clerk, one logistics administrator).

I would say that the public justification of empty labor helped me to get in contact with people who otherwise would not have wanted to participate in an interview on this subject. Doing interviews has the disadvantage that the interviewer always comes "from the outside," meaning that interviewees might have difficulty explaining the often unexpressed meaning of organizational misbehavior and take a defensive stance. In some interviews the respondents fiercely denied that half or more of their working hours consisted in empty labor. Even though I tried to make it clear in the initial contact with them that this was the only reason I wanted to talk with them, for some reason the story was different when we actually met. The trouble of finding interviewees when studying organizational misbehavior may in itself develop into a real mystery, as in Michel Anteby's study of *la perruque*, i.e. production for oneself during working hours and with company tools (the same misbehavior described by Michel de Certeau as seen in Chapter 3), where the company does not allow him to interview the workers and one of the workers even advises him not to pursue his study (Anteby, 2003). However, it is obvious that this combination of advertisement and snowball selection raises some methodological issues.

Firstly, it could be argued that what I have done is simply to vacuum exceptional cases without relevance to working life at large. Both advertisement and snowball samples may be accused of reaching only the exceptional ones (cf. Lopes et al., 1996). Granting that these are exceptional cases, which we really do not know, I would still like to argue that they are relevant as ideal types of what may generally be more widespread in lesser forms. As argued in the introduction, empty labor as such is not an exceptional phenomenon, and sometimes going to extreme cases can make clearer what is otherwise veiled in shadows. As Berth Danermark et al. put it: "The strength of experiment in natural science is that you can study, in a constructed laboratory, certain mechanisms as they appear in a purer form. An alternative, employed in social science, is to study real cases where mechanisms manifest themselves in a purer form than usual" (Danermark et al., 2002: 105). Studying critical cases turned out to be especially valuable to crystallize tactics and organizational factors behind empty labor.

Secondly, a more serious objection could be that I have not restricted the selection enough. For instance, I could have concentrated on a certain company or a certain profession. I will return to the reasons for why I chose not to do an ethnography of that type. Here, I will acknowledge only that the decision not to focus on one group was partly pragmatic, partly theoretic. As I discovered that it was quite hard to find respondents that would match the selection criterion, I decided not to add any more criteria than that. More importantly, my aim was to discern the wide spectrum of motivations and organizational factors at play, and with this in mind different contexts turned out to be helpful.

Thirdly, by turning to a website like maska.nu, the question arises: how do you avoid political bias in your sample? Have I just interviewed a group of left-wing dogmatists with little in common with other people? Since half of the purpose of this project is to study the motivations behind empty labor, this is a very legitimate question. The easy answer is, of course, that it is impossible to avoid political bias in matters like this where there is a "cultural script" (Alvesson, 2003) condemning and making it necessary to hide empty labor, and that anyone ready to talk about his or her experience of empty labor probably is not a paragon of the Protestant work ethic. On the other hand, I did actually interview several employees who appeared quite anxious to assert their work commitment. As we will see, far from all cases of empty labor derive from low commitment on the part of the employee; empty labor may be quite involuntary and it may even be experienced as a burden. Yet I have managed to interview persons who feel this way too; the snowball sampling in particular was very effective in reaching such respondents. The question of political bias can be answered only by looking at how different interviewees motivated or explained their empty labor, which I report in Chapter 6. As the reader may have discovered, the variation is great. The reason why I interviewed such a large number was precisely because I wanted to hear different stories. The group I feel that I have not been able to reach is primarily those who are too embarrassed to talk about the situation, but that is a bias shared with every interview study ever conducted.

Fourthly, whatever opinion on empty labor the respondents had prior to the interview, could it be that my view of empty labor and the morality of it influenced which stories they told me, especially considering that some of them might have heard of it in the media? Although I certainly tried not to bring out whatever I (most unconsciously) "wanted to hear," "framing the interview situation" has certainly not been completely avoided here (how could it?). However, I would say that the hard task has been the reverse, namely to break through the cultural scripts that make empty labor a shameful experience that must be defended. Although these are all textbook issues that must be developed in a study like this, I will leave them here for a moment. The reflexive shift in qualitative methodology is a welcome reaction to the "third person explanations" that ignore or even distort first person accounts while claiming to tell the "real truth" (cf. Martin, 2011), but today there is also a tendency among qualitative methodologists to over-emphasize their own importance in the interview process with lengthy accounts on the "meaning making," the "knowledge generation," the process in which "researchers and respondents jointly create social reality through interaction" (Marvasti, 2003: 29) etc. There is no need to elaborate on these intellectual subtleties. Studying empty labor with a "neutral" attitude is methodologically not a good idea if we want to avoid the defensive attitudes that the cultural scripts currently dictate. This was my experience during the first interviews in which it was hard to reach beyond the "right or wrong" issues. Howard Becker's (1967) question to the sociological community – "whose side are we on?" – here becomes tangible on a very practical level. Any interviewer who does not take sides will simply be assumed to represent the average opinion; regarding empty labor, this entails a condemning view. To be able to talk about a phenomenon that is generally conceived of as dishonorable, a certain political awareness is thus required of both the interviewer and the interviewee.

Both when interviewing and writing, the notion of "public sociology" can inspire the study of organizational misbehavior on several levels. Michael Burawoy's fundamental argument, that sociology is not of much value if it does not reach the public concerned with the same issues, seems convincing to me. It should be noted that Burawoy makes a distinction between "traditional public sociology" where the sociologist addresses the general public and uses channels of mainstream media, and "organic public sociology" in which "the sociologist works in close connection with a visible, thick, active, local and often counter-public" (Burawoy, 2005: 7). The latter type of sociology is best represented by ethnographical studies; a perfect example of a movement with interaction between the sociologists and activists to the degree that the categories blur is the feminist movement (cf. Kleidman, 2009; Turner, 1995). Even if there is no visible, thick, or local public that I particularly address here, and even if I am not doing an ethnography in a strict sense, I have been able to receive many comments and reactions on my writings from respondents and others who identify with websites such as maska.nu or who are just interested by work critical studies as such.

A final issue concerning the respondents is how I can be sure that half or more of their working hours was actually dedicated to empty labor. Something that struck me with many respondents was that estimating how much time they spent on work and on private matters was not always easy. An obvious reason is the general tendency towards blurring the borders between "work" and "leisure" – some of the interviewees did work from home on a more or less regular basis. However, it was clear that it did *not* "even itself out" among the employees I talked with. A useful way to make the estimates tangible was to ask more specifically about typical non-work activities: the minutes spent on Facebook and other internet sites, the time spent on having coffee with colleagues, time spent on "spacing out" between tasks, on smoking breaks, on private telephone calls etc. Yet another trouble when estimating how much one works is that the pattern of emptiness does not have to repeat itself on a daily basis. For many, it came in waves, sometimes in terms of days, sometimes in terms of weeks or months.

A2 Interview study versus ethnography

Labor process theory and critical management studies are mostly based on ethnographical case studies. One can see many reasons for this methodological dominance; the possibility of "triangulating" interview material with the study of actual behavior enables the observer to reach beyond the subjective sphere of the agent. Erving Goffman for one, claims "that's the core of observation. If you don't get yourself in that situation, I don't think you can do a piece of serious work" (1989: 125). Without detailing the ethnographical methodology and its limits, I will here give three reasons for why it restrains the study of empty labor.

To begin with, the differences between organizations and the forms of work behavior they entail are lost when studying only one organization. This should not be perceived as a version of the standard positivist critique of ethnography – I do not regret the loss of quantitative representation, but rather the loss of qualitative distinction. As Vincent Roscigno and Randy Hodson point out in their literature review of ethnographies that analyze worker resistance, "the wide continuum of organizational practices (from poorly to carefully organized, and from informal to highly bureaucratic), within which the micropolitical context of manager-worker relations are played out and possibly even conditioned, is largely missing" (2004: 18). In other words, while able to offer "thick descriptions" of a certain case, ethnographies often suffer from being too specific. Wide (albeit thinner) descriptions may be able to offer conceptualizations of organizational (mis-)behavior of more general relevance (for good examples, see Hochschild, 1983; Mars, 1982; Sprouse, 1992) .

Secondly, it is hard to deny the predominance of industrial work especially in labor process studies. As the service sector grows, this means that much of the empirical foundation of labor process theory is becoming increasingly obsolete. As Paul Edwards (1986: 14) asserts, the under-representation of office employees may not be disastrous for the theory of organizational misbehavior – as we shall see, the tricks of the trade in modern offices are largely the same as in the industrial studies of Donald Roy in the 1950s. However, for the conceptualization of empty labor (which is not only a matter of organizational misbehavior), there are few other sources than the interviewees themselves.

This relates to the third point. As with office workers, the manifestations of empty labor are extremely hard to observe (cf. Rothlin and Werder, 2007: 60). Since both labor and private activities normally proceed individually on the computer screen, they can be concealed in "the split second it takes to press Alt + F4" as one of the interviewees put it.[1] Part of empty labor is to simulate labor. It is hidden

---

[1] At the website atworkandbored.com (retrieved May 27, 2012), the irony of how easy it is to fake work by switching between windows on the computer screen is illustrated by a so-called panic button. When cyberslacking, visitors are advised to keep the panic button ready for whenever "the boss" might pass by. When clicking on it, the screen is filled with a chart of the "sales forecast" – presumably the ideal simulation of "work."

and must remain hidden in order to be reproduced. As Kathleen Blee comments in her study of women joining racist movements, secrecy makes it hard to survey, participate, or get access to interviewees that you feel you should ideally have to fill upcoming gaps in the interview process: "It is impossible to create an accurate sampling frame of a secretive movement" (Blee, 1996: 688). With labor increasingly becoming immaterial (both symbolically and literally, see Gorz, 2003) and individual (Allvin, 1997), it is also becoming harder to observe it more generally. In other words, even when ethnographically studying office cases of empty labor, we are completely in the hands of the employees and their readiness to share their experiences. What is work and what is not work often is a question of what takes place on the screen, and as we all know, no one would bear having an ethnographer staring over his or her shoulder for days.

A less economic way to observe empty labor is to spend a couple of years in an organization, preferably as an employee, in order to see through the labor process and the contributions of everyone involved, and also to get beneath the cultural scripts that hinder most of us from sharing experiences of empty labor. A more economic solution is to monitor all computerized activity with the type of software that some companies are now using to control distance workers (see Shellenbarger, 2012). However, there are both practical and ethical reasons not to go in any of these directions.

A3 Interviewing beyond radical skepticism

Before returning to the practical questions concerning the interview process, I will now turn to some theoretical issues that this type of interview study needs to address. Doing interviews without observational data means that we rely on our respondents – they are our windows to the world; it is through them that we can study the phenomenon at hand. The epistemological issues that permeate pure interview studies (i.e. where the main source of empirics derives from interviews) have for a long time been subject to much debate. In the well-known handbook *Research Interviewing*, Elliot Mishler discerns what he calls the "mainstream tradition of survey research interviewing" (Mishler, 1993: 2). The view of this approach that is usually taken for granted is that the interview can be regarded as an exchange of information and that the questions of the interviewer can be seen as a "stimulus" at which the interviewee simply provides a mechanical "response" (Mishler, 1993: 10). This approach deeply underestimates the importance of language, it is argued. "It is a basic assumption in much social-science research," Wendy Hollway and Tony Jefferson (2000: 8) say, "that if the words used are the same, and if they are communicated in the same manner, they will mean the same thing to numerous people in the sample."

Although this might have been true when Mishler wrote his hand-book in 1986, I very much doubt that it is "a basic assumption" among social scientists doing interviews today – especially in critical workplace studies. The "grand narrative" that reappears among our contemporary interview studies is rather that of *radical skepticism*.

Radical skepticism starts with the not-so-radical observation that numerous factors in the interview situation can influence interviewees into saying things they do not *actually* feel. The power asymmetry inherent in every interview, unconscious fears, and subtly expressed expectations of the interviewer are typical sources of distortions. In his critique of "neopositivist" approaches to interviewing, Mats Alvesson (2003: 19–24) discusses several others. The cultural script-argument draws attention to the fact that there are cultural norms regulating what is viewed as "acceptable" and "unacceptable" that influence how we perceive and talk about sensitive issues such as empty labor. One could also regard the interview situation as "identity work"; if I ask someone why he or she is engaged in soldiering or any other type of organizational misbehavior, the respondent may be more engaged in justifying or constructing a certain identity rather than in giving exact answers. There may be "moral storytelling" going on, or self-promotion; not necessarily in relation to the dominating cultural script (i.e. the glorification of work) – more local scripts including attitudes of the interviewer revealed by barely noticeable looks and head nods etc. may construct a "local" script specific for the particular interview situation (see also Silverman, 1989).

This leads us to the next step towards radical skepticism. Mishler's (1993: 52ff) understanding of the interview as the "joint construction of meaning" has since it was first formulated had an enormous impact on interviewing and qualitative methodology at large. Acknowledging the context of the interview and the interviewer as an active partic-ipant in "generating knowledge" (see Mason, 2002: 79) is easy to justify – not least in relation to the study of empty labor. When I met the respondents, it was clear from the beginning that we were going to talk about their slacking off at work. This framing of the interview doubtlessly meant that the interviewees said different things to me than they would have done at an evaluation meeting with their boss. But the notion of "joint construction of meaning" suggests something more, namely that rather than *revealing* the meaning of empty labor that the interviewee had prior to the interview, the interviewer and the interviewee are interpersonally involved in a "speech act," or in *constructing* a meaning that is no more than the product of their meeting. In other words, it can never be regarded as a genuine expression of the subject's feelings or thoughts. The reasons for why skeptics refuse to acknowledge any link between interview material and "reality" vary. Some derive their skepticism from the sources of distortion mentioned above; others go a step further by stressing the primacy of language.

The tendency to cut off whatever links there are between actuality and language is most apparent within discourse analysis (see Alvesson and Karreman, 2011), but also strong among interviewers who, like myself, are interested in *stories* as a means of communication. Two of them, Hollway and Jefferson, observe:

In the past few decades there has been a massive shift of emphasis in social theory away from assumptions that the external world can be apprehended accurately through the senses and via information-processing mechanisms to one which claims that it is impossible to know that world directly. Everything we know about is mediated by language and the meanings which are available through language never represent the world neutrally. This shift is variously referred to as the shift from 'world' to 'word,' the 'turn to language' or the 'hermeneutic turn' (that is, a move to emphasize meanings and their interpretations). (Hollway and Jefferson, 2000: 14)

The shift from "world" to "word" can be differently motivated. The benign version is to say that since it is impossible to perceive or experience anything beyond language we should not make "truth claims" about reality; the radical version is to say that there actually is nothing beyond language, that "everything is text." In organizational studies that employ a narrative approach, stories often are reduced to "sense making" or "identity construction" that either serves to reproduce organizational power structures or to challenge them (see Boje, 1991; Brown and Humphreys, 2003; Gabriel, 1995). But the notion that "language constructs rather than mirrors phenomena" (Alvesson, 2003: 13) stretches beyond skepticism; it is an ontological assertion that strangely seems to question and yet build on knowledge about the (supposedly nonexistent) "thing-in-itself."

Even more disturbingly, studies in which the meaning construction of individuals are in focus are frequently about presumably deviating behaviors. This is particularly the case of the few studies that have so far been conducted on the motivations underlying empty labor. The interest in "neutralization techniques" (Vivien and Thompson, 2005: 675), or in "the meanings they [employees] construct to rationalize their personal business on the job" (D'Abate, 2005: 1028) reveals not only that the researcher believes that these practices have no inherent meaning (which is why it must be constructed), but also that they ultimately are wrong (which is why they must, somehow, be "neutralized," or "rationalized"). The constructivist approach remains in that sense detached – what meaning there *actually* is, or what the interviewees *really* think, is, not too far from Kantian epistemology, forever hidden. However, it is easy to see which "constructions" we choose to "deconstruct," often with the explicit aim of defamiliarization, is both politically and theoretically motivated.

Here, the methodological and theoretical issues of this study converge. As we have seen, the definition of "resistance" depends to a large degree on whether primacy is given to subject or discourse. When theorizing interviews, scholars rarely relate to the much richer philosophical literature where the linguistic turn most fully took place and was debated. Particularly in critical management studies, methods and theory are often decoupled in the sense that whereas the theory may be "critical" in the sense of the early Frankfurt School, the most popular method is the type of discourse analysis that stems from Foucault, meaning that theory and method sometimes differ in the fundamental assumptions regarding subjectivity and discourse. This does not necessarily have to constitute a problem. Methodologically, the implications are more of interpretative than of practical importance. It might be said that the interviewees are merely *performing* "discursive" types of subjectivity in their accounts of empty labor, but from the existentialist perspective that Touraine represents, it could also be argued that they *enter* forms of subjectivity. The meaning of empty labor and workplace resistance might likewise be regarded as a product of joint *generation* by the interviewer and the interviewee, but it can also be regarded as *discovery* of meaning in the logotherapeutic sense of Viktor Frankl (1984 [1956]). The main difference lies in whether we attribute autonomy to the discourse or to the subject (see also Dreyfus and Kelly, 2011). Many would argue that the relationship between the two is dialectic, or that what comes first is an empirical question; sometimes individuals do formulate their own accounts, sometimes they are governed by free-floating discourses and narratives that are not their own (cf. Alvesson and Karreman, 2011). What is strikingly clear, however, is that regardless of whether the scholar adheres to radical skepticism, critical realism, or something in between, most interview studies in organizational research do seem to care about (internal) validity in the sense that the interviewees should recognize their own accounts.

Even more strikingly, the analytic chapters of interview studies share the same structure no matter what – even if it is assumed that meaning is jointly generated in the interview situation, the same type of interviewee block quotes and fragmented reports tends to be there. One could argue that this is because it is impossible to convey the full richness of an empirical material in text, including the complex interaction between the researcher and the respondent, without the risk of making it unreadable (Alvesson, 2002: 30; Miles and Huberman, 1994: 299). I would say that in the process of analysis, even the most egocentric interviewers are more concerned with what the interviewees actually say than with how exactly the speech act is mutually "constructed" etc. The idea of doing interviews originates from the notion that there are people out there whose experiences and worldviews differ from ours. Whereas in methodological debates we may indulge in the "academic sado-masochism, self-humiliation, and self-denunciation of the intellectual whose labor does not issue in scientific, technical or like achievements" (Marcuse, 2008 [1964]: 178), the act of performing an interview seems at least to aim at learning something more than any armchair sociologist could have fantasized. But if we really want to learn from our interviewees, we must distance ourselves from the third-person explanations that we have become so familiar with. Most fundamentally, this involves "taking people seriously as competent interpreters of their own lives" as Sennett (2006: 4) puts it. It is with this very simple (not to say unsophisticated) epistemology in mind that the interviews in this study have been conducted.

A4 Procedure

The *why* and *how* of empty labor make for a twofold aim that on the one hand grasps at the *motivation* of the employees and on the other hand at the *organizational conditions* and *individual tactics*. From the beginning, the question that has interested me the most is the one of motivation. However, if we straightforwardly ask "why" people behave in this or that way, i.e. if we just translate a research question into an interview question, the answers we receive risk staying within the academic frames of abstraction and intellectualization from which we come (Hollway and Jefferson, 2000: 35). A more concrete way of approaching motivation is through narrative accounts. Therefore, I have adopted a narrative interview technique that I will soon demystify for the reader.

The first time I heard of empty labor was in a story that my wife told me. While she was still in high school she got a summer job without any clear job description at a big company. Once there, they told her that she was going to work in the archives gathering documents in different folders. When she realized that they were going to isolate her in a cold basement with no windows for the next six weeks, she momentarily despaired. The archives were in a mess. No matter how hard she worked, she would not be able to deal with a fraction of the unsorted documents during the time she had. It was the type of brain-dead labor that you would not wish on your worst enemy. One day, she brought a book in her bag. That day she did not do anything except reading. When the supervisor came down in the afternoon, the door slammed and she quickly got on her feet. He did not notice anything. The next day, she brought the book again. That was the summer when she read *Anna Karenina*.

One of the most valuable characteristics of the narrative is that regardless of the plot, whether it is epic, tragic or romantic (see Gabriel, 1995), narratives share the basic structure of a beginning, middle and an end. In the beginning, we learn what initiated the event (she did not like her job); in the middle, we learn about the event itself (she started to read books during working hours); in the end, we learn how it all worked out (she read a lot). As Hollway and Jefferson contend, "while stories are obviously not providing a transparent account through which we learn truths, story-telling stays closer to actual life-events than methods that elicit explanations" (Hollway and Jefferson, 2000: 31). Whether we are "predisposed" (either by nature or socially) to think in "narrative" form – so called "homo narrans" or "homo fabulans" – is irrelevant here (cf. Brown and Humphreys, 2003: 124). The focus and search for narratives are first and foremost pragmatic – as a way of discovering meaning in experience and behavior.

A central idea in the narrative method is that the more structured "question-and-answer method of interviewing has a tendency to suppress respondents' stories" (Hollway and Jefferson, 2000: 31). The narrative approach is not only about discerning stories within the responses, it also aims at freeing the interviewee from the more or less articulated agenda of the interviewer. A typical method that I have tried to implement is to start off with an opening question and then not interfere until at least one story has been told. By verbal and non-verbal means the interviewee is instead encouraged to continue his or her story (cf. Turgeman-Goldschmidt, 2005). During the second half of the interview, the interviewer tries to fill the gaps while elaborating on the main theme, here the meaning of empty labor. This may sound tricky, and so it is:

being a player in the story-telling organization is being skilled enough to manage the person-to-person interaction to get the story line woven into the ongoing turn-by-turn dialogue using a broad class of behaviors called qualifiers, markers, and the like, that sustain storytelling across extended discourse by means of paralinguistic and kinesic cues such as head nods, postural shifts, and eyebrow raises. (Boje, 1991: 110)

I do not believe that any interviewer can honestly pretend to entirely master this skill. The idea that the interviewer is there as a mere catalyst comes close to the romantic notion of the interview that David Silverman, Alvesson, and others have criticized. In many cases, the initially taciturn approach may not work at all. I learned that the starting question did not always lead in the right direction for everyone. When I asked "Can you tell me how you experience your work situation?" some did not mention the empty hours in a sentence – despite of the fact that this was clearly stated as the theme of the interview from the beginning.

A good strategy with both the laconic and the verbose was to *concretize* the question. A very unsophisticated but effective question that

I used was: "Can you tell me a story about that?" This is a very simple tip that I got from Irving Seidman's *Interviewing as Qualitative Research*. Sometimes, it may really open up memories of a particular incident and result in detailed reconstructions of what actually happened. However, like all forms of technical interviewing advice, it does not work with everyone. As Seidman himself notes: "not everybody is comfortable with being asked directly to tell a story. The request seems to block people who may think they do not tell good stories or that story telling is something only other people do" (Seidman, 2006: 87). Five questions that I sometimes made use of to complement the first (depending on whether the respondents covered the topics spontaneously or not) were:

- Can you tell me about the last time you did not work while at work?
- Can you tell me about times when you have done little work while at work?
- Can you tell me about something you have done while not working?
- Can you tell me about when you first discovered that you could work less than supposed?
- Can you tell me about times when you were close to being exposed?

The first three questions aim to elicit stories relating to empty labor while respecting the meaning-frames of the respondents – I wanted to leave open the question of motivations and since the diversity of how people framed their stories (in the beginning) was so great, I believe that it was somewhat successful (although it is impossible to escape interviewer effects altogether). The fourth and the fifth questions were of particular importance for the second phase of the interview (which, depending on the respondent, could be considerably longer than the first). In this second part I wanted to fill the gaps from the initial stories and to approach the "how"-question – how do they do it? Here, the interview proceeded in a semi-structural way (cf. Kvale, 1997) while focusing on how and why the interviewees had so much empty labor, what they felt about their profession, their job (its purpose and organization), the company they worked for, and how it was managed. It might be argued that by asking about these "usual suspects," I produced motivations that I sought to establish. However, as the answers of the respondents make clear, the diversity of the stories elicited suggests that their accounts were not (entirely) directed by the questions.

To establish a frank, respectful and confidential interview environment was crucial for entering into the big secret of what empty labor
signifies for the majority. Whether that succeeded is an open question,
and the best judges are the interviewees themselves. Most interviews
lasted between 40 and 180 minutes, and in some cases I returned to
the respondents by phone when there was need for clarification. As
is clear in the empirical chapters, my focus shifted somewhat while I
was doing the interviews, and the how-questions became even more
important than the motivation related ones.

A5 Analysis

Based on the narrative constructs generated in the interviews and the
theoretical pre-study, I have, as one would expect, built a range of
"second-order constructs," which are my own interpretations and
abstractions. At this stage, the crucial task is to keep a clear link
between the material, the theoretical point of departure, and the analytical concepts (cf. Aspers, 2006: 28). Three students who wrote their
bachelor theses about different aspects of empty labor were involved in
the categorization process of the material. Four vocabularies of motive
were reconstructed according to five dimensions that reappear both in
the interviews and in other studies of resistance, organizational misbehavior and time appropriation (see Chapter 6). Equally important,
I discerned different organizational situations relating to the intersection of potential output and sense of work obligation in which empty
labor did emerge (see Chapter 4).

These two typologies were constructed by keeping the whole in
mind rather than fragmenting the transcripts into short pieces. This
is a strategy that narrative interview techniques employ that might
deviate some from other approaches. Narrative scholars often criticize
more "traditional" analyses where the coding process may lead to the
researcher neglecting the biographical context and sometimes from
which interview the different quotes may come. This is especially a
risk when, as I did, using a coding software such as ATLAS/ti, in
which you can code all the interviews in a single data file, create links
between the codes, merge and regroup them, until finally you have
completely forgotten which person said what and in which context.
Often the results may be "artificial aggregates that have no direct

representation in the real world of communities, social institutions, families, or persons" (Mishler, 1993: 26). A way to counter this tendency that we all move towards when faced with a mass of unstructured data is to classify the whole account of a respondent in relation to the "how" and "why" questions (Hollway and Jefferson, 2000: 68). For instance, although most of the interviewees were critical of some aspects of their jobs relating to management, very few of them actually engaged in time appropriation *in reaction* to their bosses. If we take the story of my wife referred to above, the annoying boss might have been an additional motivator, she could have said something that called for the code "bad boss," but the main reason she read books instead of filing documents was because she could not stand the monotony and meaninglessness of the job. Similarly, she might have said that reading books made her feel happier than she would have been if she had worked ceaselessly as she was supposed to, but her way of appropriating time was never a matter of "coping" as defined in Chapter 4. She did not do it in order to survive emotional depression and be able to do a good job in the future. She did not want to do a good job at all. Instead of just fragmenting the interviews into autonomous codes with the apparent risk of alienation, I worked with overall "codes" or "themes" that summarized the rationale of each interviewee. Some of these broad classifications are summarized in the typologies presented in Chapters 4 and 7.

An important concept that I used when analyzing the interviews in relation to motivation was that of *vocabularies of motive*. In one of his earlier texts, C. Wright Mills (1940) emphasizes how motives are more external than the Freudian psychology of his time assumed. This article, which is permeated with the "socspeak" that Mills (1951: 217) later would reject, is a fine example of Mills' pragmatism and of how one can study motivation while avoiding claims about the "subconscious" or "inner-self" of the respondent. Well before the "linguistic turn," Mills developed a concept of "motivation" as primarily a lingual phenomenon. This theory is more balanced than the social constructivist approach of today in the sense that it provides a more plastic notion of "motivation" – as opposed to the "systematic motive-mongering" (Mills, 1940: 911) of orthodox psychoanalysis with its assumptions of "desire," "real motives," and "rationalizations" – that does not give complete primacy to language as such.

A man may begin an act for one motive. In the course of it, he may adopt an ancillary motive. This does not mean that the second apologetic motive is inefficacious. The vocalized expectation of an act, its 'reason,' is not only a mediating condition of the act but it is a proximate and controlling condition for which the term 'cause' is not inappropriate. It may strengthen the act of the actor. It may win new allies for his act. . . . When an agent vocalizes or imputes motives, he is not trying to *describe* his experienced social action. He is not merely stating 'reasons.' He is influencing others – and himself. Often he is finding new 'reasons' which will mediate action. (Mills, 1940: 907)

With this view of motivation, the question of whether I have "really" discerned the inner feelings of the interviewees becomes superfluous: "there is no way to plumb behind verbalization into an individual and directly check our motive-mongering" (Mills, 1940: 910) and there is no need for it, either. Vocabularies of motive are always conditioned by situated forms of interpersonal agreement – "thus acts will often be abandoned if no reason can be found that others will accept" (Mills, 1940: 907). This is not to say that there is nothing beyond language, but simply that what interests us when researching motives is not which motives the person holds in the present moment or some moments ago, but rather the vocabularies of motives that reappear among the respondents. As Dorinne Kondo (1990) observes, the employee may consent, cope, and resist at different levels of consciousness at a single point in time (Collinson and Ackroyd, 2005: 321) – if we really want to analyze the personal, we will thus have to deal with all the motivational conflicts of the human psyche, and for that, just one interview per study would suffice. Furthermore, there is, as in all interview studies, no guarantee that the interviewee is speaking the truth or not withholding information. As Mills puts it: "the verbalized motive is not used as an index of something in the individual but *as a basis of inference for a typal vocabulary of motives of a situated action*" (Mills, 1940: 909). Such vocabularies are presented in Chapter 6, where I approach the question of motive in detail. Again, those who want to interpret these vocabularies as mere meaning constructions without much relation to "something in the individual" may, of course, do so; others may construct "their own" realist meaning based on the material.

Whereas the phenomenon of empty labor (in all its varieties) is the constant in all interviews, the situations in which it appears constitute the real mystery. As I argue in Chapter 6, that is primarily what makes the interpretation of the vocabularies of motive ambivalent. The working conditions, the tactics that the employee used, the organizational context including the managerial strategies in relation to empty labor are not detailed in each individual case. The main reason for this is that explaining *exactly* how an individual case of time appropriation came about would require explaining the particular labor process in detail for which there is neither space nor interest in this study. What I have attempted to do is to analyze general patterns that are repeated among the interviewees both in terms of tactics and organizational conditions; again, to provide a *wide* description rather than the thick type that captures the individual case in more detail but often misses the bigger picture.

All the data that I have made use of has been cross-checked and discussed with others who have worked with the same type of jobs or in similar fields. When studying the more general patterns of employee tactics for avoiding work, I have also tested the categories against the more detailed accounts that anonymous individuals have published at maska.nu and at a newer Danish website called dettommearbejde.dk, which is devoted particularly to the phenomenon of empty labor. Also, I make use of a survey study of empty labor that was commissioned by the Finnish newspaper *Sunnuntaisuomalainen* and performed by market research company Taloustutkimus Oy. This survey was never published in its entirety but sent to me personally, for which I am very grateful. It is one of the most thorough surveys of empty labor ever conducted, particularly since it uses multiple variables for measuring different expressions of empty labor (such as how much time you spend on reading the newspaper, on personal internet use, on corridor talk etc.). The survey was conducted in November, 2010 and done on a nationally representative sample (1077 respondents) of the Finnish adult population via an internet panel. Since the data is from Finland and the interviewees in my study come from Sweden, the statistics should rather be regarded as a point of reference than a means to triangulate.

Bibliography

Ackroyd, S. and Thompson, P. (1999) *Organizational misbehaviour.* London: Sage.

Adams, S. (1996) *The Dilbert principle: A cubicle's-eye view of bosses, meetings, management fads & other workplace afflictions.* New York: HarperBusiness.

(2008) *This is the part where you pretend to add value: A Dilbert book.* Kansas City: Andrews McMeel Publishing.

Adorno, T.W. (1950) *The authoritarian personality.* New York: Harper.

(1973 [1966]) *Negative dialectics.* New York: Seabury Press.

(1980) "Commitment." in R. Taylor (ed.) *Aesthetics and politics.* London: Verso.

(2005 [1951]) *Minima moralia: Reflections on a damaged life.* London; New York: Verso.

Adorno, T.W. and Horkheimer, M. (2010 [1956]) "Towards a new manifesto," *New Left Review* 65(Sept–Oct): 32–61.

AFP (2004) "Dead tax man goes unnoticed," *Agence France Presse* 29/1.

Allen, A. (1999) *The power of feminist theory: Domination, resistance, solidarity.* Boulder, CO: Westview Press.

Allen, S. (2005) "Doctor disciplined for leaving surgery," *The Boston Globe* 17/11.

Allvin, M. (1997) *Det individualiserade arbetet: Om modernitetens skilda praktiker.* Eslöv: B. Östlings bokförl. Symposion.

Allvin, M. and Sverke, M. (2000) "Do new generations imply the end of solidarity? Swedish unionism in the era of individualization," *Economic and Industrial Democracy* 21(1): 71–95.

Allvin, M., et al. (2011) *Work without boundaries: Psychological perspectives on the new working life.* Chichester: Wiley-Blackwell.

Alvesson, M. (2002) *Kommunikation, makt och organisation: Kritiska tolkningar av ett informationsmöte i ett företag.* Stockholm: Norstedts juridik.

(2003) "Beyond neopositivists, romantics, and localists: A reflexive approach to interviews in organizational research," *The Academy of Management Review* 28(1): 13–33.

(2008) *Tomhetens triumf: Om grandiositet, illusionsnummer & noll-summespel*. Stockholm: Bokförlaget Atlas KB.

Alvesson, M. and Willmott, H. (2003) *Studying management critically*. London: Sage.

Alvesson, M. and Karreman, D. (2011) "Decolonializing discourse: Critical reflections on organizational discourse analysis," *Human Relations* 64(9): 1121–46.

Alway, J. (1995) *Critical theory and political possibilities: Conceptions of emancipatory politics in the works of Horkheimer, Adorno, Marcuse, and Habermas*. Westport, CT: Greenwood Press.

Anteby, M. (2003) "La « perruque » en usine: Approche d'une pratique marginale, illégale et fuyante," *Sociologie du Travail* 45(4): 453–71.

Applebaum, H. (1992) *The concept of work: Ancient, medieval, and modern*. SUNY series in the anthropology of work. Albany, NY: State University of New York Press.

Arendt, H. (1958) *The human condition*. University of Chicago Press.

Aspers, P. (2006) *Markets in fashion: A phenomenological approach*. New York, NY [u.a.]: Routledge.

Bagge, P. (2005) "Många arbetslösa känner sig kränkta," *SVT* 11/10.

Baldamus, W. (1961) *Efficiency and effort: An analysis of industrial administration*. London: Tavistock Publications.

Ball, K. (2010) "Workplace surveillance: An overview," *Labor History* 51(1): 87–106.

Bark, C. (2008) "Läkarnas tid utnyttjas felaktigt," *Sjukhusläkaren* 30/4.

Barker, J.R. (1993) "Tightening the iron cage: Concertive control in self-managing teams," *Administrative Science Quarterly* 38(3): 408–37.

Baudrillard, J. (1993 [1976]) *Symbolic exchange and death*. London; Thousand Oaks: Sage.

(1995) *The Gulf War did not take place*. Bloomington: Indiana University Press.

Bauman, Z. (2004) *Work, consumerism and the new poor*. 2nd edn.; Buckingham; Philadelphia: Open University Press.

Baxter, V. and Kroll-Smith, S. (2005) "Normalizing the workplace nap: Blurring the boundaries between public and private space and time," *Current Sociology* 53(1): 33–55.

BBC (2004) "Finns miss death in tax office," *BBC News* 19/1.

Beck, U. (1992) *Risk society: Towards a new modernity*. London; Newbury Park, CA: Sage Publications.

(2000) *The brave new world of work*. Malden, MA: Polity Press.

Becker, H.S. (1967) "Whose side are we on?," *Social Problems* 14(3): 239–47.

Beder, S. (2001) *Selling the work ethic: From Puritan pulpit to corporate PR*. London, Carlton North: Zed; Scribe.

Berardi, F. (2009) *The soul at work: From alienation to autonomy*. Los Angeles, CA: Semiotext(e).

Black, B. (2009) *Three essays by Bob Black*. Seattle: Wormwood.

Blanchard, A.L. and Henle, C.A. (2008) "Correlates of different forms of cyberloafing: The role of norms and external locus of control," *Computers in Human Behavior* 24(3): 1067–84.

Blee, K.M. (1996) "Becoming a racist: Women in contemporary Ku Klux Klan and neo-Nazi groups," *Gender and Society* 10(6): 680–702.

Bloomberg 'The top 50 coffee countries', www.businessweek.com/magazine/content/10_19/b4177074227389.htm, accessed April 29, 2010.

Blue, J., Keeler, B. and Coyle, R. 'Employees waste 20% of their work day according to salary.com survey', www.salary.com/sitesearch/layoutscripts/sisl_display.asp?filename=&path=/destinationsearch/par674_body.html, accessed November, 11, 2008.

Boje, D.M. (1991) "The storytelling organization: A study of story performance in an office supply firm," *Administrative Science Quarterly* 36(1): 106–26.

Bolchover, D. (2005) *The living dead: Switched off, zoned out: The shocking truth about office life*. Chichester, West Sussex: Capstone.

Botton, A.D. (2009) *The pleasures and sorrows of work*. New York: Pantheon Books.

Bourdieu, P. (1998) *Contre-feux: Propos pour servir à la résistance contre l'invasion néo-libérale*. Paris: Liber-Raisons d'agir.

Brattberg, L. (2007) "Migrationsverkets personal porrsurfade," *Dagens Nyheter* 25/9.

Braverman, H. (1998 [1974]) *Labor and monopoly capital: The degradation of work in the twentieth century*. New York: Monthly Review P.

Bremner, C. (2013) "MEPs' fury after daily allowance challenge" *The Times* 26/6.

Brewer, M.B. and Silver, M.D. (2000) "Group distinctiveness, social identification and collective mobilization," in S. Stryker, T. J. Owens, and R. W. White (eds.). *Self, identity, and social movements*. Social movements, protest, and contention, v. 13; Minneapolis: University of Minnesota Press.

Brown, A.D. and Humphreys, M. (2003) "Epic and tragic tales: Making sense of change," *Journal of Applied Behavioral Science* 39(2): 121–44.

Brown, G. (1977) *Sabotage: A study in industrial conflict*. Nottingham: Spokesman.

Brunsson, N. (2002 [1989]) *The organization of hypocrisy: Talk, decisions and actions in organizations*. Oslo: Abstrakt forl.

Burawoy, M. (1979) *Manufacturing consent: Changes in the labor process under monopoly capitalism*. University of Chicago Press.

(2005) "For public sociology," *Soziale Welt* 56(4): 347–74.

Burawoy, M. and Lukács, J. (1992) *The radiant past: Ideology and reality in Hungary's road to capitalism*. University of Chicago Press.

Campagna, F. (2013) *The last night: Anti-work, atheism, adventure*. Winchester: Zero Books.

Carleheden, M. (1996) *Det andra moderna: Om Jürgen Habermas och den samhällsteoretiska diskursen om det moderna*. Göteborg: Daidalos.

Carroll, J. 'U.S. Workers say they waste about an hour at work each day', www.gallup.com/poll/28618/US-Workers-Say-They-Waste-About-Hour-Work-Each-Day.aspx, accessed November 11, 2008.

Casey, C. (1995) *Work, self and society: After industrialism*. London: Sage.

Cederström, C. and Fleming, P. (2012) *Dead man working*. Winchester, UK; Washington, USA: Zero Books.

Certeau, M.D. (1984) *The practice of everyday life. Vol. 1, The practice of everyday life*. Berkeley: University of California Press.

(1986) *Heterologies: Discourse on the other*. Theory and history of literature, 17; Manchester University Press.

Clawson, D. and Fantasia, R. (1983) "Beyond Burawoy: The dialectics of conflict and consent on the shop floor," *Theory and Society* 12(5): 671–80.

Cohen, M.D., March, J.G. and Olsen, J.P. (1972) "A garbage can model of organizational choice," *Administrative Science Quarterly* 17(1): 1–25.

Collins, R. (1994) *Four sociological traditions*. New York: Oxford University Press.

Collinson, D. and Ackroyd, S. (2005) "Resistance, misbehavior, and dissent." in S. Ackroyd, et al. (eds.). *The Oxford handbook of work and organization*. New York: Oxford University Press.

Contu, A. (2008) "Decaf resistance," *Management Communication Quarterly* 21(3): 364–79.

Cooke, H. (2006) "Seagull management and the control of nursing work," *Work, Employment & Society* 20(2): 223–43.

Crozier, M. (1971) *The bureaucratic phenomenon*. University of Chicago Press.

Cullen, R. (November 11, 2007), 'Aud $5b in lost productivity – is Facebook the new bane of employers' lives?', www.surfcontrol.com.

D'Abate, C. (2005) "Working hard or hardly working: A study of individuals engaging in personal business on the job," *Human Relations* 58(8): 1009–32.

D'Abate, C. and Eddy, E.R. (2007) "Engaging in personal business on the job: Extending the presenteeism construct," *Human Resource Development Quarterly* 18(3): 361–83.

Danermark, B., et al. (2002) *Explaining society: Critical realism in the social sciences*. London; NY: Routledge.

Davidsson, T. (2010) "Utanförskapelsen: En diskursanalys av hur begreppet utanförskap artikulerades i den svenska riksdagsdebatten 2003–2006," *Socialvetenskaplig tidskrift* (2): 149–69.

Debord, G. (2002 [1967]) *Skådespelssamhället*. Göteborg: Daidalos.

Deetz, S. (2003) "Disciplinary power, conflict suppression and human resources management." in M. Alvesson and H. Willmott (eds.). *Studying management critically*. London: Sage.

DiMaggio, P.J. and Powell, W.W. (1983) "The iron cage revisited: Institutional isomorphism and collective rationality in organizational fields," *American Sociological Review* 48(2): 147–60.

Ditton, J. (1977) *Part-time crime: An ethnography of fiddling and pilferage*. London: Macmillan.

Dostoyevsky, F. (1964 [1866]) *Crime and punishment*. New York: W.W. Norton.

(1994 [1864]) *Notes from underground*. New York: Vintage Books.

(2000 [1872]) *Demons*. New York: Knopf.

(2003 [1867]) *The gambler*. New York: Modern Library.

Dowding, K. et al. (2000) "Exit, voice and loyalty: Analytic and empirical developments," *European Journal of Political Research* 37(4): 469–95.

Drevfjäll, L. (2013) "Gruvanställda fuskade till sig flera miljoner" *Expressen* 18/2.

Dreyfus, H.L. and Kelly, S. (2011) *All things shining: Reading the western classics to find meaning in a secular age*. New York: Free Press.

Dubois, P. (1979) *Sabotage in industry*. New York: Peuguin Books.

Edwards, P.K. (1986) *Conflict at work: A materialist analysis of workplace relations*. Warwick studies in industrial relations, Oxford: Basil Blackwell.

Elger, T. (1990) "Technical innovation and work reorganisation in British manufacturing in the 1980s: Continuity, intensification or transformation?," *Work Employment Society* 4(5): 67–101.

Elsbach, K., Cable, D. and Sherman, J. (2010) "How passive 'face time' affects perceptions of employees: Evidence of spontaneous trait inference," *Human Relations* 63(6): 735–60.

Elster, J. (1983) *Sour grapes: Studies in the subversion of rationality*. Cambridge University Press.

(1996) *Sour grapes: Studies in the subversion of rationality*. Paris: Cambridge University Press; Ed. de la Maison des Sciences de l'Homme.

Engelberg, M. and Wegener, A. (2012) "14 jahre nichts getan, 745 000 euro kassiert," *Bild* 12/4.

Feenberg, A. (1991) *Critical theory of technology*. New York: Oxford University Press.

Fleming, P. (2005a) "Workers' playtime?: Boundaries and cynicism in a "culture of fun" program," *Journal of Applied Behavioral Science* 41(3): 285–303.

(2005b) "'Kindergarten cop': Paternalism and resistance in a high-commitment workplace," *Journal of Management Studies* 42(7): 1469–89.

(2009) *Authenticity and the cultural politics of work: New forms of informal control*. New York: Oxford University Press.

Fleming, P. and Sewell, G. (2002) "Looking for the good soldier, Švejk," *Sociology* 36(4): 857–73.

Fleming, P. and Spicer, A. (2003) "Working at a cynical distance: Implications for power, subjectivity and resistance," *Organization* 10(1): 157–79.

(2007) *Contesting the corporation: Struggle, power and resistance in organizations*. New York: Cambridge University Press.

Fleming, P. and Spicer, A. (2008) "Beyond power and resistance," *Management Communication Quarterly* 21(3): 301–09.

Foucault, M. (1971) *The order of things: An archaeology of the human sciences*. New York: Pantheon Books.

(1977) *Discipline and punish: The birth of the prison*. New York: Pantheon Books.

(1978) *History of sexuality: An introduction*. New York: Pantheon.

(1980) *Power/knowledge: Selected interviews and other writings, 1972–1977*. New York: Pantheon Books.

Foucault, M. and Trombadori, D. (1991) *Remarks on Marx: Conversations with Duccio Trombadori*. New York: Semiotext(e).

Frankl, V.E. (1984 [1956]) *Man's search for meaning: An introduction to logotherapy*. New York: Simon & Schuster.

Friedman, A.L. (1977) *Industry and labour: Class struggle at work and monopoly capitalism*. London: Macmillan.

Fromm, E. (1973) *The anatomy of human destructiveness*. New York: Holt, Rinehart and Winston.

(1994 [1941]) *Escape from freedom*. Owl Book, 1st edn. New York: H. Holt.

(2008 [1955]) *The sane society*. London: Routledge.

Gabriel, Y. (1995) "The unmanaged organization: Stories, fantasies and subjectivity," *Organization Studies*. 16(3): 477.

Gallup (2013) *State of the global workplace*. Washington, DC: Gallup, Inc.

Gardiner, M. (2000) *Critiques of everyday life*. New York: Routledge.

Garrett, R.K. and Danziger, J.N. (2008) "On cyberslacking: Workplace status and personal internet use at work," *CyberPsychology and Behavior* 11(3): 287–92.

Gartman, D. (1983) "Structuralist Marxism and the labor process: Where have the dialectics gone?," *Theory and Society* 12(5): 659–69.

Gershuny, J. (2005), 'Busyness as the badge of honour for the new superordinate working class', *Working Papers of the Institute for Social and Economic Research*, (paper 2005–9; Colchester: University of Essex).

(2009) "Veblen in reverse: Evidence from the multinational time-use archive," *Social Indicators Research* 93(1): 37–45.

(2011) "Increasing paid work time? A new puzzle for multinational time-diary research," *Social Indicators Research* 101(2): 207–13.

Gianuzzi, M. (2008) "De sätter prislapp på skitsnacket" *Dagens Nyheter* 7/8.

Gibbons, P. (2008) *Kontoret: Hur du lyfter lön utan att lyfta ett finger*. Stockholm: Alfabeta.

Goffman, E. (1956) *The presentation of self in everyday life*. University of Edinburgh Social Sciences Research Centre.

(1989) "On fieldwork," *Journal of Contemporary Ethnography* 18(2): 123–32.

Gorz, A. (1959) *La morale de l'histoire*. Paris: Éditions du Seuil.

(1967) *Le socialisme difficile*. Paris: Éditions de Seuil.

(1982) *Farewell to the working class: An essay on post-industrial socialism*. London: Pluto Press.

(1989) *Critique of economic reason*. London: Verso.

(1994) *Capitalism, socialism, ecology*. London: Verso.

(1999) *Reclaiming work: Beyond the wage-based society*. Cambridge: Polity Press.

(2003) *L'immatériel: Connaissance, valeur et capital*. Paris: Galilée.

(2010) *Ecologica*. Calcutta: Seagull Books.

Gossett, L.M. and Kilker, J. (2006) "My job sucks," *Management Communication Quarterly* 20(1): 63–90.

Gouveia, A. 'Wasting time at work 2012', www.salary.com/wasting-time-at-work-2012/, accessed September 4, 2012.

Graeber, D. (2004) *Fragments of an anarchist anthropology*. Chicago: Prickly Paradigm Press.

Grahn, V. (2011) "Kolmannes työajasta kuluu omiin taukoihin" *Sunnuntaisuomalainen* 9/1.

Gramsci, A. (1988) *An Antonio Gramsci reader: Selected writings, 1916–1935*. New York: Schocken Books.

Grant, D., Keenoy, T. and Oswick, C. (1998) "Organizational discourse: Of diversity dichotomoy and multi-disciplinarity." in D. Grant, T. Keenoy, and C. Oswick (eds.). *Discourse and organization*. London: Sage.

Green, F. (2001) "It's been a hard day's night: The concentration and intensification of work in late twentieth-century Britain," *British Journal of Industrial Relations* 39(1): 53–80.

   (2004) "Why has work effort become more intense?," *Industrial Relations* 43(4): 709–41.

Green, F. and McIntosh, S. (2001) "The intensification of work in Europe," *Labour Economics* 8(2): 291–308.

Greer, G. (2006) *The female eunuch*. London: Harpercollins Publishers.

Griffin, R.W., O'Leary-Kelly, A.M. and Collins, J.M. (1998) "Dysfunctional work behaviors in organizations." in C.L. Cooper and D.M. Rousseau (eds.). *Trends in organizational behavior 5*: 65–82.

Gustafsson, S. (2009) "Tre miljoner fildelar illegalt i sverige" *Dagens Nyheter* 12/10.

Habermas, J. (1971) *Toward a rational society: Student protest, science, and politics*. London: Heinemann.

   (1984) *The theory of communicative action, volume 1., Reason and the rationalization of society*. London: Heinemann Educational.

Hall, S. (1980) *Culture, media, language: Working papers in cultural studies, 1972–79*. London: Hutchinson in association with the Centre for Contemporary Cultural Studies, University of Birmingham.

Hannerz, E. (2013) *Performing punk: Subcultural authentications and the positioning of the mainstream*. Uppsala: Uppsala University.

Harpaz, I. and Snir, R. (2002) "To work or not to work: Non-financial employment commitment and the social desirability bias," *The Journal of Social Psychology* 142: 635–44.

Hassard, J., Hogan, J. and Rowlinson, M. (2001) "From labor process theory to critical management studies," *Administrative Theory and Praxis* 23: 339–62.

Hawkes, D. (2003) *Ideology*. London: Routledge.

Healey, J.F. (2013) *The essentials of statistics: A tool for social research*. Belmont, CA: Wadsworth Cengage Learning.

Henle, C.A. and Blanchard, A.L. (2008) "The interaction of work stressors and organizational sanctions on cyberloafing," *Journal of Managerial Issues* 20(3): 383–400.

Hirschman, A.O. (1970) *Exit, voice, and loyalty: Responses to decline in firms, organizations, and states*. Cambridge, MA: Harvard University Press.

Hochschild, A.R. (1983) *The managed heart: Commercialization of human feeling*. Berkeley, CA: University of California Press.
(1997) "When work becomes home and home becomes work," *California Management Review* 39(4): 79–97.
Hollander, J.A. and Einwohner, R.L. (2004) "Conceptualizing resistance," *Sociological Forum* 19(4): 533–54.
Hollway, W. and Jefferson, T. (2000) *Doing qualitative research differently: Free association, narrative and the interview method*. Thousand Oaks, CA: Sage.
Holmqvist, M. (2005) *Samhall: Att bli normal i en onormal organisation*. Stockholm: SNS förlag.
Horkheimer, M. (1995 [1937]) *Critical theory: Selected essays*. New York: Continuum.
Horkheimer, M. and Adorno, T.W. (2002 [1944]) *Dialectic of enlightenment: Philosophical fragments*. Stanford University Press.
Illich, I. (1978) *The right to useful unemployment and its professional enemies*. London; Melbourne: Boyars; Distributed by T.C. Lothian Pty.
Ivarsson, L. and Larsson, P. (2012) "Privata angelägenheter på jobbet," *Arbetsmarknad och Arbetsliv* 18(3): 9–20.
Ivarsson Westerberg, A. (2004) "Papperspolisen: Den ökande administrationen i moderna organisationer." (Ekonomiska forskningsinstitutet vid Handelshögskolan i Stockholm).
Jackson, T. (2009) *Prosperity without growth: Economics for a finite planet*. London; Sterling, VA: Earthscan.
Jay, M. (1973) *The dialectical imagination: A history of the Frankfurt School and the Institute of Social Research, 1923–1950*. Boston: Little, Brown.
Johansson, R. (1992) *Vid byråkratins gränser: Om handlingsfrihetens organisatoriska begränsningar i klientrelaterat arbete*. Lund: Arkiv.
Jost, J. 'Americans waste more than 2 hours a day at work', www.salary.com/sitesearch/layoutscripts/sisl_display.asp?filename=&path=/destinationsearch/par485_body.html, accessed November 11, 2008.
Kåks Röshammar, C. (2008) "Fortsatt ras för facket," *LO-Tidningen* 11/4.
Karlsson, J.C. (1986) *Begreppet arbete: Definitioner, ideologier och sociala former*. Lund: Arkiv.
(2012) *Organizational misbehaviour in the workplace: Narratives of dignity and resistance*. England; New York: Palgrave Macmillan.
Keynes, J.M. (1991 [1931]) *Essays in persuasion*. New York: W.W. Norton & Co.
Kierkegaard, S. (2004 [1846]) "Existentialism: From Dostoevsky to Sartre." in W. A. Kaufmann (ed.); New York: Penguin Books.

Kirchhoff, J.W. and Karlsson, J.C. (2009) "Rationales for breaking management rules: The case of health care workers," *Journal of Workplace Rights Journal of Workplace Rights* 14(4): 457–79.

Kleidman, R. (2009) "Engaged social movement scholarship" in V. Jeffries (ed.) *Handbook of public sociology.* Lanham: Rowman & Littlefield Publishers, Inc.

Knights, D. and Willmott, H. (1989) "Power and subjectivity at work: From degradation to subjugation in social relations," *Sociology* 23(4): 535–58.

Knöbl, W. (1999) "Social theory from a Sartrean point of view: Alain Touraine's theory of modernity," *European Journal of Social Theory* 2(4): 403–27.

Kondo, D.K. (1990) *Crafting selves: Power, gender and commitment in a high-tech corporation.* University of Chicago Press.

Korczynski, M., Hodson, R. and Edwards, P.K. (2006) *Social theory at work.* New York: Oxford University Press.

Kosík, K. (1979) *Det konkretas dialektik: En studie i människans och världens problematik.* Göteborg: Röda Bokförlaget.

Kropotkin, P. (1927 [1892]) *The conquest of bread.* New York: Vanguard Press.

Kunda, G. (1992) *Engineering culture: Control and commitment in a high-tech corporation.* Philadelphia: Temple University Press.

Kvale, S. (1997) *Den kvalitativa forskningsintervjun.* Lund: Studentlitteratur.

Ladner, S. (2009), "'Where do I hide my time?'": Time reckoning, technology, and resistance among web workers', *27th Annual International Labour Process Conference* (Edinburgh).

Langman, L. (2009) "The dialectic of selfhood." in H. F. Dahms (ed.) *Nature, knowledge and negation.* Bingley: Emerald.

Larsson, J. (2010), 'Studier i tidsmässig välfärd', *Göterborg Studies in Sociology No. 49* (Göteborgs Universitet).

Lefebvre, H. (1991 [1958]) *Critique of everyday life.* London: Verso.

Leontief, W.W. (1986) *Input-output economics.* New York: Oxford University Press.

Lindström, A. (2010) "Kommuner sparkar anställda som porrsurfar," *Expressen* 9/2.

Liu, A. (2004) *The laws of cool: Knowledge work and the culture of information.* University of Chicago Press.

Lopes, C., Rodrigues, L. and Sichieri, R. (1996) "The lack of selection bias in a snowball-sampled case-control study on drug abuse," *International Journal of Epidemiology* 25(6): 1267–70.

Lukes, S. (2005) *Power: A radical view*. 2nd edn.; Basingstoke: Palgrave Macmillan.

Lupton, T. (1963) *On the shop floor: Two studies of workshop organization and output*. International series of monographs on social and behavioural sciences; 2; London: Pergamon.

Lyon, D. (1994) *The electronic eye: The rise of surveillance society*. Minneapolis: University of Minnesota Press.

Maier, C. (2006) *Bonjour laziness*. New York: Vintage Books.

Malachowski, D. and Simonini, J. 'Wasted time at work still costing companies billions in 2006', www.salary.com/sitesearch/layoutscripts/sisl_display.asp?filename=&path=/destinationsearch/personal/par542_body.html, accessed November 11, 2008.

Marcuse, H. (1941) *Reason and revolution: Hegel and the rise of social theory*. London; New York: Oxford University Press.

   (1955) *Eros and civilization: A philosophical inquiry into Freud*. New York: Vintage.

   (1969) *Negations: Essays in critical theory*. London: Allen Lane.

   (1998) *Technology, war, and fascism*. London; New York: Routledge.

   (2005) *The New Left and the 1960s*. London: Routledge.

   (2008 [1964]) *One-dimensional man: Studies in the ideology of advanced industrial society*. London: Routledge.

   (2009 [1968]) *Negations: Essays in critical theory*. London: MayFlyBooks.

Mars, G. (1982) *Cheats at work: An anthology of workplace crime*. London: Allen & Unwin.

Marsden, R. (1993) "The politics of organizational analysis," *Organization Studies Organization Studies* 14(1): 93–124.

Martin, J.L. (2011) *The explanation of social action*. New York: Oxford University Press.

Marvasti, A. (2003) *Qualitative research in sociology*. London: Sage.

Marx, K. (1976 [1867]) *Capital: A critique of political economy. Vol. 1*. Harmondsworth: Penguin in association with New Left Review.

Marx, K. and Engels, F. (1998 [1848]) *The Communist manifesto*. London: ElecBook.

Maslow, A.H. (1943) "A theory of human motivation," *Psychological Review Psychological Review* 50(4): 370–96.

Mason, J. (2002) *Qualitative researching*. London; Thousand Oaks, CA: Sage.

McGregor, D. (1960) *The human side of enterprise*. New York: McGraw-Hill.

McKevitt, S. (2006) *City slackers*. London: Cyan Books.

Méda, D. (2008) *Le temps des femmes: Pour un nouveau partage des rôles*. Paris: Flammarion.

Meyer, J.W. and Rowan, B. (1977) "Institutionalized organizations: Formal structure as myth and ceremony," *American Journal of Sociology* 83(2).

Miles, M.B. and Huberman, A.M. (1994) *Qualitative data analysis: An expanded sourcebook*. Thousand Oaks, CA: Sage.

Miller, D. (2002) "Turning Callon the right way up," *Economy & Society* 31(2): 218.

Miller, E.J. (2007) *The effect of rewards, commitment, organizational climate and work values on intentions to leave: Is there a difference among generations?*; New York: ProQuest Information & Learning.

Mills, C.W. (1940) "Situated actions and vocabularies of motive," *American Sociological Review* 5(6): 904–13.

(1951) *White collar: The American middle classes*. New York: Oxford University Press.

(2000 [1959]) *The sociological imagination*. New York: Oxford University Press.

Mills, J.E. et al. (2001) "Cyberslacking! A wired-workplace liability issue," *The Cornell Hotel and Restaurant Administration Quarterly* 42(5): 34–47.

Mishler, E.G. (1993) *Research interviewing: Context and narrative*. Cambridge, MA: Harvard University Press.

Morrill, C., Zald, M.N. and Rao, H. (2003) "Covert political conflict in organizations: Challenges from below," *Annual Review of Sociology* 29(1): 391–415.

MOW International Research Team (1987) *The meaning of working*. Organizational and occupational psychology. London: Academic Press.

Mumby, D. (2005) "Theorizing resistance in organization studies," *Management Communication Quarterly* 19(1): 19–44.

Newton, T. (1998) "Theorizing subjectivity in organizations: The failure of Foucauldian studies?," *Organization Studies* 19(3): 415–47.

Nicolaus, M. (1970) "Proletariat and middle class in Marx." in J. Weinstein and D.W. Eakins (eds.). *For a new America; Essays in history and politics from studies on the Left, 1959–1967*. New York: Random House.

Noon, M. and Blyton, P. (2007) *The realities of work: Experiencing work and employment in contemporary society*. Basingstoke: Palgrave Macmillan.

O'Doherty, D. and Willmott, H. (2001) "Debating labour process theory: The issue of subjectivity and the relevance of poststructuralism," *Sociology* 35(2): 457–76.

Offe, C. and Heinze, R.G. (1992) *Beyond employment: Time, work and the informal economy.* Cambridge: Polity Press.

Olausson, A. (2012) "Skopanställda: Var tionde fuskar med svaren" *Arbetaren* 31/5.

Ones, D.S. and Viswesvaran, C. (2003) "The big-5 personality and counterproductive behaviours." in A. Sagie, S. Stashevsky, and M. Koslowsky (eds.). *Misbehaviour and dysfunctional attitudes in organizations.* New York: Palgrave Macmillan.

Parkinson, C.N. (1957) *Parkinson's law, and other studies in administration.* Boston: Houghton Mifflin.

Patton, M.Q. (2002) *Qualitative research and evaluation methods.* Thousand Oaks, CA: Sage Publications.

Paulsen, R. (2008) "Economically forced to work: A critical reconsideration of the lottery question," *Basic Income Studies* 3(2): 1–20.

    (2010) *Arbetssamhället: Hur arbetet överlevde teknologin.* Malmö: Gleerups.

Penney, L.M., Spector, P.E. and Fox, S. (2003) "Stress, personality and counterproductive work behaviour." in A. Sagie, S. Stashevsky, and M. Koslowsky (eds.). *Misbehaviour and dysfunctional attitudes in organizations.* New York: Palgrave Macmillan.

Piven, F.F. and Cloward, R.A. (1977) *Poor people's movements: Why they succeed, how they fail.* New York: Pantheon.

Pouget, É. (1913 [1898]) *Sabotage.* Chicago: Charles H. Kerr.

Power, M. (1997) *The audit society: Rituals of verification.* London; New York: Oxford University Press.

Proudhon, P.J. (1876 [1840]) *What is property?*; Princeton, Mass.: Benjamin R. Tucker.

Rådahl, E. (1990) *Löftesfabriken: Samhall i närbild.* Stockholm: Pandemos.

Ray, C.A. (1986) "Corporate culture: The last frontier of control," *Journal of Management Studies* 23(3): 287–97.

Riedy, M. and Wen, J. (2010) "Electronic surveillance of internet access in the American workplace: Implications for management," *Information & Communications Technology Law* 19(1): 87–99.

Robinowitz, C.J. and Carr, L.W. (2006) *Modern-day Vikings: A practical guide to interacting with the Swedes.* Boston, MA: Intercultural Press.

Roos Holmborg, N. (2009) "Sju uppgsagda på LFV efter att ha porrsurfat" *Dagens Nyheter* 5/5.

Roscigno, V.J. and Hodson, R. (2004) "The organizational and social foundations of worker resistance," *American Sociological Review* 69: 14–39.

Rothlin, P. and Werder, P.R. (2007) *Boreout! Overcoming workplace demotivation*. London: Kogan Page.

Roy, D. (1952) "Quota restriction and goldbricking in a machine shop," *The American Journal of Sociology* 57(5): 427–42.

(1953) "Work satisfaction and social reward in quota achievement: An analysis of piecework incentive," *American Sociological Review* 18(5): 507–14.

(1954) "Efficiency and "the fix": Informal intergroup relations in a piecework machine shop," *The American Journal of Sociology* 60(3): 255–66.

Røyseland, H. and Vikås, M. (2010) "Lege på vakt gikk på Iron Maiden-konsert" *Verdens Gang* 12/8.

Runciman, W.G. (1966) *Relative deprivation and social justice: A study of attitudes to social inequality in twentieth-century England*. Berkeley: University of California Press.

Russell, B. (1996 [1935]) *In praise of idleness and other essays*. London: Routledge.

Sagie, A., Stashevsky, S. and Koslowsky, M. (2003) *Misbehaviour and dysfunctional attitudes in organizations*. New York: Palgrave Macmillan.

Sanne, C. (2007) *Keynes barnbarn: En bättre framtid med arbete och välfärd*. Stockholm: Formas.

Schor, J.B. (1991) *The overworked American: The unexpected decline of leisure*. New York: Basic Books.

(2010) *Plenitude: The new economics of true wealth*. New York: Penguin Press.

Schutz, A. (1967) *The phenomenology of the social world*. Evanston, IL: Northwestern University Press.

Scott, J.C. (1985) *Weapons of the weak: Everyday forms of peasant resistance*. New Haven: Yale University Press.

(1989) "Everyday forms of resistance." in F.D. Colburn (ed.) *Everyday forms of peasant resistance*. Armonk, NY: M.E. Sharpe.

(1991) *Domination and the arts of resistance: Hidden transcripts*. London: Yale University Press.

(2012) *Two cheers for anarchism: Six easy pieces on autonomy, dignity, and meaningful work and play*. Princeton University Press.

Scott, R. (1998) *Organizations: Rational, natural, and open systems*. 4th edn.; Upper Saddle River, NJ: Prentice Hall International.

Seidman, I. (2006) *Interviewing as qualitative research: A guide for researchers in education and the social sciences*. New York: Teachers College Press, Columbia University.

Sennett, R. (1998) *The corrosion of character: The personal consequences of work in the new capitalism*. New York: W.W. Norton.

(2006) "Preface." in A. Buonfino and G. Mulgan (eds.). *Porcupines in winter: The pleasures and pains of living together in modern Britain*. London: The Yound Foundation.

Sewell, G. (2008) "The fox and the hedgehog go to work," *Management Communication Quarterly* 21(3): 344–63.

Sewell, G. and Wilkinson, B. (1992) "'Someone to watch over me': Surveillance, discipline and the just-in-time labour process," *Sociology* 26(2): 271–89.

Sewell, G., Barker, J.R. and Nyberg, D. (2012) "Working under intensive surveillance: When does 'measuring everything that moves' become intolerable?," *Human Relations* 65(2): 189–215.

Shellenbarger, S. (2012) "'Working from home' without slacking off," *The Wall Street Journal* 11/7.

Shelley, P.B. (1839) *The complete poetical works of Percy Bysshe Shelley*. New York: T.Y. Crowell.

Silverman, D. (1989) "Six rules of qualitative research: A post-Romantic argument," *Symbolic Interaction* 12(2): 215–30.

Simmel, G. (1906) "The sociology of secrecy and of secret societies," *American Journal of Sociology* 11(4): 441–98.

(1981) *Storstäderna och det andliga livet*. Göteborg: Korpen.

Skeggs, B. and Wood, H. (2008) "The labour of tranformation and circuits of value 'around' reality television," *Continuum: Journal of Media & Cultural Studies* 22(4): 559–72.

Skjervheim, H. (1971) *Deltagare och åskådare: Sex bidrag till debatten om människans frihet i det moderna samhället*. Stockholm: Prisma.

Sloterdijk, P. (2001 [1983]) *Critique of cynical reason*. University of Minnesota Press.

Smith, A. (2007 [1776]) *An inquiry into the nature and causes of the wealth of nations*. Petersfield: Harriman House.

Snow, D.A. and Benford, R.D. (1992) "Master frames and cycles of protest." in A.D. Morris and C. Mclurg Mueller (eds.). *Frontiers in social movement theory*. New Haven: Yale University Press.

Solanas, V. (1967) *Scum manifesto*. Pétroleuse Press.

Sprouse, M. (1992) *Sabotage in the American workplace: Anecdotes of dissatisfaction, mischief, and revenge*. San Francisco: Pressure Drop Press.

Standing, G. (2011) *The precariat: The new dangerous class*. London: Bloomsbury Academic.

Stewart, P. (2008) "Le mythe de la 'fin du collectivisme'" in S. Bouquin (ed.) *Résistances au travail*. Paris: Éditions Syllepse.

Svahn, C. (2012) "Nämndeman lade patiens," *Dagens Nyheter* 13/9.

Sverke, M. and Hellgren, J. (eds.) (2002) *Medlemmen, facket och flexibiliteten.* Lund: Arkiv förlag.

Swedberg, R. (2003) *Principles of economic sociology.* Princeton University Press.

Swidey, N. (2004) "What went wrong?" *The Boston Globe* 21/3.

(2010) "For a fallen surgeon a higher power," *The Boston Globe* 28/2.

Tanner, J., Davies, S. and O'Grady, B. (1992) "Immanence changes everything: A critical comment on the labour process and class consciousness," *Sociology* 26(3): 439–53.

Taplin, I.M. (2006) "Managerial resistance to high performance workplace practices." in V. S. P (ed.) *Research in the sociology of work, vol. 10, The transformation of work.* Amsterdam: JAI.

Taylor, F.W. (1919) *The principles of scientific management.* New York; London: Harper & Brothers.

Taylor, L. and Walton, P. (1971) "Industrial sabotage: Motives and meanings." in S. Cohen (ed.) *Images of deviance.* Harmondsworth: Penguin.

Taylor, P. and Bain, P. (2003) "'Subterranean worksick blues': Humour as subversion in two call centres," *Organization Studies* 24(9): 1487–509.

Tellström, R. (2005) "From crispbread to ciabatta." in D. Goldstein and K. Merkle (eds.). *Culinary cultures of Europe.* Council of Europe Publication.

Thompson, E.P. (1967) "Time, work, discipline and industrial capitalism," *Past and Present* 38: 56–97.

(1995 [1978]) *The poverty of theory, or an orrery of errors.* London: Merlin Press.

Thompson, P. (1983) *The nature of work: An introduction to debates on the labour process.* London: Macmillan.

(2009) "Resisting resistance: Moving the debate on" (Edinburgh: 27th International Labour Process Conference).

(2011) "The trouble with HRM," *Human Resource Management Journal* 21(4).

Thompson, P. and Ackroyd, S. (1995) "All quiet on the workplace front? A critique of recent trends in British industrial sociology," *Sociology* 29(4): 615–33.

Thompson, P., Warhurst, C. and Callaghan, G. (2001) "Ignorant theory and knowledgeable workers: Interrogating the connections between knowledge, skills and services," *Journal of Management Studies* 38(7): 923–42.

Tilgher, A. (1931) *Work: What it has meant to men through the ages.* London: George G. Harrap.

Topham, G. (2012) "Air passengers' lives will be put at risk, pilots warn," *The Guardian* 6/6.

Touraine, A. (1971a) *The May movement; revolt and reform: May 1968–the student rebellion and workers' strikes–the birth of a social movement.* New York: Random House.

(1971b) *The post-industrial society: Tomorrow's social history: Classes, conflicts and culture in the programmed society.* New York: Random House.

(1983a) *Solidarity: The analysis of a social movement: Poland, 1980–1981.* Cambridge University Press.

(1983b) *Anti-nuclear protest: The opposition to nuclear energy in France.* New York; Paris: Cambridge University Press; Editions de la Maison des Sciences de l'Homme.

(1995) *Critique of modernity.* Oxford: Blackwell.

(2000a) "A method for studying social actors," *Journal of World-Systems Research* 6(3): 900–18.

(2000b) *Can we live together? Equality and difference.* Stanford University Press.

(2005) "The subject is coming back," *International Journal of Politics, Culture, and Society* 18(3): 199–209.

Townley, B. (1993) *Reframing human resource management.* London: Sage.

(1997) "Beyond good and evil: Foucault and HRM." in A. McKinlay and K. Starkey (eds.). *Foucault, management and organization theory: From panopticon to technologies of self.* London: Sage.

(2008) *Reason's neglect: Rationality and organizing.* New York: Oxford University Press.

Townsend, K. (2004) "Management culture and employee resistance: Investigating the management of leisure service employees," *Managing Leisure* 9(1): 47–58.

(2005) "Electronic surveillance and cohesive teams: Room for resistance in an Australian call centre?," *New Technology, Work and Employment* 20(1): 47–59.

TT (2006) "Hovrättsdomare varnad för att han struntar i arbetstider" *Ystads Allehanda* 18/7.

(2013) "Gruvarbetare på lkab miljonfuskade" *Dagens Industri* 18/2.

Turgeman-Goldschmidt, O. (2005) "Hackers' accounts: Hacking as a social entertainment," *Social Science Computer Review* 23(1): 8–23.

Turner, J. (1995) "Economic context and the health effects of unemployment," *Journal of Health and Social Behavior* 36(4): 213–29.

Vardi, Y. and Weitz, E. (2004) *Misbehavior in organizations: Theory, research, and management.* Mahwah, NJ [u.a.]: Erlbaum.

Vaught, C. and Smith, D.L. (1980) "Incorporation and mechanical solidarity in an underground coal mine," *Work and Occupations* 7(2): 159–87.

Veblen, T. (2001 [1921]) *The engineers and the price system*. Kitchener: Batoche Books.

    (2008 [1899]) *The theory of the leisure class*. Ebook #833: Project Gutenberg.

Verton, D. (2000) "Employers ok with e-surfing," *Computerworld* 34(51): 1.

Vivien, L.K.G. and Thompson, T.S.H. (2005) "Prevalence, perceived seriousness, justification and regulation of cyberloafing in Singapore: An exploratory study," *Information & Management* 42(8): 1081–93.

Vivien, L.K.G., Thompson, T.S.H. and Geok Leng, L. (2002) "How do I loaf here? Let me count the ways," *Communications of the ACM* 45(1): 66–70.

Wakefield, J. (2008) "Google your way to a wacky office," *BBC News* 13/4.

Wallace, D.F. (2011) *The pale king: An unfinished novel*. New York: Little, Brown and Co.

Warhurst, C. and Nickson, D. (2007) "A new labour aristocracy? Aesthetic labour and routine interactive service," *Work Employment Society* 21(4): 785–98.

    (2009) "'Who's got the look?' Emotional, aesthetic and sexualized labour in interactive services," *Gender, Work & Organization* 16(3): 385–404.

Warhurst, C. et al. (2012) *Are bad jobs inevitable? Trends, determinants and responses to job quality in the twenty-first century*. Hampshire: Palgrave Macmillan.

Warren, S. and Fineman, S. (1997) "'Don't get me wrong, it's fun here, but...' Ambivalence and paradox in a 'fun' work environment." in R. Westwood and C. Rhodes (eds.). *Humour, work and organization*. London: Routledge.

Waterfield, B. (2012) "German civil servant says he 'did nothing for 14 years'," *The Telegraph* 12/4.

    (2013) "Fury caught on film as MEPs 'sign in and slope off'" *The Telegraph* 25/6.

Weber, M. (1978 [1922]) *Economy and society: An outline of interpretive sociology*. Berkeley, CA: University of California Press.

    (1992 [1904]) *The Protestant ethic and the spirit of capitalism*. London: Routledge.

Weeks, K. (2011) *The problem with work: Feminism, Marxism, antiwork politics, and postwork imaginaries*. Durham: Duke University Press.

Weman, J. (2011) *Åtgärdslandet: Arbetsförmedlingens svarta bok*. Stockholm: Federativ.

West, A. (2007) "Facebook labelled a $5b waste of time" *The Sydney Morning Herald* 20/8.

White, M.C. (2012) "You're wasting time at work right now, aren't you," *TIME* March 13, 2012.

Willis, P.E. (1981) *Learning to labor: How working class kids get working class jobs.* New York: Columbia University Press.

Willmott, H. (1993) "Strength is ignorance; slavery is freedom: Managing culture in modern organizations," *Journal of Management Studies* 30(4): 515–52.

   (1994) "Theorising agency: Power and subjectivity in organization studies." in J. Hassard and M. Parker (eds.). *Towards a new theory of organizations.* New York: Routledge.

Wood, H. (2005) "Texting the subject: Women, television, and modern self-reflexivity," *The Communication Review* 8: 115–35.

Wright, E.O. (2010) *Envisioning real utopias.* London; New York: Verso.

Zenou, T. (2011) "Svenskarna slösar bort sin arbetstid" *Dagens Nyheter* 22/5.

Žižek, S. (1989) *The sublime object of ideology.* London; New York: Verso.

   (2009) *First as tragedy, then as farce.* London: Verso.

Index